Ann Hadley
April 2008

Tears in the Dark:
A Journey of Hope

D0533194

'clearly an important story, emotional and revealing'
Ken Loach, film director

'very powerful'
Playwright Tony Marriot, writer of 'No Sex Please We're British'

'This is a very powerful and extraordinary account of your life'
Portman Entertainment

'I found *Tears in the Dark* very moving' **Regent Productions**

'a very powerful moving story . . . engaging' **Working Title Films**

'*Tears in the Dark* is a moving and powerful story all the more so because it is true' **BBC Film and Drama**

'A tragic story with an uplifting conclusion . . . very powerful'
Specific Films

'Your story is very moving and very powerful'
London Weekend Television

'Thank you for your powerful autobiography, you have clearly led an interesting and unusual life . . . very powerful' **Virgin Publishing**

'very inspiring' **Twickenham Film Studios**

'this story is clearly extremely powerful and very moving'
Catherine Wearing, BBC producer

'a powerful and compelling story' **Yvonne Hewett, Director**

'deeply, deeply moving' **Erica Wolfe-Murray, Touch Production**

'An exceptionally vivid account of a child's journey through the care system. The voice of the child is clearly heard. Mark's intolerable pain, bewilderment, fear and insecurity are vividly recalled . . . This book is essential reading for social workers, and those in allied professions . . . Mark's progress also re-affirms the power of counselling, and people's ability to recover. We are privileged that Mark has been able to share his story with us.'
Paula Evans, Social Worker

'Mark Edwards' emotional and gripping book has something to say to most of us. To professionals: Please give children what they need, namely, love, permanence and security. To parents and carers: Listen to your children and give them of yourselves. And to children: Remember, however the adults treat you, you are lovable and capable.'
Peter Crompton, Psychologist, Counsellor and Trainer

Tears in the Dark:
A Journey of Hope

by Mark Edwards
with Joan Histon

Authentic

Copyright © 2004 Mark Edwards

12 11 10 09 08 07 06   10 9 8 7 6 5 4

Reprinted 2004, 2005, 2006
Authentic Media
9 Holdom Avenue,Blectchley, Milton Keynes MK1 1QR, UK
and 129 Mobilization Drive, Waynesboro, GA 30830-4574, USA
www.authenticmedia.co.uk
Authentic Media is a division of Send the Light Ltd.,
a company limited by guarantee (registered charity no. 270162)

All rights reserved. No part of this publication may be reproduced,
stored in a retrieval system, or transmitted in any form or by
any means, electronic, mechanical, photocopying, recording
or otherwise, without the prior permission of the publisher
or a licence permitting restricted copying.
In the UK such licences are issued by the Copyright Licensing
Agency, 90 Tottenham Court Road, London, W1P 9HE

The right of Mark Edwards to be identified as the author of this work
has been asserted by him in accordance with the Copyright, Designs
and Patents Act 1988.

British Library Cataloguing in Publication Data
A catalogue record for this book is available from the British Library

ISBN 1-85078-545-7

Unless otherwise stated Scripture quotations are taken from the
HOLY BIBLE, NEW INTERNATIONAL VERSION
Copyright © 1973, 1978, 1984 by the International Bible Society.
Used by permission of Hodder and Stoughton Limited. All rights
reserved. ÔNIVÕ is a registered trademark of the International Bible
Society. UK trademark number 1448790

Cover design by River
Typeset by Textype, Cambridge
Print Management by Adare Carwin
Printed and Bound in Denmark by Nørhaven Paperback

In memory of
Pastor David Coombs
Chester City Mission
1973 to 1984

Contents

Foreword   ix

PART ONE

Chapter 1   3
Chapter 2   12
Chapter 3   21
Chapter 4   38
Chapter 5   47
Chapter 6   61
Chapter 7   76
Chapter 8   94

PART TWO

Chapter 9   111
Chapter 10   121
Chapter 11   133
Chapter 12   149
Chapter 13   160
Chapter 14   176

PART THREE

Chapter 15	191
Chapter 16	205
Chapter 17	215
Chapter 18	226
Chapter 19	236
Chapter 20	251
Chapter 21	263
Chapter 22	272
Chapter 23	281

Foreword

For some people the Christian path is smooth and natural. For others it's tough and (as they say) 'character forming'. Here's a story of faith, courage and stubborn determination – and that's just on God's side! Mark has posed God a few problems in his time but has emerged with a buoyant confidence in his Lord and an effective ministry in the Church. Central to the story have been key relationships which are explored here with honesty and sensitivity. Above all we become aware of the lasting strength of two key partnerships – with Mark's wife Lesley and with a God of infinite hope.

This is a fascinating story – read it and never despair again!

Rt Revd John Pritchard,
Bishop of Jarrow

PART ONE

Chapter 1

'I'm telling you, Billy, either those damn kids go or you can pack your bags and clear off!'

I gripped the kitchen door handle nervously as her voice echoed along the corridor from the living room.

'But they're my kids, Maggie.' My father's voice was softer and pleading and I had to strain my ears to hear him. 'I can't keep fostering them out every time the going gets tough. I have to try to make a home for them.'

'Aye, but not this home! It's me that's watching out for them, feeding them, and it costs a pretty penny, I can tell you!'

'But Maggie . . .'

'Don't Maggie me!' Her voice suddenly softened. 'It was you I took on, Billy, not your kids.'

Slowly, I unclenched my fingers. My knuckles had turned stiff, but it was a pleasant pain, better than the one gnawing away inside me. Shivering, more from the fear of being caught listening than with the cold, I crept along the corridor back to the small boxroom I shared with my younger brother, Paul. Crawling into his bed for warmth, I pulled the blankets tightly around me. He stirred. His dark brown hair fell over his face and big brown eyes opened wide and stared at me.

'What's the matter, Mark?' he whispered.

I shook my head, too frightened to tell him that we might be on the move again, but he knew. His bottom lip quivered and he snuggled in closer, clinging tightly to me, the way he had on so many occasions.

It seemed as though there'd been uncertainty around us for as long as I could remember. When we were very small there'd been arguments and friction between my mum and dad, and then one day they took my mum away to the hospital.

'She's got a sickness in her head,' the social worker told us. I didn't really understand what she meant, but I was frightened. I remember her pulling a face when she picked Paul up. He was only a toddler at the time.

'Ugh! He smells and he's wet himself!' she said, and she grimaced as she held my hand to take us to our first foster home. 'Scruffy little street urchin', she called me. I didn't know what that meant either, but I remember feeling very ashamed, as if there was something wrong with me.

After the divorce we were all placed into separate foster homes. There were times when we were able to spend a brief period with Mum, between hospital stays, or with Dad, between jobs, but it always ended up the same way, back to being fostered. Sometimes they would have to drag me kicking and screaming from the house, I was so frightened, but my behaviour upset Paul so much I started trying to control my own fears and comfort my little brother instead.

There were five of us altogether. The twins, Shene and Jenny, were fifteen, Maxine was thirteen, I was eight and Paul was the baby, he was only six. The sad thing was, with so much coming and going, we hardly saw our sisters, so we never really knew what family life was all about.

The sound of my father's footsteps coming along the corridor silenced Paul's whimpering and, hardly daring to breathe, we waited for him to come through the door.

It creaked open and he stood silhouetted against the passage light. People said I was like him: wiry and with a mop of black hair that insisted on flopping over my eyes. The sound of a song that was continually being played on the radio at that time drifted through the open door of the living room and the words seemed to etch themselves deeply into my mind. *I'm nobody's child. Nobody loves me, nobody cares.*

I remember the words because for the first time it seemed somebody, albeit a singer, was reflecting how I was feeling. But I had been unable to formulate how I felt into words until now.

'Boys?'

I lifted my head to show him I was awake, but I was too frightened to say anything.

'Get dressed quickly,' he said gruffly. 'I'm taking you to your Aunt Violet.' He dragged the familiar small brown suitcases from underneath the beds and began throwing in our belongings. Paul and I slid out of bed. Our toes curled with discomfort on the cold linoleum and we shivered as we pulled on our clothes.

Maggie didn't even come to the door to wave us goodbye as we left the meagre warmth of her house and took the long walk in the cold night air to my father's sister's home.

Within the hour we were knocking on Aunt Violet and Uncle Frank's front door.

'Glory me!' Aunt Violet exclaimed, throwing her big, plump hands across her ample bosom. 'What are you doing here at this time of night? Come in! You poor kids.' She turned on my father angrily. 'You can't keep dragging these kids from pillar to post like this, Billy!'

'I know! I know! But what was I to do? Maggie won't have them. Their mum's back in . . .'

'Aye well, let's get these bairns to bed first. I dunno what your uncle'll have to say about this, but come on in, chucks. You'll all have to squash in the little bedroom, but you'll not have to mind that. Brrr . . . you feel cold!' She wrapped her ample arms affectionately around us and my cold nose squashed on to her flowered pinny. It had a warm, comfortable smell about it. I suddenly felt very tired and made no objections to Aunt Violet fussing around us with hot milk and blankets, putting us to bed.

I curled up on a mattress on the floor of the little bedroom beside Paul, warm, drowsy and comforted by the motherly affection from Aunt Violet. Tomorrow, I decided, was another day. I'd worry about it when it came.

The following morning my father woke us very early. Bleary-eyed, we sat with a cup of tea and a slice of bread and marmalade on our mattresses on the floor. Then he wrapped us in our warm outdoor clothes, and an hour later we were sitting, shivering nervously, on our suitcases outside the Social Services Department, waiting for it to open. My father paced the pavement anxiously, smoking cigarette after cigarette.

'I wish we could stay with Aunt Violet,' I said apprehensively.

'Eh?' He stopped pacing. 'Oh yes. So do I, Mark. So do I, but they've not got the room to have you both. Ah! About time. Here they come.'

The key holders arrived and Paul and I followed my father along the cream and green glossy corridors, carrying our suitcases. Our footsteps echoed on the clean, tiled floors until eventually we came to a brown door with frosted glass on the top.

'Wait here, boys.' My father disappeared inside the office and we sat down on our suitcases and listened to the sound of muffled voices from behind the door. Suddenly it opened, and the familiar figure of Miss Vernon, our own special social worker, came out.

'Hello, Mark and Paul.' Her voice was warm and gentle. 'Your dad tells me you both need to be fostered out again, just for a short time, until he finds somewhere for you all to live.' She hesitated before asking, 'How do you feel about that?'

'Well . . .' Being two years older than Paul, it was always left to me to speak for us both. 'Well . . .' How did I feel about it? I tried very hard to stop the knot of fear running down my back. 'Could we not go and live with my Aunt Violet?'

Miss Vernon knelt down on the cold tiles beside us. She was an older lady. I could tell by the way her hair was starting to go grey. She'd been our social worker since I was three and Paul had still been in nappies and had replaced that other horrible one who'd called me a scruffy little street urchin. She was very forthright and bossy with grown-ups, but with Paul and me she always asked us what we wanted and listened when I spoke.

'It would be nice if you could go and live with your Aunt Violet, Mark, and I'm sure she would love to have you, but she hasn't room in her house.'

I struggled to control the great big lump in my chest that was making it difficult for me to breathe. Paul started crying softly and Miss Vernon reached out to hold his hand. 'I want you to be very brave, boys. We're going to find another foster home for you while your dad looks for a job and a place for you all to live.'

Another foster home! The lump in my chest grew bigger and tighter. The last foster parents spent all their time telling us how grateful we should be to them and the ones before that still gave me nightmares. I shuddered. I could usually manage to block what had happened with them out of my mind, but today I was tired and upset anyway. The great big lump rose up from my chest, into my throat and exploded into hot tears that spilled down my cheeks. 'I don't . . . don't . . . want to be . . . fostered. Not . . . not again! Please, Da . . . Dad!' I sobbed.

He placed his big hand on my shoulder and with the other he stroked Paul's hair. 'Now, now, boys. It's only for a short time. Just till I get a job and somewhere to live. Then I'll come and get you.'

'No . . . no you won't!' I sobbed, moving away from him. 'You'll leave us like . . . like you did the last time!'

He reached out his hand, but I didn't want him to touch me. I couldn't trust him to come back for me and Paul, and even if he did, there'd be other nights of being woken, thrown out of our lodgings, taken to Aunt Violet, then back to Social Services to be fostered out again. More foster homes! More schools!

'It's always like this!' I sobbed. 'It's always . . . horrible!'

'Leave them with me, Mr Edwards,' I heard Miss Vernon say. There was a mumble of conversation, which I tried to ignore. I hated them whispering about what they were going to do with us. Then Miss Vernon took us by the hand and led us, still sobbing, down the corridor, my father following, then into the car park around the back of the building.

'In you go, boys,' she said briskly, opening the back door of her red Mini. 'I think you'll like the place I'm going to take you to this time. Here, I'll put your suitcases in the boot.'

I didn't dare turn to look at my father, but I was aware of him standing a short distance from the car, watching

Miss Vernon take control of the situation the way she usually did.

She slid behind the steering wheel. 'Are you all right in the back?'

'Ye . . . yes.'

Miss Vernon started the engine and as she slowly drove out of the car park both Paul and I turned to look out of the back window. The lonely, dejected figure of my father stood waving us goodbye, tears running down his face.

I've discovered you can only cry for so long. Eventually the lump in your throat disappears, the tears dry up and for a while the pain goes away, until something else horrible happens. Then the whole process starts all over again.

The soothing voice of Miss Vernon from the front of the car helped ease the ordeal of waving goodbye to my father and the apprehensions we always had over a new foster home. This would be our fourth.

'We'll be all right, won't we, Mark?' Paul whispered, sliding along the seat towards me. His face was dirty and tear stained.

'Of course you'll be all right,' Miss Vernon interjected. 'Mr and Mrs Tait are very nice people. You'll like them. They've two children of their own, Laura and David, they're fourteen and fifteen.'

'Is it far away?' I ventured.

'Bless you, no. Twenty miles at the most, and I'll pop in from time to time to see how you're getting on.'

'Every week?'

'No . . . no, perhaps not every week, but quite often.'

Well, that was better than nothing.

The gentle motion of the car soon rocked Paul to sleep. I sat silently, looking through the window, watching the early morning traffic in the city centre flash past, then we were out into the countryside with fields and trees. Occasionally I'd glance into the driver's mirror and catch Miss Vernon's eye, and she'd smile reassuringly at me.

Eventually we pulled up at a semi-detached house on the outskirts of the next town. A man was bending over the bonnet of his car in the driveway, tinkering with the engine. It looked quite a pleasant place, really. There was a bus stop and fields opposite and I could see more fields behind the row of houses. I gave Paul a shake to wake him while Miss Vernon collected our cases from the boot of her car.

'Here we are, boys,' she said as we climbed out. 'Look, can you see the budgies at the side of the house? Mr Tait keeps an aviary and there's a big garden at the back with strawberry bushes.' She handed us the cases and as she led us down a long garden path the front door opened and a comfortably plump middle-aged lady with slightly greying hair, a smiling face and wrinkles at the corners of her eyes came out to greet us.

'Hello. You must be Mark and Paul,' she said jovially. 'My name is Mrs Tait, but you can call me "Mum" if you like.'

We didn't speak. I held tightly on to Paul's hand and refused to take my eyes off the garden path.

'They're a little upset and tired' Miss Vernon whispered, as though I couldn't hear. 'Apparently they were thrown out of their lodgings with the father last night.'

'Ah!' said Mrs Tait. She reached out her hands and took ours firmly into hers. 'Are you hungry? It's scallops for dinner today.' She led us up the steps and into the house. 'Do you like scallops?'

I shrugged. I didn't really know what scallops were, but I suddenly realised I was ravenously hungry. 'I'd rather have chips,' I said.

'Chips it is, then.' She led us into a big room with a brightly burning fire and a settee covered in colourful cushions. 'Would you like a few biscuits and a drink of orange juice while I talk to Miss Vernon?'

I nodded, and a few minutes later Paul and I were left to warm ourselves in front of the living room fire and ease our pangs of hunger with orange juice and biscuits, while Mrs Tait and Miss Vernon talked about us in one of the other rooms.

'Mark?'

'What?'

It was quiet in the living room. The fire crackled behind the fireguard and a big clock ticked softly on the mantelpiece.

'Is it . . .' I watched apprehensively as a few crumbs from Paul's biscuit fell on the floor. I hoped we wouldn't get into trouble for making a mess. 'Is it going to be all right? Is it?'

I didn't answer him. How was I to know? I was only eight. My mum had been taken away from me. My dad had had to send me away. I didn't know where my sisters were and Maggie didn't want me. Perhaps there was something wrong with me?

'Is it?' Paul asked nervously, tugging my sleeve and almost making me spill my juice. I put my arm around my little brother.

'Don't worry, Paulie. I'll take care of you. It'll be all right. You'll see.'

Chapter 2

'Wow! Look at the size of that combine harvester, Paul.' I straddled the stone wall and sat watching, fascinated, as the corn was gathered in.

'Wow!' Paul echoed, climbing up beside me. 'It's coming towards us as well.'

The roar of the combine harvester drew closer and a suntanned farmer with a round, smiling face, a cloth cap and shirt sleeves rolled up past his elbows waved cheerfully at us. 'Like a ride, boys?' The huge machine ground to a halt beside us.

'Really?' I couldn't believe anyone could make such a generous offer.

'Of course. Climb up here beside me and hold on to that rail.'

We covered a good part of the field before the harvester gave a shudder and stopped not far from the farmhouse.

An hour later, laden with potted plants, covered in straw and cow dung and smelling like a farmyard, we shouted our farewells and ran happily across the fields home.

It seemed as though day after day of that summer was spent in the endless enjoyment of playing in the fields or in the stream at the bottom of the Tait's big garden. The quaint little village school wasn't so bad either. Unfortunately my education was a little bit behind that of the other children, which did nothing to boost my ego, but I overheard the teacher telling the headmaster that I was doing quite well, considering where I was from, and he thought the extra reading lessons Mr and Mrs Tait were giving me were starting to pay off.

The biggest relief was when Paul stopped wetting the bed. Those first few nights with the Tait family, he'd been terrified when he'd woken and found he'd wet the sheets. Maggie used to give him a good hiding, but all Mrs Tait said was, 'Not to worry, Paul. We'll soon have them washed. Our David used to do this all the time.' She'd strip the bed and even used to give us a packet of crisps or a biscuit and send us out to play.

They were nice people, Mr and Mrs Tait, but strict, the same as they were with their own children. They weren't averse to giving us a hard smack if we were really naughty, but we didn't mind that. It gave us a sense of being cared for and treated like the rest of the family, and we soon got used to the house rules.

The 'glass in the back door' episode was the real testing time. I accidentally broke a large pane of glass when rushing out of the back door to play with the Tait children down by the dyke.

'Don't slam the door!' Mr Tait shouted.

Too late! There was a shattering of glass as the pane smashed on the floor. Mr Tait had to replace it.

'Close the door gently until the putty sets, Mark,' he warned, standing back to admire his handiwork. I didn't. There was another loud crash and the new pane fell out. Mr Tait sighed, then patiently set about mending it once again, this time using some expensive, multi-coloured patterned glass, which he said he'd got hold of when it fell off the back of a lorry. I never quite understood how it was still in one piece if it fell of the back of a lorry, but never mind. The following day, in my haste to get out to play, I slammed the back door behind me and his beautiful multi-coloured glass fell out and shattered on the floor yet again. I learned a new set of swear words that day! Otherwise he was a quiet man.

As we raced home across the fields from the farm after our ride on the combine harvester, dirty and smelling of farmyards, we spotted Miss Vernon's red Mini standing in the driveway.

'Miss Vernon! It's Miss Vernon!' Paul shrieked, and raced into the house. Placing my potted plants on the doorstep, I carefully – very carefully – closed the kitchen door behind me and followed him inside.

Miss Vernon, looking crisp and efficient in a pale pink summer ensemble, sat primly on the edge of the settee. Her face lit up when she saw us and she held out her arms in greeting. So it really was her own fault she got covered in cow dung!

There seemed so much news to give her. When we eventually ran out of steam, her question to us came like a bolt out of the blue. 'How would you feel about staying with Mr and Mrs Tait on a more permanent basis, boys?'

Time seemed to stand still as my eyes met and wordlessly held Paul's across the room. I was suddenly aware of the clock ticking monotonously on the mantelpiece and Mrs Tait clashing dishes as she prepared our tea in the kitchen.

'But . . . will we still see our own mum and dad and sisters again?' I asked hesitantly.

'Gracious me, of course you will! They can visit you whenever they want.'

'What about us going to stay with them?'

Miss Vernon pursed her lips. 'Well, that might be a little difficult. Your father is still living in lodging with Mrs . . . er, Maggie, and although your mother is out of hospital she and her new husband only have a small bungalow, so there's not really much room.'

I glanced across at Paul. His bottom lip was trembling.

'Well boys. What do you say? No more moving around. No more changing schools and having your education interfered with. Instead you'll have a proper home and a settled family life with Mr and Mrs Tait.'

Paul looked at me, waiting for me to make a decision for us both. How could I? How was I to know what was best? I thought of the Cubs' football match, the holiday at the seaside with the Tait family, feeding the calves at the farm, catching tadpoles with Laura and David in the dyke at the bottom of the garden, and slowly, very slowly, nodded my head.

'Splendid!' Miss Vernon beamed and held out her arms to us. 'All I have to do now is send the official papers to Mr and Mrs Tait for their signatures and this will be your new permanent home. OK, boys?'

We joined her on the settee, grinning happily at each other. Yes, I'd made the right decision.

'Everything's going to be fine,' she said, squeezing us. 'Just you wait and see.'

It seemed as though those happy, lazy days of summer drifted into autumn without us noticing. There were always regular weekly events to look forward to. Cubs, football, helping the farmer or Sunday school. We enjoyed Sunday school, even if there were more girls than boys. We learned all about God loving us and being our heavenly Father, but I didn't reckon much on that! Fathers abandoned you when they couldn't get work or when their girlfriend didn't want you because you wet the bed or you were too much trouble. No, I didn't reckon much on God, but our Sunday school teacher was young and had a big happy smile and told us great stories from the Bible about God's son, Jesus. I liked him much better. He could coax a frightened little man that nobody liked out of a tree by asking, 'Zacchaeus, can I come back to your house for a cup of tea?' Then he brought a little girl who was dead back to life again, so he must have liked children, and he had lots of pals who were fishermen. The only trouble was that they killed him and nailed him to a cross, and when he was dying he shouted up to his dad, 'Why have you abandoned me?' Paul and I were abandoned, so I knew just how he must have been feeling. Yes, I liked Jesus.

It seemed no time at all before there was a buzz of excitement as we prepared for the Christmas festivities. Our playground had turned into a skating rink, the football pitch a mud bath, and the delicious smell of mince pies and Christmas puddings from Mrs Tait's kitchen promised it would be a good Christmas.

The first snow of the year fell softly over the fields as we arrived home carrying a large green Christmas tree. We decorated it with tinsel and brightly coloured lights, then we went singing with the Sunday school and scoffed so many mince pies we could hardly manage the big supper when we returned home.

A white Christmas had heralded in an Arsenal football kit for me, a Liverpool kit for Paul, leather footballs, boxing gloves, toy guns, soldiers, books and sweets. I sat in front of the warm flickering coal fire early Christmas morning, listening to the squeals of delight from the rest of the family as they ripped open their parcels, and wallowed in the waves of contentment that flooded over me when I thought of that special day when documentation would come through, and days like this with the Tait family would be on a more permanent basis.

'OK, Mark?' Mrs Tait, still in her dressing gown and with two curlers in the front of her hair, sat on the floor beside me.

I nodded. 'Thank you.' It seemed such a small word to say for all the lovely things around us. 'This is the best Christmas ever!'

Soon the first of the yellow daffodils began bursting forth in the front gardens of the row of semi-detached houses. They towered high above the colourful crocuses in the bright morning sunshine and there was a feeling of spring in the air.

Paul and I gave 'Mum' a cheery wave as we jumped on the bus for another day at school. Our chatter with the rest of the boys was about the impending soccer match that evening against the Cubs from the next village.

'We'll thrash 'em ten nil!'

It was a nightmare trying to keep my mind on morning assembly and I wondered how on earth I would get through the rest of the day. However, in the afternoon, while I was at model making class, I was distracted by the sound of two cars driving into the small playground. I strained to see out of the window and was surprised to see a red Mini followed by a larger Ford Escort come to a halt by the old bicycle shed. It couldn't possibly be Miss Vernon's Mini, could it? What would she be doing at our school on a Wednesday afternoon?

Both car doors slammed as the occupants got out. It was Miss Vernon all right, and the other lady looked vaguely familiar as well. I left the clay duck I'd been making and wandered over to the window to take a closer look. Now I recognised her. She was Mrs Robins, the educational psychologist Mrs Tait had taken us to see last week. We'd spent most of the morning doing silly things like putting square pegs into holes, and I'd been asked a lot of strange questions like what a certain picture on a card reminded me of, what did I think of Mr and Mrs Tait?, and did they ever smack us, and how and where? The psychologist in her white coat and big glasses kept writing things down and humming to herself. Anxiously I watched Miss Vernon and the psychologist walk towards the headmaster's house, which stood at the other side of the playground.

It was just a small jab of anxiety at first. Not enough to dampen the excitement of the forthcoming match, so I pored intently over my clay duck, trying to ignore it.

A few minutes later the classroom door opened and the headmaster came in with a serious expression across his face. He started whispering to Mrs Clark, the teacher, who nodded and frowned and occasionally glanced in my direction. Eventually she turned to me. 'Mark Edwards, would you leave your clay model please and go with the headmaster.'

I tried to suppress the rising panic. Had Paul had an accident? Had something happened at home? I followed the headmaster out of the classroom and as I glanced back was alarmed to see Mrs Clark clearing the clay duck from my desk. Obviously I wasn't expected to return.

The headmaster briskly crossed the playground to his house and I had to trot to keep up with him. As we reached his gate I was relieved to see Paul standing in the lobby. We glanced at each other uneasily, too scared to voice our concerns.

'Come in, boys, come in.' He ushered us into his living room. A brown fluffy cat lay on a thick-pile rug in front of an open fire and a big bunch of yellow daffodils stood on a low table at the side of the settee, where Miss Vernon and Mrs Robins sat.

'Hello, Mark, Paul. Sorry to take you both away from your lessons.' Miss Vernon was forcing herself to be cheerful, I could tell. My stomach knotted up.

'Something's happened to Mum and Dad Tait, hasn't it?'

Miss Vernon shook her head. 'No, Mark. They're fine. Now collect your coats and school bags, we're going on a little trip.'

'I have them here.' The headmaster's wife bustled in with our belongings.

'Right! Off we go! Come along, boys.' Miss Vernon stood up and made towards the door. 'Mark, you can come in my car. Paul will go with Mrs Robins.'

They were splitting us up!

'No!' I grabbed Paul by the scruff of his neck and hauled him back to stand next to me, but he needed no persuading. 'What's happened?' I could hear the fear in my voice. 'Tell me!'

Miss Vernon took my hand. 'You'll just have to trust me, Mark. Come along now!'

'No! No!' Something was wrong. Very wrong! I tried to push her away but her grasp tightened. I started yelling and lashing out, and out of the corner of my eye saw Paul trying to free himself from Mrs Robins to come to my aid.

'Please calm down, both of you!' Miss Vernon raised her voice, then suddenly let go of me, and I almost fell over the cat. Mrs Robins let go of Paul and he backed away from her, scowling.

There was a pause. Then Miss Vernon said, 'Mark, Mr and Mrs Tait can't look after you any more.'

There was a horrible silence in the room. I remember thinking *What about my soccer match tonight?*, but my tongue seemed to be stuck to the roof of my mouth.

'Please try to be brave, boys,' Miss Vernon said gently.

'Where are you taking us?' I whispered.

Miss Vernon crouched down and took one of my hands in hers. She reached out to hold one of Paul's hands, but he stepped back.

'You're being taken to a children's home,' she said quietly. 'At least until we can find a new foster home for you.'

Blind fear made me scream 'No! No!' and I tried to pull away from her. Somewhere in the background I could hear Paul crying. Then the headmaster, his wife, Miss Vernon and Mrs Robins dragged us, screaming and struggling, out to the cars. As both cars roared out of the playground I felt as if my perfect world had been shattered.

Chapter 3

I sat in the back of Miss Vernon's car with my chin resting on my chest in an attempt to hide the tears that were streaming down my face. Occasionally I glanced behind to make sure the blue Ford Escort with Paul and Mrs Robins inside was still following.

As we sped past familiar scenes that had been my home for two years I began to wonder if all this could be some horrible nightmare coming to haunt me and that when Miss Vernon pulled up at the Tait's house I would wake up to find Dad busy in the aviary, Mum making tea in the kitchen and David and Laura doing their homework in the living room. However, as we reached the row of semi-detached houses with their long gardens and bright yellow daffodils and she made no attempt to slow down, I let out a cry of alarm.

'Calm down, Mark,' Miss Vernon soothed, glancing through the rear-view mirror. 'It's going to be all right, you'll see.'

'You said we could stay!' I sobbed, pressing my face to the window. 'You said we could stay!'

She didn't say anything and I glimpsed, through a blur of tears, my home gradually disappearing from sight. I curled up on the back seat of the car, too frightened even to cry.

Ivy Cottage Children's Home wasn't nearly as pretty as its name suggested. It was a large, flat, red-brick building with dozens of identical windows. There was a football lying in the middle of a spacious lawn and an old bicycle propped up against a tree. Miss Vernon pulled up at a big brown front door.

'This is to be your new home, at least until I can find you a foster home,' she said gently. 'Trust me. It'll work out.' She attempted to reach over to squeeze my hand, but I pulled back. Trust her? Never! Not after all her promises!

Paul jumped out of Mrs Robins' car and ran over to me. His cold fingers entwined themselves around mine. A normal day at school had turned into a nightmare and no one had stopped to explain what was going on or to offer us any substantial reassurances.

Mrs Robins pressed the doorbell and a moment later an unsmiling, short, dark-haired woman in a plain dull grey dress opened the door. The only bright thing about her was a colourful flowered apron.

'You must be Mark and Paul?' she said, without a flicker of interest. 'Come on in. My name is Aunty Freda.'

With a jolt I realised that we must have been expected.

Miss Vernon and Mrs Robins left us with empty words of reassurance and Aunty Freda took us into the dining room for our tea, where fifteen to twenty curious children bombarded us with questions: 'How long will you be here?' 'Where have you come from?' 'Are your mum and dad dead?' It was a relief to be allowed to watch television before another Aunty, Aunty Gwen, led us upstairs to a room at the end of a long landing. This was our bedroom, which, she informed us, we would have to share with two other boys, Richard and Brian. It was a plain room with plain cream walls, no pictures. The four beds, two each side of the room, facing each other, were covered with plain bright yellow bedspreads with tassels on the end. A large wardrobe stood behind the door and a small chest of drawers with a mirror on top separated each bed. A couple of dull green rugs covered the brown linoleum and a draught from the open fire escape door wafted the faded flowered curtains across an untidy shelf, scattered with books, jigsaws and a few toys.

'How old are you both?' Aunty Gwen asked us brightly as she closed the fire escape door and locked it. I liked Aunty Gwen. She had a round, chubby face, like Mum Tait's.

'I'm ten and Paul is eight.'

'Well then, you will go to bed at eight o'clock, Mark, and Paul goes at a quarter to eight. Come on, I'll show you where the bathroom is, you can put your pyjamas on, then I'll give you your numbers. We have numbers on all our things so we know what belongs to who.' She smiled down at our anxious faces. 'Don't worry. I know it must seem strange for you, but it won't always feel like this. You'll soon get used to it.'

The bed with number fourteen painted on it, my bed, was beside the fire escape door. After she'd left us I sat on the edge of it, silently watching Paul making faces at himself in the mirror on his chest of drawers. Had it only been this morning we'd stood at the bus stop, waiting for the school bus, watching the yellow daffodils wave in the bright morning sunshine, excited over the forthcoming football match? They'd have finished the game by now. I wondered who had won. Had it only been this morning Mum Tait had given us our dinner money and happily waved us goodbye? Why didn't she want us back? What had we done wrong? I tried to work it out, but there was too much confusion in my head.

'I *hate* this place!' Paul spun around to face me, his teeth clenched in anger.

'Keep your voice down,' I warned.

'I don't care! I don't flaming well want to be a number, neither!' He picked up his tooth mug from his bedside table and hurled it against the bedroom wall. There was a clatter as it bounced off the radiator.

'Stop it, Paul!' I hissed. 'You'll get us into trouble.'

I crawled inside the crisp white sheets and closed my eyes, although I knew I'd never be able to sleep. Too much had happened that day and there was too much to worry about for tomorrow. A few minutes later Paul crawled in beside me and promptly burst into tears. I gave him a hug. 'It's all right, Paulie. If we stick together we'll be all right.'

'I'll not be able to sleep.'

'Yes you will.'

We lay silently for a while. Then Paul said, 'Mark, how long will we be here for?'

'I don't know.'

There was silence for a while. 'I don't want to be fostered out again, Mark.

'Neither do I.'

'Why do you think they took us away from Mr and Mrs Tait?'

I shook my head. 'I don't know.'

'Do you think we did something wrong?'

'I don't know.'

'What about our clothes and toys and . . .' There was a sudden clatter as the door burst open and our two roommates charged into the bedroom.

'Hi!' The boy with sandy-coloured hair and number twelve on his pyjamas greeted us in a friendly manner. The other one hung back shyly. 'I'm Richard, he's Brian.'

Both boys looked about the same age as us. They hung their dressing gowns on pegs marked twelve and thirteen, then Richard leapt into the bed beside mine.

'Aunty Freda'll kill you if she finds you both in the same bed,' he informed us.

Not wishing to get into trouble, Paul reluctantly slid out of my bed and, shivering, padded across the cold linoleum to the bed marked number eleven. As soon as he was between the covers, Brian switched off the light, dived into the bed next to Paul's, and silence descended upon our room.

The familiar lyrics of that song I'd heard at Maggie's ran through my mind. *I'm nobody's child. Nobody loves me, nobody cares.* I turned my head into the pillow and pulled the blankets up over me. For some strange reason the Jesus I'd learned about at Sunday school and whose life had proved to me that he cared for children and little people that no one else wanted sprang into my mind. For the first time in my life, I prayed. 'Please, Jesus! Help me and Paul. Help us!' Then I cried until, utterly exhausted, I fell asleep.

Breakfast seemed a rather regimented affair. There was a set time to arrive at the table, certain children were to serve the porridge and tea, and others had clear up. After breakfast we were called into the office to see Uncle Andrews and his wife.

Aunty Andrews had a long, thin face, fair curly hair and peered at us through a pair of half-moon shaped glasses as we entered. She sat behind a big desk covered in papers, but when she smiled she didn't look too fierce. Uncle was a thickset, middle-aged man with very large dark bushy eyebrows. He sat in a big leather chair by the window and smiled pleasantly at us.

'Nice to have you with us, boys,' Aunty Andrews said in a soft Scottish accent. 'You do know that you will have to stay here until your social worker can find another foster mum and dad for you, don't you?'

The very thought of having to discuss our uncertain future with these two strange people made my mouth go all dry inside.

'Don't you?' she repeated.

'Yes.' Paul, standing beside me, nodded.

'Well, until that happens, we've decided it would be best for you to attend the local primary school along with the rest of the children in the Home.' She pushed the half-moon glasses further up her nose and smiled kindly, but I was aware of being carefully scrutinised, and I shuffled uneasily. 'Because there are seventeen children in the Home, we have a list of rules and regulations, which enables us to run a smoother and more efficient Home. To break any of these rules will result in punishment. Do you understand?'

We nodded.

'On Saturdays you will each receive fifty pence pocket money. Out of this, twenty pence will be saved towards your summer holidays for spending money. The rest you can spend as you wish.'

That didn't sound too bad. We'd have left this place by the time the summer holidays came around, so that probably meant we had a full fifty pence to spend as we wanted.

'You will have various chores to do', Aunty continued, 'from setting the tables, washing dishes, peeling the potatoes to cleaning the water closet pipe in the boys' toilet.'

My heart sank. It all seemed so harsh and strict.

'There will be a member of staff to check you bath yourself properly and you will also be expected to go and sit on the toilet after meals and stay there until a member of staff has come to check to see if your bowels have moved.'

Highly embarrassed by such explicit instructions regarding the toilet, I averted my gaze to my shoes. Then

I glanced at Paul. He'd stopped listening to what Aunty Andrews was saying and was staring out of the office window, watching the crocodile of children with their coats and school bags following Aunty Gwen up the long drive.

'Paul, would you pay attention, please?' Aunty Andrews said it gently, but he jumped, and I could see fear in his eyes.

My protective instinct rose up for my little brother. I wanted to reproach her. *Can't you see he's scared by all these rules and regulations? We're both scared! Don't you understand how we feel?* But, like Paul, I was too frightened to say anything. Frightened I'd get into trouble, or that they'd separate us or send us off somewhere else again. So I continued staring down at my shoes.

'Have you any questions?' she asked softly.

Questions? Of course I had questions! Why were we promised a proper home and proper family with the Taits, then dragged away without any explanations? Had we done something wrong, or was it just that Mr and Mrs Tait didn't want us any more? Why wouldn't someone tell us? We had to leave our clothes and toys, my Arsenal football kit, the Cubs and our friends, our football matches and all the things we'd come to love. *Why? Why? Why?* But I didn't say any of these things. I just stood quietly, staring down at my shoes, crying and confused inside. So Aunty Andrews dismissed us. We were to have the morning off school so we could settle in and explore our new home.

We wandered wordlessly outside into the warm morning sunshine. I sat on one of the swings. Paul ambled over to the sandpit and started digging.

What must it be like to belong to a proper family, I wondered? To be cared for by somebody warm and gentle who would love you and listen to how you feel? That would never happen if we were fostered out again.

There was no security in being fostered. Giving love, like we'd done with the Tait family, and getting love back was a dangerous thing to do, because at any moment people from Social Services, like Miss Vernon or Mrs Robins, could come along and swipe it all away. It was too painful to let that happen again. Far too painful! In my agitated state I found I was now swinging so high I could almost see over the garden wall. I stretched my neck, but I couldn't quite see what was over the other side. I clung tightly to the rope and brought myself into a standing position, but whatever was over the other side was protected from my curious gaze. I resumed my sitting position thoughtfully. That was what I wanted. A great big high wall of protection around myself so that no one would ever be able to climb over and hurt me ever again. I thrust my legs forward and, clinging tightly to the ropes, leant back. When the swing had swung forward as far as it would go, I thrust my body forward and my legs back, putting all my effort into making the swing go higher and higher, and with each surge of the swing I built my imaginary wall of protection. No one else could protect me. Not my parents: they were either sick, jobless or didn't care. Not Social Services. They didn't know what they were doing! I mean, why take us away from a foster home we were happy in? What had we done wrong? Not even Jesus could protect us. He certainly didn't have any control over my parents, Maggie or Social Services! Perhaps we didn't deserve help? No! I would be better off taking control of my own life, and Paul's, from now on and forgetting about everyone else. I could do it! *I could!* Higher and higher I swung until my back ached and my hands were sore from clinging so tightly to the ropes.

After a while my legs grew tired and the swing began to slow down until eventually I skidded to a stop. There was no need to strive any more. My new resolution was in place.

As it turned out, the local primary school wasn't so bad. The headmaster seemed to be a kind, patient sort of man, and to my delight I found I was sharing a desk with a boy about my age, Gary, also from the children's home.

'How long have you been in the children's home?' I asked him in the playground during break time.

'Me and my brother Robin have been there about two years. It's not a bad place once you get used to it. You can have quite a good laugh, but you have to watch Aunty Freda. She's strict, won't think twice about slippering you, and I should know!' He rubbed his bottom and grinned cheekily at me. 'Aunty Gwen's OK though. She never seems to catch me.' He nodded toward three boys playing at the far end of the playground. 'Uncle's good. He doesn't stand for any bullying, and those three over there, the Clark brothers, are always getting a spanking.'

The eldest Clark brother, Ian, looked over towards me and Gary. He had a miserable face very like his two younger brothers, but he was lankier and spottier. I made a mental note to keep myself and Paul out of their way, which was easier said than done. Before long both of us had experienced bullying from one or all of these brothers.

I didn't plan to run away during those first few weeks at Ivy Cottage. It just seemed like a good idea at the time, a way of making someone sit up and take notice of how unhappy I was at being bullied, of how lost and bewildered I was by all that had taken place.

I was wandering aimlessly around the shops by myself at the time, spending my pocket money on a few sweets at Woolworths and a bag of chips at the chip shop. Paul and his new friend, Robin, were at a football match. Suddenly I spotted one of the notorious Clark brothers across the road. My first inclination was to turn in the other direction, but on the spur of the moment I shouted across to him. 'Hoy! Martyn!'

He glanced nervously around, caught sight of me, then to my surprise darted into Marks & Spencer. Puzzled, I crossed over, nipping in between the slow-moving vehicles, and followed him into the large department store. Catching up with him, I gave him a sharp dig. 'Hoy! What's up with you? Didn't you hear me shout?'

He looked sheepish. 'Uncle's after me. That's why I ran when you shouted. I thought he'd sent you to find me.'

A Clark brother or not, we suddenly found ourselves united in a common plight to escape from the children's home. We wandered through the ladies' underwear in silence for a while.

'Want a chip?'

He nodded. 'I'm starving.'

We finished what was left of the chips.

'What'll we do now?' Martyn glanced around warily before wiping his greasy fingers over a pair of large silky bloomers.

'I thought I could go to Boston,' I said. 'My dad lives there. I think he should know how horrible it is in the home.'

'But it's miles away.'

I sucked my salty fingers. I hadn't thought of that. An assistant made her way purposefully towards us, so we made a hasty departure.

'We'll hitch,' I said decisively.

An hour later, having bus-hopped to get us out of town, we found ourselves in the open countryside. My heart lifted as we strode purposefully along the quiet country road, confidently waving our thumbs in the air to hitch a lift from a passing car or lorry. The day was beginning to turn out quite well. A lukewarm sun had come out, drying the roads and taking the dampness out of the air, and making it pleasant to walk. There was a smell of freshly ploughed fields and vegetation. Once more I had taken control of my own life. I deliberately didn't dwell on what Paul would do once he'd heard I'd run away. He'd have to cope until I could get Dad to help us. I stopped and turned around to see how far we'd come. Thanks to our jumping the buses, the town lay a good few miles behind us, and as far as the eye could see either side and ahead of us were farmhouses, barns, fields, trees and hedges.

'Hey! Look!' I followed the direction of Martyn's grubby finger. A ramshackle hut lay half hidden through the trees.

'Come on.' Scrambling through the undergrowth, we crept up to the hut, then, standing on a wooden crate, we peered through a grimy window covered in cobwebs, still glistening with the morning dew. Pieces of rusted machinery, tools and boxes surrounded a dirty wooden bench, but it was the two full bottles of beer that caught our attention. We grinned at each other, delighted, obviously both of the same mind.

A moment later there was a shattering of glass as we hurled a brick through the window. In the distance a dog barked, but otherwise there was no indication we'd been heard. Clearing the remnants of glass from the frame and using our coats as protection from splinters of wood and glass, we clambered through the window and made a beeline for the beer bottles. Holding the bottle firmly with both hands, I turned my head away and smashed the bottle top on the side of the wooden bench. A few minutes later we were satisfying our raging thirsts by swigging frothy beer from the broken bottles. It was cold and fizzy and went down extremely well with the remnants of an unwrapped toffee I found in my coat pocket. I cut it in half with a hacksaw we found in the corner and I shared it with Martyn. There were bits of fluff and hair on it and brown grease from the saw, but we didn't mind.

We felt amazingly refreshed by the time we'd finished our feast and were in a considerably happier frame of mind. It didn't seem to matter too much that no one stopped to give us a lift after that. We were in that happy haze that only a couple of pints of beer on an empty stomach can bring. Unfortunately we discovered that a couple of pints of beer on an empty stomach could bring more than just a happy haze. By mid-afternoon my head was aching and I was feeling extremely sick.

'It's the beer,' I said, retching into the hedgerow. 'It must have turned bad.'

Martyn belched. 'Oh God! I feel awful!'

By now the sun had disappeared and the grey sky hanging threateningly overhead had chilled us off. I shivered and zipped up my coat. 'I wonder how far we have to go now?' I stopped and pulled off my shoe. My feet were really sore and the hole in my sock was causing my shoe to rub painfully against my heel.

We wandered slowly passed a few stone cottages with neat fences and purple rockery flowers. I glanced anxiously up at the dark grey sky. 'It's going to start raining soon. I hope someone stops to give us a lift.' My eye lighted on an old bicycle standing at the side of one of the cottages. 'Martyn! How about borrowing that?' I pointed to the bicycle. 'We can always return it when we get to Boston.'

Martyn glanced furtively around. 'Go on, then.'

A moment later I was hurtling down the hill towards the village with Martyn sitting on the seat, clinging to my shoulders.

'We did it!' I shrieked, wobbling dangerously as we came to the crossroads. I wasn't sure how to stop, so we didn't. We just went straight over. 'At least, I did it!' I bragged. 'I took all the risks.'

'No you didn't. Look!' A pint of milk appeared in front of my nose and Martyn cackled in my ear, making me wobble precariously close to the ditch. We came to a shaky stop outside a deserted garage. Dropping the bike on the ground we sat on the grass and hungrily gulped down the bottle of milk between us. It tasted cold and smooth as it slid down my throat.

'Gruuuump!' I belched as I slurped the last dregs of milk, then hurled the empty bottle behind the hedge.

We discovered going downhill was fine, but pushing the bike uphill was quite another matter, so a few miles further on we dumped it at the side of the road, all previous moral notions of returning it to its rightful owner forgotten, although I did have a few pangs of guilt about our actions, which only goes to prove some of my Sunday school teaching on right and wrong must have had an effect somewhere along the line.

By now it was well past teatime and we were ravenously hungry, my legs ached intolerably and Martyn had developed a blister. On top of that my tongue was covered with fur, my head was aching, and I was growing colder by the minute.

We were so used to cars flashing past us as though we didn't exist that we were more than amazed when an old blue Ford Cortina pulled up a few yards ahead of us and a middle-aged lady poked her head out of the window. 'Need a lift anywhere, boys?'

We stared at her in amazement. 'Come on!' I said, pulling myself together.

She was a very countrified-looking lady with a tweed skirt, stout flat shoes and thick jacket. 'Where are you heading?' she asked. She was very well spoken.

We climbed into the back of her car and sank wearily back into the warm upholstery. 'Oh . . . er . . . Boston,' I said. 'We're going to my dad's house.'

'My goodness! You're a long way from Boston,' she said, revving up and increasing her speed.

'Yes, well, er . . .' I glanced anxiously at Martyn.

'My granny's car broke down a few miles back,' he said, without a flicker of hesitation. 'She had to take it into the garage. The man said it would only take him an hour to put it right so Granny suggested we set off walking to Boston and . . . and . . . er . . .'

' .... and she would catch us up,' I chipped in. I knew I shouldn't tell lies, but it sounded a pretty plausible story. I couldn't help but feel quite proud of myself.

'Won't she worry if she doesn't catch you up?' the lady said. I couldn't quite make out whether it was interest or disbelief she was expressing.

'No!' To get out of this warm comfortable car and walk again was unthinkable. 'She said that if the bus came along or anyone stopped to offer us a lift we could take it and she'd see us there, at Dad's place.'

'Oh?' This time there was no doubt: she sounded suspicious. 'Have you an address to go to in Boston?'

Martyn raised an eyebrow at me. 'Yes,' I said, and was able to give her my dad's address without any difficulty. After all, I'd lived there, on and off, with him and Maggie.

The lady was quiet for quite a while. Then she said, 'I'm going into Boston so I'll take you to your father's house.'

Waves of relief flooded over me. I lay back against the tartan rug and groaned at my aching legs. I was unbelievably tired. I wondered what Paul was doing. I hoped that once we got to Dad's house he'd send for Paul and we'd all be together again. I closed my eyes and ceased wondering as the gentle rocking motion of the car and my extreme tiredness brought a welcome blanket of sleep over me.

I was abruptly shaken awake some time later by Martyn. 'Mark! Dad's address. What is it again?'

I glanced out of the window. It was almost dark and the streetlights were coming on. I realised I was on vaguely familiar territory and able to direct the lady to the council estate where Dad and Maggie lived. 'That's it!' Excited, I pointed to a row of semi-detached houses. 'That's his house over there.'

We pulled up at the side of the road and Martyn leapt out of the car. 'Thank you ever so much.'

The lady gave a friendly wave and we watched her car move slowly down the road.

Martyn frowned. 'Do you think she believed us?'

I shrugged. 'Who cares. We're here now. Come on.'

Eagerly we walked up the short garden path and knocked on the door. There was no answer. We knocked again, loudly, but it was obvious Dad and Maggie weren't at home.

'Drat! If my dad's not in I suppose we could go to my Aunty Joyce's house. That's Maggie's daughter. She just lives across there.' I surveyed her unlit house anxiously.

We'd just crossed the road when a police car with flashing blue lights screeched to a halt outside my dad's house. Martyn's fingers dug into my arm.

'I bet that old bat in the car rang them!' he spat. 'You can't trust anybody these days!'

I looked around frantically for some means of escape. I refused to be caught now. Not when I was so close to my dad!

'Mark! Martyn!' A thickset policeman climbed out of his car and spotted us standing on the pavement. 'Come on, lads. I think we better take you back to the children's home, don't you? There are a lot of people worried about you.'

I almost felt Martyn's defeat as he let go of me. His arm fell to his side and his body slumped, but I wasn't beaten! Not yet, anyway! A child's bicycle was propped up against Aunty Joyce's hedge. As Martyn turned and slunk towards the police car, I spun away from him, the remaining dregs of adrenaline giving me the energy I needed to grab the handlebars, leap on to the bike and pedal as fast as I could away from the flashing blue lights. I would *not* be taken back! Not now! Not when I'd come all this way to see my dad!

The handlebars of the child's bike wobbled and to my humiliation I saw the wheel was buckled and the tyre flat. I heard the engine of the police car behind, then it caught up and kept pace with me. I glared furiously at it. Martyn sat in the back, looking scared and dirty.

'I don't think you're going to get very far on that, do you, sonny?' the policeman said, winding down his window.

Tears of frustration prickled behind my eyelids, but I wouldn't give in. I steered away from him, then, throwing the bike on to the curb, I ran back to my dad's house and, sobbing with tiredness and frustration, hammered on the door again.

The police car reversed and the policeman climbed out. 'Come on, Mark. How about coming back with your mate, eh?'

Wearily I turned towards the policeman, defeated.

It should have been a thrill having a ride in a police car, but it wasn't. They even switched the flashing lights on for us and let us wear their hats, but I refused to be patronised. When we arrived at the police station the sergeant offered us bars of chocolate while we waited for

Social Services to arrive. Martyn guzzled his hungrily but I shook my head. 'I don't want no chocolate!'

Miserable, I curled up in the corner. It was late and dark. I was tired, hungry and scared stiff because I knew I'd be in big trouble when we got home, so I turned my back on their kind gestures and stared stubbornly at the empty cream glossy walls of the police station.

That evening I had to go and stand before Uncle and Aunty Andrews, but our meeting didn't quite turn out the way I expected. I had thought they would spend time listening to our reasons for running away and perhaps promise to put everything right. However, it seemed as though nobody could really be bothered to listen to our views on anything. They were more intent on expressing theirs! Strangely enough it was the rest of the children who were the greatest encouragement. They wanted to know what we'd done and how far we'd travelled, and so we began expanding on our story to the rest of our brothers and sisters to such an extent that for the next few weeks we were heroes and adventurers. It gave me a good feeling, being so popular, and helped ease the burning pain at the back of my mind that once again there'd been nobody there when I'd needed them.

Chapter 4

I never thought for one moment that I would find myself happy at Ivy Cottage, but as the warm summer nights lengthened and we were allowed extra time to play out in the garden our new playmates became more than just numbers on towels and toothbrushes: they became brothers and sisters, and we began to enjoy having such a big family, even though it meant sharing the love and attention given by the houseparents between seventeen of us. Slowly but surely, Paul and I settled into this new and more stable environment.

Miss Vernon called occasionally to see us. I was still fond of her. After all, I reasoned, she had always tried to help us in the past. But I was wary. I no longer threw my arms around her neck to welcome her as a friend. Friends don't let you down. Friends don't make promises they can't keep. Miss Vernon had done both, and I didn't feel I could trust her as much as I used to. However, I conceded, she had probably been forced into taking us away from Mr and Mrs Tait, because she was bound by the rules and regulations of the Social Services system, just as we were bound by the rules and regulations set down for us by the children's home. But I was still left with a lot of unanswered questions racing around in my head.

When she called she gave us news of our family. Our sisters had been fostered out into different homes. Dad was still unemployed and with Maggie and my mum was still in and out of hospital. She and her husband had moved, but their new home was only a small one-bedroom bungalow, so there wasn't really any room for us.

'But don't worry, boys,' Miss Vernon reassured us. 'I'm doing all I can to find a new foster home for you.'

I wasn't quite sure whether I wanted that. Deep down I longed to be part of a real family, like we were with Mum and Dad Tait, Laura and David. People who loved us and were willing to give us a permanent home and a sense of security. That surely would be better than being stuck in a children's home. Or would it? What if we just got settled in a new foster home and they took us away again? It was all very unsettling. In fact, I was glad when Miss Vernon waved us goodbye after each visit so we could focus our thoughts away from our uncertain future and on to more pleasant issues. Like the summer holidays, for instance.

For two weeks every year the children took their annual holiday in a large house in the seaside town of Mablethorpe. The excitement in the children's home surrounding this holiday was contagious, and for the first time in my life I found I was really looking forward to something and I wasn't disappointed. I discovered Mablethorpe was all that Gary and the other children had said it would be. The fair proved to be full of scary rides, slot machines, candyfloss, ducks to catch on the end of a long pole with a prize every time. Sometimes we took a boat out on the lake in the park and raced each other, or there were donkey rides on the beach. There was always someone wanting to crab hunt or play football. By the end of the first week we were all as brown as berries and for the first time I really felt as though I belonged to Ivy Cottage Children's Home.

The holiday came to an end far too quickly and a new term at school began. Paul and I celebrated our ninth and eleventh birthdays and then, unexpectedly, Miss Vernon called to see us.

'It's a Mr and Mrs Bradshaw,' she explained as we sat around the table in the empty dining room. 'They've two children your ages and they're very keen to foster. How do you feel about letting them take you out to see how you all get on together?' She looked from me to Paul then back at me again. 'Well? What do you think?'

What did I think? I was sick of thinking! I had just started to feel comfortable with my new brothers and sisters in the children's home, and now this! Was it worth being uprooted again? I was aware of Paul watching me closely, waiting for me to make the decision. I not only had myself to consider. I chewed my lip thoughtfully.

The strict discipline and rules and regulations were a real pain. I hated them! If we were fostered out again we'd be doing away with all that, and you never know, it might just work out this time. It would be nice to belong to someone again. Mr and Mrs Bradshaw might even be as nice as Mr and Mrs Tait.

'When will they come?' I asked.

Miss Vernon smiled. 'Tomorrow if you want, Mark.'

I looked at Paul. I could tell he wanted them to. 'OK.'

Mr and Mrs Bradshaw were very nice people. I liked them straight away. They were both very tall and slim. He had a moustache and was extremely smart, even in casual clothes. Mrs Bradshaw had twinkling blue eyes, long brown hair tied back with a colourful scarf and what looked like very expensive jewellery. They both smiled and joked a lot and tried to make us feel at ease when they took us back to their home for tea and to meet their children.

'What do you think?' I asked Paul after their fourth visit.

'I think they're nice. I like them.' Paul was more absorbed in the toy tank they'd bought him, which, according to him, fired real shells.

'Mmm.' I examined my armoured car. 'They buy great presents. I think they've got a lot of money don't you?'

He nodded. 'Do you . . . do you think they want us?' He said it almost as though he didn't care, but I could tell he did.

'I don't know, Paulie. It's hard to tell. They seem to like us and they seem to be serious about fostering.' I was frightened to hope.

'I think . . . I think I would like to be fostered by them.'

I raised my eyebrows, surprised. Paul usually waited for me to make the decisions. 'Yes, I think I'd like to be fostered by them as well,' I said. 'So don't go and mess things up by doing something stupid. Right?'

November 5th, Guy Fawkes Night, at Ivy Cottage was one of the highlights of the year. We'd spent the last two weeks collecting branches and firewood for the bonfire in the garden and making a guy for the top. We had a magnificent display of fireworks, which Uncle was going to set off for us, and our own personal packets of sparklers. In the kitchen there were baked potatoes, roast chestnuts, soup, hot dogs with all the 'bits' and marshmallows on sticks. The weather forecast said it would be cold but fine. It promised to be a perfect evening, especially for me and Paul, who had been allowed our own special guests – Mr and Mrs Bradshaw.

Uncle had just lit the bonfire in the garden when Aunty Gwen called for us. 'Mark! Paul! Mr and Mrs Bradshaw have arrived.'

Excitedly we raced to the front door to greet our guests. 'I helped make the guy,' Paul informed Mrs Bradshaw.

'Really?' She smiled down at his eager face. She really was very pretty.

'And we've got lots to eat,' I said. 'Would you like to come into the back garden and see the bonfire?'

Mr Bradshaw laughed. 'I'd love to come, Mark.' He placed two nicely wrapped parcels on the hall table and winked. 'These are for you and Paul. You can open them later, son.'

Son! Son! I laughed excitedly, stammered my thanks, then dragged them out into the cold night air where the bonfire was crackling and spitting and sending bright orange and red flames high into the dark clear sky. Warmly wrapped in our scarves and gloves and big heavy coats, we stood around the bonfire watching Uncle set off rockets and Catherine wheels, and laughing at the girls every time a banger cracked. All the time I was conscious of Mr Bradshaw standing beside me with his hand resting lightly on my shoulder. I reached out with my long stick to cook my roast chestnuts, the fire warming my cold face. I waved across at Paul and Mrs Bradshaw, standing on the other side. They held sparklers and were laughing over some private joke. Contented, I licked my fingers, sticky with the homemade toffee Aunty Gwen had cooked, and a wave of happiness washed over me as I gazed around at my friends and savoured the promise of a new bright future with these two lovely people.

'Hot dogs and soup indoors after I've set off these Catherine wheels, children!' Uncle shouted. 'How does that sound?'

A great cheer went up and a few minutes later Paul and I had joined the stampede of children charging towards the house for more food. I was so engrossed in devouring a massive hot dog smothered in tomato sauce, onions and mustard that at first I didn't notice Mr and Mrs Bradshaw were missing. I looked around the sea of faces squashed in the kitchen.

'Paul! Where are the Bradshaws?' I shouted over the heads of the other children.

He shook his head. 'I haven't seen them since we came in the house.'

I pushed my way through the congestion of hungry children to the hall door where I was just in time to see them coming out of the office with Aunty Andrews. They all looked extremely solemn.

'Ah! Mark.' Aunty Andrews spotted me standing with a fistful of hot dogs in a bun. 'Mr and Mrs Bradshaw have to go now. Would you go and find your brother and meet me in the office, please.'

I glanced at Mr Bradshaw. He smiled then averted his eyes. 'What's wrong Aunty?'

'Just do as I say, Mark. Go and find your brother and come to my office.'

I sensed something was wrong. My stomach lurched and suddenly I didn't feel like my hot dog anymore. Mrs Bradshaw dabbed her nose with her handkerchief and stared at her shoes. I turned abruptly, pushed my way through the huddle of bodies standing behind the door, and grabbed Paul.

'Get off! Get off! What's the matter with you?' Paul struggled to release himself.

'Don't ask! Just come!' I hissed fiercely. He recognised the urgency in my tone and didn't need a second warning.

As we headed towards Aunty Andrew's office I heard the Bradshaws' car pull away from the front door. My heart sank. They hadn't even stayed to say goodbye. Feeling slightly sick, and it wasn't due to too many hot dogs, I knocked on the office door, then we walked in to Uncle Andrew's 'Come in, boys.' We sat down nervously on the low settee in the corner of the room. Uncle sat in his usual big leather chair in front of the window and Aunty Andrews sat behind her desk, her half-moon glasses resting neatly on the end of her nose. She played with her pen in a preoccupied sort of way before smiling kindly at us and saying, 'Mark, Paul, I'm afraid I have some bad news for you.'

That old familiar knot of tension began growing in my stomach. 'I don't want to know,' I said, frowning and shaking my head. 'I don't want to know.'

Aunty Andrews came from behind the big desk and sat down on the small stool beside us. 'I'm afraid that for various reasons Mr and Mrs Bradshaw can't go through with their plans to foster you,' she said softly. 'I'm sorry, boys. I'm so sorry.'

'I don't believe you,' I said shakily. 'You're lying. You must be lying.'

Uncle came over and perched on the chair opposite us. 'I'm sorry, boys, but it's true.' He rested his big hand on my shoulder. 'I know how upsetting this must be for you.'

'We did something wrong, didn't we?' I persisted. 'We did something they didn't like?'

Paul bust into floods of tears. 'I thought they was . . . going to . . . to foster us!' he sobbed. 'They bought us presents . . . and . . . and . . .'

'No, Mark, neither of you did anything wrong,' Uncle answered. 'It wasn't your fault. You mustn't blame yourself, or Paul.'

'Then why?' I stood up. The knot had moved from my stomach up to my chest, making it difficult for me to breath. I couldn't believe we were being rejected again.

'This can't be happening!' My voice raised in anger. 'Not again! No! No!' I turned to run out of the door, but Uncle grabbed my arm.

'Calm down, Mark!'

As I struggled to release myself the knot in my chest exploded into fury. 'I hate you! I hate them! I hate! Hate . . .'

Uncle shook me. 'Mark! Mark!'

Paul flung himself on Uncle. 'Let my brother go!'

'Calm down, both of you!' Aunty struggled to make herself heard above our shouting.

'I don't ever want to be fostered again!' I screamed, hysterically. 'Do you hear me? Never . . . ever . . . again!'

'Yes, I hear you, Mark,' Aunty said softly, resting her hand gently on my head. I backed away from her. 'I hear you and you don't have to be. I shall speak to your social worker and suggest you stay here with us until you're sixteen. Is that what you would like?'

'I don't care! I hate Miss Vernon! I hate her!' I broke down into uncontrollable sobs. Paul stood beside me, his eyes wide with fear. I was usually the strong one. The one who kept us together. I pulled my arm sharply away from Uncle and, still sobbing, violently flung open the office door. Through a haze of tears I saw Uncle reach out to grab me again.

'Let him go, Uncle,' I heard Aunty say. 'Let him work it out of his system. He'll come around eventually.'

As I raced up the stairs I heard Paul quietly sobbing after me, 'Mark! What'll we do, Mark? Mark! Don't go.' But there seemed to be a knot in my head now, the same as the one that had been in my chest, and I couldn't think. I just knew I had to get away from everybody. Even my little brother.

As I raced past Richard on the stairs he called, 'Hey! What's wrong with you, Edwards?', but I ignored him and ran into the bedroom, slamming the door behind me. I flung myself on to the bed and buried my head in the pillow. The pain was so bad I felt as though my head would explode.

'I hate . . . hate . . . hate . . . *you*, God! *Do you hear me?* I'll never forgive you! Never! *Never!*' And that old familiar song reverberated around my head with the pain. *I'm nobody's child. Nobody loves me, nobody cares.*

Chapter 5

He was dark brown, furry, had grey ears and stood about twelve inches high. His blue-brown glassy eyes stared unwavering into mine, forming an instant bond of friendship. Someone had knitted him a bright red waistcoat and a pale yellow hat with a green pom-pom on top.

'Merry Christmas, Mark.' Aunty Gwen ruffled my hair as she passed. I beamed up at her.

'Is he for me?' I lifted the teddy bear from his Christmas wrappings.

'Yes, he's all yours, Mark.'

I stroked the soft fur, then, conscious that boys my age don't play with teddy bears, nonchalantly pushed him back into his wrappings as though I didn't care. But I knew I did. There was something about this second-hand teddy bear that had appealed to me the moment I'd spotted him at the local Christmas fair a week ago. He'd needed somebody to want him, somebody to care for him, but I'd forced myself to walk away from the stall because I had no money. Perhaps Aunty Gwen had seen how much I liked him and had bought him for me? But now wasn't the time to cuddle him. Not with all the other children squealing with excitement as they unwrapped their Christmas presents. I opened my other parcels. I had a few books, a board game, sweets and a pair of gloves. They were all gifts donated from churches for children in care.

My mind flashed back to a previous Christmas with the Tait family, when I'd been given my lovely Arsenal football kit and all those other wonderful new toys, but I didn't dwell on it. To be truthful, there was so much going on in the children's home in the way of parties and outings and present making for each other that I actually found very little time to mope around after that dreadful Guy Fawkes Night. I was too busy enjoying myself. I hadn't even found time to get into trouble!

'That must be a record,' Aunty Gwen had remarked with a twinkle in her eye. Gary and I had gained the reputation of being the main mischief-makers.

Teddy became a permanent fixture in my bed. In fact, when I found out that most of the other children took a doll or cuddly toy to bed with them, I didn't feel so silly snuggling up with my teddy bear. That was until Barry came on the scene. He was one of the older boys. He was nearly sixteen, and was always complaining that he didn't had any flared trousers or shirts with big collars, so he was out of fashion. His greasy black hair always seemed to hang like a shaggy dog's over his spotty face and he rarely smiled. Gary said he thought he was weird. I couldn't make my mind up about him. But during the last couple of weeks he had seemed to put himself out to buy me sweets or give me a hug.

I bumped into him as I came out of the steamy bathroom late one night.

'Whoops! Off to bed with your teddy bear then, Mark?'

I knew my face was turning red with embarrassment. 'Yes,' I said, concentrating hard on fastening the buttons of my pyjamas.

'Here, let me help you with that.' He fastened the last two buttons on my jacket and I had to let him because he was blocking my way into the corridor. 'I suppose you need something to cuddle and keep you warm, eh?'

I nodded.

'Can't have been easy for you, coming to the children's home.' He placed his hand on my shoulder and I stepped back into the steamy bathroom.

'It's all right. I'm getting used to it.' I was rather puzzled as to why this older boy should bother showing such concern over me.

He stepped into the bathroom after me and closed the door behind him. 'What you need is a cuddle from someone real. Not a teddy bear,' he whispered, reaching out and gently pulling me towards him. He was hot and sweaty and smelled heavily of aftershave. I stood perfectly still, confused and a little embarrassed as to what was happening, as his hands moved slowly over my shoulders, gently squeezing my arms and fondling my face. Then he bent his head and whispered indistinguishable words in my ear. I didn't like it! His breath was hot. I stepped back, pressing my shoulder blades hard up against the bathroom wall. The weight of his heavy body pressed up against mine, then his hands began groping my body, fondling, squeezing where they shouldn't. This was horrible! Horrible! A surge of sheer panic gripped me. I opened my mouth to scream but he pressed his hand firmly across my lips to silence me.

'Shhh!' he spat. 'Be quiet!'

How could I be quiet? What was happening to me wasn't right. It was repulsive! It made me feel sick! I struggled to get out of his grasp, but as his grip tightened and his body pushed mine roughly against the cold, tiled wall, my mind reacted and began to shut out what was happening to me. Far away in the distance I heard a muffled scream. It seemed to echo around the small bathroom over and over again. I caught a glimpse of two figures struggling through the steamy bathroom mirror. The small one was writhing, his face twisted, eyes filled with terror, and his mouth was open. With a shock I realised it was me, and the voice screaming was mine. Then there was the sound of banging on the bathroom door and Aunty Freda shouting something, but even though my brain was too confused to take it in I knew I wanted Aunty Freda to get to me more than anything else. Then I heard Uncle's deep voice and a moment later the bathroom door was forced open. I don't remember anything else after that.

They told me I needn't be afraid of Barry any more because he'd been sent away immediately to a 'special home' for disturbed older children. 'Forget about him,' I was advised. 'Forget all about it.' So I did. I buried it behind my brick wall with all the other hurtful, painful memories and I allowed my life to resume its normal and secure routine.

Every Sunday a group of us would accompany Uncle and Aunty to the local Methodist church. It was very boring. I only went because I had to. After all, what had God done for me? Nothing! He was probably too busy sorting out wars and famines started by grown-ups to be bothered with what was happening to children like me and Paul, so I didn't bother singing the hymns and got up to as much mischief as I could.

Unfortunately my behaviour was so disruptive that the minister barred me, Gary and two other boys from his Sunday service and as punishment we were sent to the Baptist church. This was much better. They had a Boys' Brigade, and it was worth sitting through a Sunday service just to be allowed to be part of that. In fact, the Sunday service wasn't too bad, as far as Sunday services go. Every so often there was a baptismal service, and Gary and I would sit on the edge of our seats, clinging to the balcony rail, watching the people being dunked and hoping and praying they'd drown somebody. Much to our disappointment they never did!

As I grew into adolescence, God became a vague figure in the background that I even less than vaguely believed in, despite my regular visits to church. I couldn't identify with either the Fatherhood of God because of my experience of fathers or the love of God because of the lack of love in my own life. I struggled to find answers to questions like 'Who am I?' 'If God is a God of love, why have so many awful things been allowed to happen to me?' 'Why does nobody want me?' 'Why has God cruelly snatched away the few kind people who have shown any interest in us?'

There were compensations of having to go to church, however. As I reached the age of fifteen and girls replaced toys, our weekly jaunt to the Baptist church took on a new meaning, but not necessarily a spiritual one.

We had a short visit from Dad once. He said he was almost certain to get the job he'd applied for, and before we knew it we'd all be together again, but I was almost glad to see him go. I was afraid of any more disappointments. Mum paid us the occasional visit, and my oldest sister, Shene, and her new husband, Graham, often invited us to spend the weekend with them, as did my other sisters, Jenny and Maxine. These were the first feelings of really being wanted that I'd experienced and it felt good to have someone to belong to.

Marked changes took place at Ivy Cottage as well. Our bedrooms no longer had plain cream, painted walls, faded rugs and brown linoleum. They'd been decorated with colourful patterned wallpaper, fitted carpets and new bedspreads. The whole place had a more cheerful, homely feel. We were even allowed to put pictures up on the walls. I plastered my corner of the bedroom with a full-length poster of the actress Lindsay Wagner in her role as Jamie Sommers, the superwoman with bionic limbs. I adored her! At that vulnerable age of fifteen, this beautiful lady fulfilled my wildest fantasies, and epitomised for me everything a member of the opposite sex should be. It was wonderful having a full-length poster of her looking down at me in my bed every night.

Unfortunately I was still no great shakes at school. 'Limited ability' were the words constantly hurled in my direction and the PE teacher shook his head despairingly at my ability at games. Even though I attended remedial literacy classes, I'd never been able to catch up with my year group, and would frequently be left to struggle on alone while the teachers concentrated on the brighter pupils. Now, heading towards the frightening prospect of my CSE examinations, I persevered to understand the work set before us. Although Aunty Freda had never been my favourite Aunty, for once she came up trumps, and spent hours with me and my homework. 'He hasn't got it in him,' I overheard her tell Uncle Andrews as I peered through the keyhole of his study. 'I can't see Mark amounting to much at all. Shame, really.'

I arrived back at the home late one September afternoon to find a female figure standing at our kitchen sink. The first thing I noticed was her tight blue jeans, or rather the shape that was poured into them.

Aunty Freda bustled in. 'Oh, Mark, this is Aunty Lindsay, the new houseparent. Say "hello", then go and get changed. And Mark, remove your school bag from the kitchen table, please.' I ignored her. I couldn't take my eyes off the newcomer.

She turned and smiled at me. She was the most beautiful thing I had ever seen. She was young, about twenty-three or twenty-four, and had tawny, shoulder-length hair, which curled around a perfect oval face. She had deep blue eyes, long dark lashes and a sensuous, wide smile. The long, loose, pale blue jumper she wore couldn't conceal her trim and sexy figure. Although she bore no great physical resemblance to my heroine, Lindsay Wagner, it could very well have been her standing in front of me. The similarities in the name and the smile, just the way my heroine in her poster smiled down at me in my bed each night: it was like my fantasies had been brought to life.

'I, er . . .' I could feel my cheeks turning red. 'Er . . .' I found my tongue. 'Hi!' Then, to my own acute embarrassment, I turned and fled.

It was Lee who started the argument later that evening. Lee and I had never got on since we'd set the bins alight in the park one day, and when he began taunting me about fancying Aunty Lindsay, I completely lost my temper.

'Right, you've asked for it!' I stormed angrily up the stairs after him with Gary hard on my heels, and just missed getting my nose broken when he slammed the bathroom door in my face. I hammered on the door. 'When I get in there, Lee, your head is going down the loo!'

The only response from behind the door was a 'Yeah!' and the toilet being flushed.

'What's all this racket about?' I didn't need to turn around to see who it was.

Gary answered for me.

'Just fooling around, Aunty Lindsay.'

I remained with my back to her, silent, hoping she'd go away.

'Well, perhaps you'd be better off fooling around outside, don't you think so?'

'Yes, Aunty.' Gary gave me a nudge and without even a glance in her direction I turned and, brushing past her, muttered to Gary, in a loud enough voice for her to hear, 'Who the hell does she think she is?'

'I heard that, Mark. Would you come back here, please?'

I ignored her. Gary glanced at me apprehensively as we heard her footsteps behind us.

'Just a minute, young man, I want a word with you.' She gave Gary a wave of dismissal as she grabbed me firmly by the shoulder and turned me to face her. 'Didn't you hear me telling you to come back?'

I glared at her, blatantly challenging her to reprimand me. Her lovely blue eyes held and probed questioningly into mine. 'Why are you staring so defiantly at me, Mark?'

I didn't answer, but my glare wavered at the softness in her voice and I dropped my head and stared at the carpet.

'I hope we can be friends, Mark, I really do, but when I ask you to do something I don't expect to be ignored. Do you understand?' She put her finger under my chin and lifted my head. I kept my eyes lowered.

'I'm sorry,' I muttered.

She smiled. 'That's all right, Mark. I'll overlook it this time, but don't ignore me again.'

It only took a matter of days for Lindsay to become the most popular houseparent at Ivy Cottage, but then she didn't have too much competition. The others were either too old, too strict or too fat, whereas Lindsay was just perfect. She often took over from Aunty Freda in helping me with my homework. She would sit beside me at the dining room table, smelling warm and scenty as she explained what was obviously beyond my comprehension. Occasionally our shoulders would brush and she'd laugh at some of the things I said, or she'd listen sympathetically when I talked about the difficulties of schoolwork or disappointments with my parents.

Watching her closely at the Guy Fawkes fireworks display held on the village green a few weeks later was like bringing to life all the fantasies I'd held for my heroine Lindsay Wagner. My Lindsay looked lovely. She'd pulled a bright green woollen hat firmly over her long tawny hair and a matching scarf was wrapped twice around her neck. The warmth of the bonfire had brought a flush to her cheeks. I couldn't take my eyes off her. She gave one of the younger children a gentle rebuke for venturing too close to the fire and held on to the child's arm. Inexplicably, I found myself being envious of the close physical contact between her and the child. Suddenly she turned, and as I caught her eye a warm tingle ran through my whole body. She smiled, and I found myself smiling back. It seemed as if we stood like that for ages before she was forced to turn away because of the demands from one of the younger children. That was the trouble really; they were always demanding her attention.

It was a wonderful evening. We set off bangers to scare the girls and I flirted with Lindsay, as much as a fifteen year old knew how to. Then later that evening Gary and I pinched her hat, and she entered into the spirit of the game, laughing and joking with us as she chased us around the field trying to get it back. Then it all turned sour. It was my fault really. I didn't mean to become disruptive. All I was trying to do was gain her attention, but as usual I took the whole thing too far.

We were being driven home in the minibus at the time and I thought I'd try my new trick on her. Standing up behind her, I placed one hand on her head then brought the other one forcibly down on top of it, making a sound like an egg being cracked. I hadn't meant to hurt her. I was just carried away by the excitement of the evening, but Lindsay gasped with pain and, wincing, dropped her head into her arms. She remained like that for only a moment, then, turning angrily around, she snapped, 'Why did you do that? You stupid boy!'

For some ridiculous reason I thought she was still joking with me, the way she had been all evening. I stood up, leant forward and laughed loudly in her face. Furious, she turned on me and raised her hand. I don't know if she meant to hit me. I think it was meant to be more like a cuff around the earhole, but in an unsteady bus I somehow received a resounding slap across my face. Stunned, I flopped back in my seat, while Lindsay, obviously still hurt and shaken, wordlessly turned her back on me and sat down. Hurt and confused, I glared at the back of her head for the rest of the journey.

Eventually the driver pulled up at the children's home and we filed off. Lindsay turned to face me as the last child left. She had the grace to look slightly apologetic. 'Mark, that smack was . . .'

I swung angrily around. 'You're just like everybody else!' I couldn't stop my voice from shaking. 'You pretend to care, but you don't! I hate you! Do you hear me? I hate you!'

I missed supper that evening. The last thing I wanted to do was face Lindsay, so I made up an excuse and lay on my bed looking at the ceiling and allowing the warm feelings I'd had for her earlier to turn sour. I should have known better than to start trusting Lindsay. I'd sworn never to let anyone get that close to me again! I rolled over in my bed and shut my eyes tightly, but the image of her standing at the bonfire with her cheeks glowing in the firelight haunted my dreams for the rest of the night.

The next few weeks I spent trying to avoid her. If she walked into the television room I'd walk out. If I saw her walking towards me in the corridor I'd change direction. I refused, absolutely refused, to forgive her! Besides which, I was secretly gaining some strange form of pleasure when I saw her watching me, as if she was trying to fathom out why I was behaving like I was. I didn't actually know why I behaved that way; all I knew was that here was someone whose very presence sent my emotions into turmoil and I was confused because I didn't know how to handle them.

Unfortunately our paths had to cross at some time and that time happened to be when I was on kitchen duty. She was standing with her back to me at the sink washing dishes and gave me a friendly 'hello' in greeting. Deliberately ignoring her, I picked up a tea towel and began drying dishes, sadistically enjoying the uncomfortable silence in the kitchen. Spotting the remnants of tomato sauce on one of the dishes she hadn't washed properly, I venomously threw it back into the sink. Dirty frothy water splashed all over her jumper. She jumped back, but must have decided to ignore my action, because she continued washing up in silence. I didn't like being ignored! Picking up the stack of plates I'd just dried, I dropped the whole lot into the kitchen sink. Water spilled over the top, on to Lindsay, the floor and her shoes. She turned on me, fuming.

'I've just about had enough of you, young man!'

I hurled the wet tea towel at her. 'Then dry the flaming dishes yourself!' I yelled, and stormed out of the kitchen.

'You have a job to do like everyone else, Mark! Now come back here and sort these dishes out!'

Ignoring her, I darted into the boot room and slammed the door behind me. She followed me inside. I tried to dodge past her but she grabbed my arm.

'Let . . . me . . . go!' I struggled to get out of her grasp.

'Mark! Mark, listen to me! I'm sorry if I've hurt your feelings. I truly want to be your friend, but you keep treating me with such utter contempt. Why?'

Why? I didn't know why. I broke free and raced up to my room before she caught the tears spilling down my face.

I knew my behaviour would draw Uncle's attention to me eventually, so it came as no surprise when I was summoned into his office a few days later.

'Mark, it has come to my attention that you're having problems with Aunty Lindsay?'

He spoke kindly, but I was embarrassed. This was something I could not talk about.

'I'm speaking to you, Mark.'

'Yes,' I muttered.

'Do you want to talk to me about it?'

I shook my head.

Uncle paused for a moment before he said, 'We need to ensure a smoothly run home, Mark, and being insubordinate to Aunty Lindsay, or sulky when she gives time to the other children, or stubborn when she asks you to do something, just causes friction and jealousies. This behaviour really cannot be tolerated in this house.'

I tried to focus on my brick wall. Tried to ignore the whirlwind spinning around my head. How had Uncle come to know all this? Had somebody told him? Who had told? Gary? No it wouldn't be Gary. Lindsay? Lindsay!

'I'm fully aware all this nonsense started because Aunty Lindsay had cause to discipline you on Bonfire Night, which, I might add, she has every right to do. Do you understand?'

I nodded again.

'Good.' Uncle smiled at me and in a gentler tone added, 'Now then, run along, and don't let me hear any more reports of you having an attitude problem with Aunty Lindsay. But I'm sure after our little talk that won't be the case, will it, Mark?'

'No, Uncle.'

'Good.' He rose to his feet and opened the door, indicating quite clearly the interview was at an end.

I ran out of the back door and into the cold dark December evening to 'my' tree. The one at the bottom of the garden by the brick wall. I clenched my fists and hammered on its rough trunk. *How could she tell Uncle on me like this? Why does it hurt so much?* The tears began streaming down my face, a welcome release from my deep emotions. I rested my forehead against the cold, hard bough. Why did no one seem to care how *I* felt? *Me?*

The one person who seemed to care has . . . has . . . bloody well betrayed me . . . like everyone else! I hate her! I hate her! A Sunday school story unexpectedly flashed through my mind. There was one man who knew exactly what it was like to have someone around you, helping you with your work, pretending to be your friend, only to discover that that friend could betray you without a second thought. Except that Judas had been paid thirty pieces of silver! Did Jesus feel as horrible as this when he realised he'd been betrayed? I slid down the trunk of the tree and lay sobbing on the wet grass. I didn't notice the dampness soaking through my trousers nor the chill in the winter air. I was conscious only of a gnawing pain inside me.

Eventually I calmed down, exhausted by my mental ordeal of hating. A glimmer of light filtered through the downstairs curtains of the living room where the children sat watching television. One or two lights shone in the bedrooms upstairs where the smaller children had retired early or were playing. Everyone was involved in doing his or her own thing. No one was missing me. No one wanted me. I wasn't important in anyone's life.

'Mark?'

I lifted my head. She was walking towards me, her coat wrapped around her shoulders to keep her warm from the cold December evening. She came up to where I lay and stood looking down at me, then, kneeling down, she reached out her hand and rested it on my shoulder. 'What's wrong, Mark?' she asked gently.

'You reported me to Aunty and Uncle didn't you?' I glared angrily at her.

She shook her head. 'No, Mark. I didn't report you to anyone.'

'I don't believe you. You betrayed me. You told Uncle and Aunty on me.' I stood up and shrugged her hand off my shoulder. The dampness had soaked through my clothes and I was shivering with the cold, but I didn't care. This hollow empty vacuum inside was almost a friend to me by now. The vow that I'd made on the swing, that I'd never let anyone get behind my brick wall to hurt me again, came to mind. How was it that Lindsay had wheedled her way in? How? A surge of anger at my own weakness and her cleverness rose to the surface. 'Get lost, Aunty Lindsay!' I shouted. 'Stop pretending you care! I've lived without anyone caring for fifteen years. I don't need it now!'

Even through the darkness I could see the hurt in her eyes. What was wrong with me that I could hurt the one thing in my life that I loved with such passion and depth? I turned and ran indoors.

Chapter 6

Ten days before Christmas Uncle announced that he and Aunty Andrews would be going to Wales for four days to visit relatives. As Aunty Freda was also taking a few days' leave and Aunty Gwen was sick, Aunty Lindsay would be left in charge. A residential social worker was coming in to help her.

'But I don't want you to worry, children,' he said. 'We'll be back in time for all the Christmas festivities.'

I wasn't worried! I was absolutely delighted at this unexpected change of routine.

'Meanwhile,' he continued, 'I would like you to do as much as you can to help Aunty Lindsay and Hazel, the social worker.' He frowned at us, warningly. 'And no upsetting cook or the domestic staff while we're away. Do you hear me?'

We nodded, attempting to look as angelic as possible in case he changed his mind and stayed.

The following evening Fram asked me if I would give him a hand with his paper round. I hesitated. Dominaco Fragalie, or 'Fram' as he was generally called, was a dark swarthy lad of Italian origin whose mother, obviously under the impression they never fed us at the children's home, frequently invited me back for the most enormous helpings of dinner. Fram had become a good friend. So had his mother!

'Well . . . we're supposed to ask permission if we're going to be late back from school, but extra money . . . Yeah! OK then.'

Unfortunately it was nearly seven o'clock by the time we'd finished. Guiltily I crept in through the front door and tiptoed towards the staircase.

'Mark!'

I jumped. The kitchen door stood open and Lindsay was seated at the table, writing. One glance at her angry face was enough. I took to my heels and fled upstairs, slamming the bedroom door behind me. Then I sat on the bed, nervously waiting for the inevitable. Her footsteps thudded up the stairs. On the spur of the moment I leapt up, grabbed the key to the fire exit door and swung it open. A blast of cold air swept into the room. I stepped outside, but in a few short strides Lindsay had grasped my arm and hauled me back inside. She was stronger than I imagined, and you didn't need an academic qualification to work out she was absolutely furious. I struggled, spurred on by obstanacy, but she held me firmly with one hand while the other slammed the door behind me. 'Now then, young man!' She pushed me towards the bed. 'Explain yourself!'

Angry at being reprimanded like a child, I sat on the bed with my back to her and gazed down at my hands, black with newspaper print. I had no intention of telling her.

'I'm waiting for an explanation, Mark. Didn't you realise we'd be worried sick when you didn't come in for tea?'

I turned my head slowly in her direction and smirked, secretly pleased that she'd been worried. She didn't like that. Her voice rose in anger.

'You could at least have had the decency to come into the kitchen to offer me an explanation. Instead you rush straight upstairs like a silly stubborn child!'

Child! Never in my wildest fantasies would Lindsay Wagner, my heroine, call me a child!

'God knows I've tried to understand you over the last few weeks, but all you ever do is treat me with utter contempt!'

Tried to understand me? I wished I could believe that. I rested my chin in my hands and sat hunched on the bed staring at my poster. The slightest indication that I was responding could knock down the wall of protection I'd been building over the last few years. I'd never let her in. I'd never let her hurt me. Never!

She sat on my bed, covering my grazed, ink-stained hands with hers. 'Mark, I know you hate me.'

Hate her? Slowly I lifted my eyes to meed hers. 'Leave me alone.'

'No, Mark, I will not leave you alone,' she said gently. 'Whether you believe me or not, I happen to care about you.'

'And I suppose your idea of caring is smacking me around the face for no good reason and reporting me to Uncle and Aunty!' I snapped.

'You know I didn't deliberately slap you across the face. I reacted because you were extremely disorderly in the bus and I was there to keep order. Besides which, you had hurt me. However, I didn't report what had happened. There was no need to. You made it so obvious yourself that I was actually reprimanded for being too soft with you!'

'Oh yeah, I'm sure!' My tone of sarcasm obviously angered her and her patience snapped.

'What you need, Mark Edwards, is a good hard spanking!'

If what I needed was a good hard spanking then why didn't she give it to me? If she cared for me she'd give me what I needed, but I didn't say anything.

She took a deep breath. 'Right!' she snapped. 'As I'm as mad as hell and you're not in the frame of mind to talk, I'm leaving. I've neglected the other children long enough. I suggest you change out of your school uniform then come to the kitchen for something to eat, and as punishment for tonight's behaviour you're grounded for the rest of the week. Is that clear?'

Without waiting for me to respond she stood up and marched out of the bedroom. She didn't care! She was ignoring me again, and I didn't like to be ignored! I would *not* be ignored! In a spate of uncontrolled fury I jumped up, snatched the wooden hairbrush from my bedside table and hurled it through the open bedroom door towards her receding figure. To my horror it narrowly skimmed past her head and landed on the hall floor with a clatter. I held my breath and for a split second there was a stunned silence, then, shaking with either fright or anger, I'm not sure which, she picked up the hairbrush and moved menacingly back into my bedroom. For a moment I though she was going to spank me with it.

'Go on, Lindsay,' I willed her. 'Spank me! Show me you care for me by giving me what you think I need the most. Go on!'

'You stupid, stupid child!' she shouted, brandishing the brush in my face. Her knuckles were white around the handle of the brush and she was shaking with anger. 'Count yourself lucky this didn't hit me, otherwise I might have done something I would have regretted!' She slammed the brush down on the bedside table. 'For goodness' sake, Mark, grow up, will you? Violence isn't going to solve the problem you have with me. Now! Get changed and go downstairs for dinner.'

Without another word she turned and marched out of my bedroom and I could tell by the sound of her footsteps thudding down the stairs that she was still mad with me.

I threw myself full length on to the bed in remorse. What had I done? What on earth had possessed me to throw that bloody brush! I closed my eyes, but the tears fell anyway. I punched my fury into my pillow until I had no energy left, then, covering my face with my dirty hands, I wept into them, wishing I was a million miles away.

When the tears had dried up I lay back on my pillow, staring at the ceiling. If I hated her so much, why did I feel like this? I moved my head so that I could see my poster. 'I don't hate her, do I?' I asked my heroine. She didn't answer – she just smiled provocatively back at me. 'I love her, don't I? I really love her.' The realisation left me feeling more confused than ever.

It was hunger more than the threat of more punishment that drove me downstairs for tea. Hazel, the residential social worker who'd come to help us out, was in the kitchen tidying up. She was young, the same age as Lindsay, but was married and more experienced in childcare work. She was very pretty, had long blonde hair and a soft Irish accent. We all thought she was lovely.

'There you go, Mark,' she said, handing me a plate of baked beans on toast. 'The kettle will be boiled in a minute and I'll make you a cup of tea.'

Tears stung behind my eyelids at the kindness in her voice. It was quiet in the dining room and a relief to have space to myself. I finished my meal, closed my eyes and, wrapping my fingers around the hot mug, drank my tea. I heard the younger children running upstairs to play before bedtime and the television being turned on for some programme or other. Then I heard Lindsay's voice carrying clearly through the closed serving hatch between the kitchen and dining room.

'Whew! I'm shattered! I'll give myself half an hour then I'll start bathing the little ones.'

'You look just about all in,' Hazel remarked. 'Coffee?'

The kitchen chair scraped briefly across the tiled floor. Lindsay must be sitting down at the kitchen table. 'I'd love one, please. What a day!'

There was silence for a while, then the kettle whistled and crockery rattled.

'Penny for them,' Hazel said.

'Mmm? Oh, I was just thinking over the episode between Mark Edwards and me. I'm at a complete loss to know what to do about the boy.'

Another chair scraped across the floor. 'Want to talk about it?' Hazel must be sitting up at the kitchen table as well.

Lindsay sighed. 'Perhaps it might help. I had to reprimand him over some minor incident eight weeks ago, Bonfire Night. He was playing some stupid, disruptive game on the bus, which ended up in me receiving a nasty bang on the head. In my attempts to restore order, I turned to push him back into his seat. Unfortunately it developed into a slap across the face, harder than I intended. I apologised, but since then he's refused to speak to me, he goes out of his way to avoid me, he's awkward, stubborn, moody and really angry. Then tonight when I went upstairs . . .'

I sat with my hands wrapped around my mug of tea, unashamedly listening to Lindsay give an account of the events of the evening.

Hazel gave a sharp intake of breath. 'Did the hairbrush hit you?'

'Fortunately for Mark it didn't, but if it had I could have done something I might have regretted.'

'Like what? Smack him?'

'Yes.'

Hazel chuckled. 'I can't imagine you walloping a fifteen year old. He's almost your size.'

'It's not funny, Hazel. Mark may be fifteen years old but mentally he's a lot younger and physically his body is underdeveloped. I remember studying maternal deprivation at college in psychology. Mark is a classic case of being a late developer because of the emotional problems he encountered in his early childhood. I've tried to be pleasant to the boy but he just doesn't respond. I know he's hurting inside and I want to help, I really do, but . . .' She sighed and there was silence from the kitchen.

Then Hazel said, 'Teenagers can be awkward to deal with at times. They tend to swing from high to low for no apparent reason. How did you find him before that episode in the bus?'

'He seemed a pleasant enough lad. A bit moody and mischievous but . . . what are you grinning at?'

'It's just occurred to me that it's not beyond the realms of possibility that Mark has developed a crush on you.'

'What?' Lindsay's voice rose in astonishment. 'Never in this world!'

'I'm serious. Think about it. A new, good-looking, trendy houseparent breezes into the establishment like a breath of fresh air and doesn't look unlike that poster he has of Lindsay Wagner above his bed. You unintentionally upset Mark, on whom you've already made a strong impression, and in your attempts to put things right you single him out for special attention. The problem is, Mark may have some kind of emotional blockage that prevents him trusting your attempts at kindness.'

There was silence from the kitchen.

'Mmm. Could be. It would make sense. I only hope the confrontation we had earlier hasn't done more harm.'

'On the contrary. A darn good telling off was probably what was needed, and you can't appear to show favourites. It's not fair to the other children.'

'So what do you suggest?'

'I suggest you don't single him out for special attention any more. Play him at his own game. Ignore him.'

'He could see that as a rejection.'

'Is it working, you giving him special attention? No. Try it. See what happens.'

'Mmm.'

It was at that point I decided I'd better escape to my bedroom before I was discovered.

I felt isolated during those days leading up to Christmas. It was a self-imposed isolation, and wandering around the cold, wintry garden with its leafless trees and barren flowerbeds only added to my exile. The sky darkened overhead and I shivered as a chill wind whipped across the lawn, threatening snow. I fastened the top button of my coat. I caught a glimpse of Lindsay hurrying into the kitchen, her long tawny hair bouncing around her shoulders as she bustled around helping cook with last-minute preparations for dinner. She paused momentarily to glance out of the steamy window. She couldn't fail to see me. I turned my head away and tried to imagine what the garden would be like when the sun regained its warmth and the crocuses and daffodils came out. It was hard to imagine the garden being anything other than desolate and uninviting.

It was obvious Lindsay had taken Hazel's advice and was 'playing it cool'. Perhaps she was hoping I would respond to her in my own time and in my own way, but that was the trouble. I didn't know how. I longed to call out to her and say that I was sorry, but each time I saw her I seemed to clam up. Somewhere inside I was crying out for her to notice me, but she didn't, and I didn't know how to communicate my desperate need for love and attention. No one had ever taught me how to do that.

Everyone was chattering excitedly over their midday meal that day, speculating on what they would get for Christmas. Of course, no one really knew, as most of the presents were donated by various charities, but we were always allowed to ask for something small from the limited funds available to the children's home. The rest of the conversation was about the afternoon excursion to the cinema for us older children to see a film about the Swedish pop group Abba.

'I bet you're going to sit next to Lindsay, Mark,' Rachael whispered provocatively across the table.

I glared at her over a spoonful of treacle pudding, horrified that the relationship between Lindsay and me had even been noticed. 'Shut your bloody mouth!'

'Shut your own or I'll slap your face!' she hissed.

'Oh? You and whose bloody army?' The note of sarcasm evoked an infuriating smirk, which did nothing to improve my temper. In a moment of insanity I flicked my spoonful of treacle pudding across the table towards her.

She didn't see it coming and it hit her full in the face. 'You . . . you . . . sod!' she screamed.

Gary, sitting next to her, grabbed one of her long curly bunches and pulled. 'And this bloody arm'll ram its fist down your big fat gob if you don't stop needling. OK?'

Without warning, Carol pushed her chair back, and, reaching across the table, grabbed a handful of Gary's thick black hair. 'Leave . . . her . . . alone!'

'Ow! Leggo of my bloody hair!'

As I made a dive for Carol in support of my friend, Paul and Robin, seeing their brothers about to start a scrap, dived in as reinforcements and I suddenly found myself being dragged halfway across the table with the remnants of my treacle pudding. I landed head-first on the floor with the tablecloth over my head. There was a resounding crash as the crockery followed me.

'What on earth . . .' I heard Lindsay's astonished voice above the sudden babble of excitable children as our dining room turned into the battlefield for World War Three. I pulled the tablecloth off my head and looked around. The place was a shambles. Broken crockery, upturned sugar bowls, spilt milk and dollops of treacle pudding were being trampled into the dining room carpet as Hazel and Lindsay attempted to separate the troops intent on destruction.

'Right! Would someone care to enlighten me as to how this little escapade started?'

No one spoke. We all eyed each other accusingly.

Hesitantly Rachael broke the silence. 'It was my fault, Aunty Lindsay. I said something to Mark and . . . and . . . made him . . .'

Carol interrupted. 'Then I grabbed Gary's hair and it all seemed to get a bit out of hand, as it were.' She shrugged her shoulders and raised her eyebrows as if to say 'You know how these things happen.'

Lindsay turned on Gary. 'And you, young man. What was your part in all this?'

Gary pulled a comb out of his pocket. 'Just got carried away, Aunty. Sorry about that.' His face twisted in disgust as a piece of treacle pudding fell out of his hair and on to the floor. Carol smothered a giggle and there were titters of amusement around the room.

Lindsay took a deep breath. 'Think yourselves very lucky I don't cancel your trip to the pictures. Now, if you've finished your meal you can all go, except this table! You can stay and clear up this mess.'

That afternoon as I sat watching the Abba film, listening to them singing about about having so much to say but feeling unable to say it, I realised that was just how I was feeling. There was so much I wanted to say to Lindsay but felt totally unable to say it. Waves of deep despair engulfed me.

The film ended, the cinema lights came on, and there was a clatter of seats as the audience stood up and made its way towards the exits. We joined the other children in the foyer then made our way out into the cold evening air.

The streetlights were starting to come on and there were cries of delight as we realised the first snowflakes of winter had fallen while we'd been inside. Chattering excitedly about the film, the children began the long walk back home. Sullenly I brought up the rear.

'Hurry up, Mark. Don't dawdle. It's starting to snow quite heavily!' Lindsay called. Then, linked either side by two of the girls, the party continued on its way.

Being all screwed up inside can do funny things to you. Common sense should have told me that home was the place where it would be warm and cosy, where there'd be laughter and excitement so close to Christmas and where Paul and my Christmas presents would be waiting for me. But somehow or other I found myself darting into the park when no one was looking and walking briskly across the green towards the playground. The snowflakes were beginning to soak through my trousers and my chin was frozen against the biting wind, but the discomfort outside was nothing compared to the discomfort going on inside me. Why wasn't everything clear and simple? I turned to look at my solitary set of footprints across the virgin-white snow. I could see where they came from and where they were heading. Why wasn't my mind like that? In fact, why wasn't my life like that? Nothing had ever been clearly marked out for me. *Why?* Why did I hate Lindsay and try to avoid her, yet at the same time long to be near her? Why did I want her to notice me, yet shun her when she did?

I crossed the white lawns and headed towards the pond. What was the good of going to church to pray to a God who made no attempt to make my life any better or less confusing? I glanced around me. The park was deserted and looked different, all white with grey trees. I felt like the sole survivor on a strange planet. Even the ducks had found shelter from the cold winter evening. The pond had a thin covering of ice below the snow, which cracked when I pressed it with my toe. I wondered how deep it was. It was too cold to stand around, so I wandered aimlessly towards the swings, lonely and still without the children playing on them. Clearing the middle one of snow, I sat down and started swinging slowly backwards and forwards.

They would be worried about me back at the children's home by now. Lindsay would be anxiously questioning the other children as to who had seen me last. Paul would be fretting. They might even call in the police. These thoughts didn't give me much pleasure, but then again I didn't feel any sense of guilt either. In fact, I was confused as to what I actually did feel. About Lindsay. About my family. About everything!

I don't know how long I swung in the cold evening air with the snowflakes falling gently around me. It seemed like a very long time and I should have been frozen stiff, but somehow I no longer felt the cold. I was in a world of my own making, until suddenly I noticed an alien figure in a dark blue duffel coat and green woollen hat and scarf following my footprints. My heart leapt with a mixture of fear and excitement. Lindsay! I jumped off the swing and stood dithering by its side.

'Mark!' Her call had the ring of anger to it. Jerked into action I started running in the opposite direction, toward the bowling green. There was a look of either fury or exertion on her face. I couldn't tell which, so I kept running, faster, faster! Glancing behind, I saw Lindsay sprinting after me. The ground was slippery underfoot, but even so, if I'd kept my eyes on where I was running I would have seen the upraised root of the tree. A moment later I lay sprawled across the ground. I heard Lindsay panting a few yards behind me and struggled to get to my feet. Suddenly my legs were grabbed in a rugby tackle and I was brought down with such force that all the breath was knocked out of me. I lay panting on the wet snow with Lindsay, gasping for breath, on top of me. Gradually her grip on my legs loosened. Seizing the opportunity, I rolled over and kicked out as hard as I could. There was a gasp of pain as my boot caught her shoulder and another gasp as my second kick caught her in the ribs. Suddenly she leapt on top of me. I curled up in defence.

'You stupid, stupid boy!' she screamed, and gave me a resounding slap across my back. Her eyes blazed with anger then she winced and curled up in pain. 'What the hell do you think you're playing at?'

I wrapped my arms around my head and hot burning tears, which seemed to come so easily these days, started running down my cold face. Lindsay watched me for a while and I was vaguely aware my crying seemed to drain the anger out of her. Then she dropped her arms to her sides despondently and moved over to sit beside me. She was quiet for a long time before she said softly, 'You're wrong, you know, Mark. I don't want to hurt you like other people have done.'

The pain that had been tearing me apart for so many weeks was released into a long wail of anguish. Lindsay knelt beside me and, wrapping her arms around me, pulled me close to her. Strands of her wet curly hair fell across my face as I clung to her, warmed and reassured by the physical contact. Was this what it was like to have someone care for you?

The snow fell silently around us for what seemed like forever. Eventually she whispered gently, 'Mark, I know you feel I've betrayed you, but please don't hate me.'

I wiped my wet sleeve across my face and, struggling to control my sobbing, stammered, 'I . . . I . . .'

She brushed the snow off my hair. 'Shhhh . . .'

'I . . . don't . . . hate you.' My voice was hardly above a whisper, even to myself.

'You don't?'

I shook my head. 'I'm . . . so . . . so confused . . . I . . . I . . .'

She gave me another reassuring hug. 'Try telling me.' The warmth from her voice seemed to be having a gentle melting effect on that cold block of ice that had been growing inside me for the last few weeks.

'I . . . think . . . I think . . .'

'Yes?'

'I think . . . I love you.' There! I'd said it. A huge sob racked my body.

She didn't say anything. Not at first. She just held me and let me sob into her wet coat. Then after a while, when I'd quietened down somewhat, she released me and when I looked up I saw she was smiling at me. She wiped the tears from my face with her wet glove and said softly, 'I'm glad you told me, Mark.' Then she gave a forced laugh. 'Just look at us! We're beginning to resemble two snowmen.'

I gave her a watery smile and there was a comfortable silence between us before she said, 'We'll try again, shall we, Mark?'

I nodded. A chance! A second chance!

'Come on then. Let's go home. If we sit on this wet ground any longer they'll have to get a blowlamp to thaw us out.' She smiled at her feeble joke and I smiled back. 'There!' she said. 'That's better.'

As we walked home together through the park, a warm sensation flowed through my veins. I glanced sideways at Lindsay as she shook snow from her green woollen hat and I couldn't help but reflect that it hadn't been a blowlamp that had thawed out the cold enmity between us but a bitterly cold snowy evening a few nights before Christmas. The time when a baby called Jesus came into this world, bringing love and peace.

Chapter 7

I knew Lindsay was going away to her parents for the Christmas period and I was anxious to explain in greater detail the depths of my feelings for her before she left. However, as I had neither the courage nor the vocabulary to address her directly, I decided a letter might be a good idea. So later that evening, after I'd dried out and warmed up, I found a corner in the dining room, tore a page out of my school exercise book and began to write.

Dear Aunty Lindsay,

I am writing this letter because I know I have caused you a lot of problems since you started working here and I really want to say how sorry I am.

When you slapped me around the face on Bonfire Night I felt humiliated and it made me realise you weren't any different from everybody else who'd hurt or betrayed me and I was just beginning to think you were. Sometimes I hated you, yet at other times I've wanted to talk to you, but each time I approached you I seemed to knot up inside.

Please don't give up on me, because I do feel bad about the way I've behaved. I hope we can be friends and I hope you don't think I'm silly writing to you.

Love,
Mark

I folded the letter neatly in half, crept upstairs and, glancing around to make sure the corridor was empty, crouched down and pushed it underneath her door.

Suddenly, out of the corner of my eye, I saw a gawky figure hurdling through the air towards me. Before I had a chance to sidestep he propelled into me and sent me crashing against the wall. There was a roar of laughter as I angrily untangled myself from Gary's arms and legs. I gave him a hard thump on the back.

'What did you do that for?'

'Couldn't resist it when I saw you crouching there,' he chortled. 'What are you up to anyway, you pervert?'

'Nothing, I'm . . .'

'What are you boys up to outside Aunty Lindsay's room?' Hazel came upon us so suddenly we jumped.

'Mark's just coming to my room so I can lend him my algebra book. He wants to do extra homework during the holidays.'

That was what I liked about Gary. He could always come up with an answer no matter how inconceivable it might seem. Hazel raised her eyebrows questioningly and shook her head. She wasn't that naive.

I didn't see Lindsay the following morning. I'd arranged to go to town with Fram for last-minute Christmas presents and inevitably I was asked back to his house for an enormous plateful of meatballs and spaghetti. By the time I'd waded through my second helping and staggered back to Ivy Cottage it was well into the afternoon.

I raced up to my bedroom and there, propped up against my hairbrush on my chest of drawers, was a pale pink envelope with 'Mark' scrawled across it in big bold writing. Lindsay! I'd have recognised the handwriting anywhere. Quivering with nervous anticipation I sat on the edge of the bed to read it.

Dear Mark,

By the time you receive this letter I will have left to visit my parents for the Christmas holidays but I had to write to say I was absolutely delighted to receive your letter. I'm sorry if I've hurt you. I never meant to and I realise how difficult if must be for you to talk to me after our bad start. But please try. I don't bite, you know!

As far as I am concerned it's all in the past and forgotten. And Mark, of course I will never give up on you. I want us to be friends. So let's put all this behind us so that when I come back after Christmas we can start afresh. OK, buster?

Finally, no, I don't for one minute think that you are silly writing to me. It was very sweet of you. Have a smashing Christmas, Mark.

Take care and behave yourself.

Love,
Aunty Lindsay XXXXXXXX

Tears of sheer happiness welled up in my eyes. I read and re-read my precious letter before carefully folding it, placing it back in the envelope and hiding it under the old T-shirts at the back of my chest of drawers. Then, taking a deep breath, I went downstairs to join the others in welcoming Uncle and Aunty back home. It looked as if it was going to be a good Christmas after all!

In the weeks that followed my thoughts were totally centred around Lindsay. She had shown she cared enough not to give up on me the way so many others had done in the past and I responded to the gentleness and concern of this houseparent by falling deeply in love with her. Sometimes loving her felt wonderful and exhilarating but at other times it was painful and frustrating having a love I could never verbally express. A schoolboy crush – that's all she thought it was. She had no idea of the intensity of my love, so saw no need to discourage me from seeking her out, which I did at every possible opportunity.

I loved every minute we spent in the quiet dining room after dinner, just the two of us, working and discussing some problem with my schoolwork. I volunteered for extra chores if I knew she'd be on duty and couldn't bear it when she had a day off.

She attended the evening service at the Baptist church, so I started going as well, just to be with her, and after the service we'd slowly wander home chatting about the sermon. Lindsay appeared to have a very deep faith in God. I knew I could never love or trust him the way she did, but that didn't bother me. I also knew Lindsay would never love me in the same way as I loved her – however, that didn't bother me either, because at last I had found what I had been searching for all my life. Love!

Winter receded and spring burst forth in an array of crocuses in the garden at Ivy Cottage. Uncle cleaned and mended the lawnmower and with the evenings growing lighter the children took every opportunity to linger outside before bathtime. Hazel became pregnant and Aunty Gwen decided she would only work part-time, so there were changes afoot for the staff at Ivy Cottage as well.

During those months my love for Lindsay became the subject of mockery amongst the other children. It was painful enough loving her, but the very thought of the entire household knowing and laughing about it was unbearable. School became a nightmare. Lee, who I'd never really got on with anyway, made sure everyone, but *everyone*, knew I was infatuated with the houseparent. Fram, Gary and Paul kept telling me to ignore the crude, sometimes insulting jibes, but the amused glances, whispers and giggles when I came into a room were like knife stabs that seemed to cut my insides to ribbons. The deep humiliation of being made to feel my love was abnormal tore me apart so much that I began to retreat into my own little world, seeking isolation from the cruelty behind my protective brick wall. I ought to have been focused on the forthcoming exams that summer, but somehow I couldn't seem to concentrate. I became so chewed up about it that I began to find it difficult to eat. Food seemed to stick in my throat and make me feel sick and I would scrape half my meal on to Paul's plate when no one was looking.

Paul surveyed me with a worried frown. 'You look like shi . . . !'

'Shut up!'

He shook his head at me and didn't bother me again, but I could see him watching me anxiously and I knew I was starting to keep him, Brian and Richard awake at night with my nightmares. They were becoming more frequent and more horrific as the days turned into weeks and the nights seemed to grow longer as I tossed and turned, sleepless, fretting and bathed in sweat. On more than one occasion I'd brought one of the houseparents racing into the bedroom with my screams of 'Lindsay! Lindsay!' I was aware something very horrible was happening inside me but it seemed there was nothing I could do about it. It was frightening.

Uncle and Aunty Andrews called me into their office one evening.

'Mark, dear, sit down,' Aunty said, indicating the settee in the corner. 'There's something we'd like to discuss with you.'

Hesitantly I sat down and she and Uncle smiled reassuringly at me. 'Mark, we'll come straight to the point. You seem to be having problems with Aunty Lindsay again. Is that right?'

'No,' I answered sullenly. 'I don't.'

Uncle and Aunty glanced at each other, then Uncle got to his feet. 'Perhaps "problem" was the wrong word to use,' he said. 'You seem to feel the need to be near her all the time.' He raised his eyebrows questioningly and waited for me to answer. I didn't. Taking my silence as an indication he had made the correct assumption, he said, 'Mark, you are only sixteen. Aunty Lindsay is seven or eight years your senior and these affections you have towards an older member of staff are just not *normal*. Now, Aunty Lindsay tells us it's nothing more than a schoolboy crush, but we've been watching your behaviour and for your own good as well as for the good of the home and the children who live here you must try to suppress this . . . this *infatuation* you have for her. Don't you realise how hostile you've become to the other houseparents and children? This is no way to keep a happy, smooth-running home, *and* you're putting extra strain on Aunty Lindsay.'

'But she likes being with me.' I was horrified at their implication that I was putting extra strain on her.

'I dare say she does, but then Aunty Lindsay is a sociable person and likes being around all the children.'

I fought against the wave of jealousy.

'The headmaster telephoned us this morning, Mark. He believes this problem is affecting your studying. He says you're leaving your school dinners and isolating yourself from the other children. He's extremely concerned about you.'

I snorted through my nose. 'Since when has anyone really been concerned about me?'

I saw Aunty and Uncle glance at each other before Aunty said, 'Would you like to talk to us about this problem, Mark?'

I shook my head and stared out of the window.

'Are you sure?'

I nodded. I knew they were only trying to be kind, but there was nothing they could do to help me. Nothing!

'Mark, dear, we thought it advisable to make an appointment for you to see the doctor.'

That shook me. 'The doctor! What for?'

'Because we're all concerned, especially over the nightmares you've been having.'

It was useless denying it, but I was blowed if I was going to admit to it either. Uncle must have picked up my apprehension because he came over and patted my shoulder reassuringly. 'Come on, lad. Don't look so worried. All teenagers have their ups and downs. With a bit of luck, you'll get to the doctor's and back before tea.'

Tea? I couldn't face tea! But a bit of luck? Yes, I could do with some of that!

'Stress!' the doctor said. 'Probably nothing more than stress over exams, perhaps stress reaction from a difficult childhood, with a little bit of teenage rebellion and attention seeking thrown in. Nothing to worry about.'

Doctors! What did they know? What did anybody know? Nobody could guess what it was like to love someone so much that it hurt, then to be told it was nothing more than a schoolboy crush. Nobody could guess what it was like to have your love joked about, whispered about in corners, and to be treated as though you were abnormal for loving someone seven years your senior. What was the point of loving if it caused all this pain? At church they taught us that God is a God of love, but then these church folk lived in a dream world of their own. The real world wasn't like that. It was full of pain, rejection, betrayal, humiliation and always wishing for something better. But that 'better' never materialised. Not for the likes of Paul and me. We could hope and dream and wish for the rest of our lives, but it would never get any better than this, and if that was the case . . . why bother living?

Abstractly I fingered the scalpel in the school laboratory. The blade was shiny and sharp. Sharp enough to dissect frogs in the lesson we'd had earlier and put them out of their misery. Sharp enough to ...

'Mark! Mark Edwards!' The teacher's voice seemed to come to me through the fog of cotton wool that had been thickening in my head all morning. 'Mark! What on earth is the matter with you? Didn't you hear me speak to you?'

I surfaced back into the real world and stared blankly at the biology teacher.

'The scalpels and knives, Mark. Would you collect then in for me, please? Store them in the cupboard at the back of the classroom, lock it, and give me the key.' She peered into my face with a worried frown. 'Are you all right? You look a bit pasty.'

I nodded before silently making my way around the classroom gathering in the scalpels and knives.

It was dark in the cupboard, but a faint light from the partially open door filtered through, allowing me to search for the boxes that held the scalpels and knives. I paused in my search, struggling to gather my thoughts away from this muffled, surreal world in which I found myself but which, in some peculiar way, I liked, because it offered a release from the pain of reality. I jumped as the school bell shrilled, marking the end of the lesson. There was a clatter of feet and babble of voices as my classmates left, slamming the classroom door after them. Then silence. I dropped the scalpels and knives into their boxes.

'Mark? You're not still putting those things away are you? Good gracious boy! The time it takes . . .'

Somewhere in the background the biology teacher's voice nagged on and on and on ...

'I could have had the whole job done myself in . . .'

I stealthily lifted a scalpel out of the box and pushed it in my pocket. But it was no good without a blade. Where was the blade box again?

'If you think you can waste time clearing up here just to miss your next lesson . . .'

With surprisingly steady hands I picked up two new blades, still in their wrappers.

' . . . you'd better think again!'

I pushed them into my pocket just as the cupboard door opened. I stared innocently at the biology teacher. She hesitated; obviously unsure what to make of me, then rather uncertainly said, 'Off you go to your next lesson, Mark.'

As I closed the biology room door after me I overheard her say to one of the other teachers, 'Strange boy, Mark, at the moment. I can't fathom him out at all,' and I smiled to myself. A slow, secret smile. Doctors, houseparents, friends, teachers. None of them could fathom me out. Perhaps that was just as well. I couldn't seem to fathom myself out either! Which only went to prove that my brick wall of protection was doing its job. The only problem was that lately I was having difficulty catching a glimpse over it and into the real world myself.

Alone in my bedroom that evening I sat on the bed with the fog of cotton wool thickening in my head and examined the scalpel and blades.

'Be careful of the scalpel,' the biology teacher had warned. 'It's extremely sharp.'

Slowly I lifted the weapon up to eye level. Sharp? I ran my finger carefully over the blade. Yes. It was very sharp. Sharp enough to dissect frogs. Sharp enough to ...

I turned it over and over, examining it carefully from every angle, then, gripping the handle firmly with my right hand, turned my left hand over, palm up, and lay the blade on my wrist. The steel was cold. This was what people did to end their pain and misery, wasn't it? Cut their wrists. I pressed very gently on to the blue vein that seemed to stand out more than any of the others. One sharp slash across the wrist would be painful, but it would be quick, better than ... than ... I sat staring at the slight indentation made on my skin by the blade, then suddenly and for no accountable reason my left hand started to tremble uncontrollably. Beads of sweat ran down my forehead and a rushing sound, like the sea pounding against the rocks, seemed to surge through my head. Frightened, I dropped the scalpel to the floor as though it were a piece of red-hot coal and sat trembling, horrified at the thoughts that had been running through my mind. Then, making a conscious effort to push the thoughts as far away from me as possible, I focused on the comforting noises of the house all around me. There was the clatter of pans and dishes in the kitchen as cook prepared dinner and the smell of cabbage and rice pudding. I could hear the children's programmes on the television downstairs and shouts and cheers from outside in the garden where a noisy game of football was in progress.

The clanging of the gong startled me as it resounded through the house. Aunty Gwen shouted 'Teatime!' as though the gong hadn't been loud enough and doors slammed and footsteps clattered down the stairs and through the passage as hungry children raced into the dining room.

Slowly I bent down and picked up the scalpel. The fog in my head was clearing again, at least enough for me to ask, why had I pinched a scalpel? It didn't make sense. Opening the bottom drawer of my bedside table, I slid the offending object and the two blades between two T-shirts at the back. That would have to do as a hiding place until I could find somewhere safer.

I hurried downstairs. I'd been reprimanded on more than one occasion for being late or for not eating the food in front of me so I didn't want to get into trouble again. Quickly and as unobtrusively as possible I slid into my seat. Lindsay glanced across at me. She must be wondering what had kept me and I knew she'd ask, but not, I hoped, in front of the other children. I couldn't stand being made the focus of attention, not again.

'Quiet children! Robin! Would you like to say grace, please?'

Robin giggled and nudged Paul. The room went very quiet, waiting for the few words that were more than a blessing, but a starting pistol for hungry children. Robin stood up and all heads bowed in anticipation. *'Grace!'* he said loudly, then he and Paul bust into hysterical laughter.

'Very funny, Robin,' Lindsay reprimanded. 'Now would you say it again, but properly this time, please?'

'For what we are about to receive may the Lord make us truly thankful.'

There was a clatter of knives and forks as hungry children dived into their food. I moved a sausage around my plate and tried a small mouthful of potato. I wasn't very hungry.

'Aunty Lindsay, can we have the record player on, please?' Carol waved her fork in the air to catch Lindsay's attention. 'It's all set up ready to play.'

I should have realised something was amiss when she and Rachael sniggered and glanced in my direction.

'Yes, all right. Gwen, would you flick the record player switch please?'

No one had realised they'd turned the volume up, and as the words to 'Puppy Love', one of the latest pop records, bellowed out across the dining room, every eye turned in my direction and there were shrieks of laughter.

Gary took one look at my furious face and aimed a sharp kick under the table towards Carol and Rachael. 'You bitches! You did that on purpose, didn't you?'

There was something rather delightful about Rachael's howl of pain.

'What on earth is going on over there?' Lindsay shouted. 'And turn that racket off. I thought we were meant to be sitting quietly listening to music.' Her words were lost in a howl of anguish from Carol as Gary's second kick of vengeance caught her on the shin. Robin and Paul cheered him on.

'Be quiet!' Lindsay stormed across to our table. 'You really are the most troublesome table! I don't know what's going on, but this sort of behaviour over mealtime isn't good enough. Mark! Eat up!'

'I'm not hungry!' I glowered at my bangers and mash. I couldn't bear to look at her, not with that song droning loudly on in the background.

'You usually like sausages. Will someone shut that noise off *now?*'

I shook my head stubbornly. 'I'm sick of sausages. I hate potato. And if anyone tries to make me eat this flaming garbage I'll throw up all over them!'

Abruptly the music stopped, but Lindsay kept her voice raised. 'Young man, if you keep up this angry tone of voice with me, you'll be in big trouble!' Her face was flushed and angry. 'I don't know what's going on with you this time, Mark, but I'm sick and tired of this continual moody behaviour!'

There was a deathly hush in the dining room. Every eye turned in our direction and I willed the floor to open up and swallow me. Bursting with indignation I retaliated the only way I knew how. 'And I'm sick of being ordered around!' I jumped to my feet and my chair fell over with a clatter.

'Sit down this instant and get on with your dinner!' she ordered.

'I'm not eating your bloody sausages and mash and I don't care what you or anyone says!' I shouted. Bravely I looked her straight in the eye, pleading with her in this one silent gesture not to humiliate me in front of everyone. But I knew she didn't understand the significance of 'Puppy Love'. It was more than I could stand. Stumbling over my chair, I fled out of the dining room, and taking the stairs two at a time ran into my bedroom, slamming the door after me. I stood in the middle of the floor, shaking.

That rushing sound started up in my head again and the rapidly thickening fog of cotton wool welcomed me back into its strange and surreal world. It wrapped itself around my mind in a form of protection from the painful reality in which I lived. I asked myself why I should have to live with all this pain. I shouldn't have to, should I? In fact, I wouldn't! My feet seemed to wander over to the chest of drawers almost without me knowing it. I opened the bottom drawer and fumbled between my T-shirts. My fingers closed over the scalpel. I pulled it out and stared at it.

If you're going to do it, get on with it. My pain seemed to urge me on. Somewhere at the back of my mind I knew this train of thought was wrong. There'd been enough moral and Christian influences in my life to tell me otherwise, but none of it was of any consequence at that moment. Paul was of no consequence. God was of no consequence, not in my surreal world with my own pain so overwhelming. I sat on the bed and held the scalpel to my wrist. It was a familiar, almost comforting gesture, because I had been there before.

Quick! Before they come in and find you!

Yes! Yes, I would do it. Then they'd be sorry. They'd feel bad over the way they'd been treating me! I hesitated. But it would hurt. Wouldn't it?

Just for a moment, one quick moment, then there'd be no more pain – ever!

I heard the sound of muffled footsteps coming up the stairs.

Quick! Do it!

I stared at the indentation on my wrist.

Do it now!

The bedroom door was flung open and Lindsay marched in, slamming it behind her. 'Now listen to me, Mark Edwards . . .' Her face paled at the sight of the scalpel in my hand. 'M . . . Mark . . .' She licked her lips. 'Give me the scalpel, Mark,' she said softly.

'Leave me alone!' The voice didn't sound like mine. It had a desperate ring to it.

Lindsay took a step towards me.

Quick! Do it now before she makes a grab for the scalpel!

'Mark, the only person you're punishing is yourself. Can't you see that?'

It was lies! It was all lies! Couldn't she see I wasn't punishing myself; I was setting myself free! Free from continual rejection and humiliation!

'You don't understand!' I could hear the sob of anguish in my voice. I pressed the scalpel hard against the vein on my wrist. It hurt. 'They, you, everybody has made my life . . . hell! Day after day . . . after day . . . after . . .' She made a move towards me. 'Stay away! I'll do it! You know I will!' I stood up and backed towards the window with the scalpel still pressed firmly against my wrist.

'Mark, just put down the scalpel and then we can talk about it.'

'Talk? Talk?' My voice had an unreal screech to it.

'Yes, Mark. Talk,' she said gently. She held out her hand and slowly walked towards me. 'Whatever's troubling you – we can talk about it. Share it. Really we can.'

I shook my head and glanced down at my wrist. A tiny drop of blood had marked the blade, but there wasn't a deep cut and hardly any pain.

'If we talk, then I can understand what's troubling you.' Her voice sounded closer. I glanced up sharply, but before I had a chance to react she'd reached out and grabbed my wrist.

'No!' I struggled to keep the precious instrument that gave me control to choose between life and death, but Lindsay was strong. Through the corner of my eye I caught a glimpse of the poster of my heroine, the bionic woman, Lindsay Wagner, above my bed and fantasy and fiction blended as I wrestled. I felt the softness of her body brushing against mine as we fought. The knife waved wildly in the air as I struggled to gain control. Lindsay was panting, her breath hot against my face as we scuffled, our bodies locked in conflict. If she wasn't careful she'd be the one cut with the scalpel, not me, and I wouldn't want to hurt her. Not my Lindsay! I loosened my grip fractionally. My arm twisted and I gasped as a sudden searing pain shot across my hand.

Lindsay cried out, 'Oh my God!', then, loosening her hold on me, stared at the blood pouring from my thumb, horrified. Deep red spots fell on the carpet. The awful pain seemed to drag me back from that half-real world and I let out a wail of anguish.

Taking a handkerchief from her jeans pocket she gently placed it over the wound. 'Calm down, Mark. It's going to be all right. Quickly now, into the bathroom.' She ushered me out of the bedroom, along the corridor and into the bathroom. 'Hold your hand over the sink. I'm going to call Aunty Freda. Stay calm now. Everything's going to be all right.' She raced out of the bathroom urgently calling, 'Freda! Freda!'

I bent over the sink, watching the deep red blood trickle on to the white ceramic. Then, lifting my head, I looked at my reflection above the basin. A thin, ghostly face with deep, haunted eyes stared back. Thick black hair that badly needed a trim at the barbers fell in an unruly fashion over my forehead. I looked awful! I heard Aunty Freda racing up the stairs and a moment later she rushed into the bathroom with Lindsay.

'What have you been up to, Mark?' Her tone was more one of alarm than anger.

I didn't answer. I was starting to feel sick.

Within minutes she'd wrapped my hand in a clean towel, thrown my coat around my shoulders, left instructions for Lindsay to inform Uncle what had happened and was ushering me into her car to take me to the casualty department at the local hospital.

Two hours, six stitches and a very long lecture later, Aunty Freda brought me home and indulged me in hot sweet tea and chocolate biscuits in the empty dining room. She allowed Paul to come in to see I was OK. Once he was reassured I was still in the land of the living, she sent him off to watch *Star Trek* with the other children before bedtime, and I was left alone.

I wandered over to the window and stared at Uncle's disastrous attempts to grow a few flowers and vegetables in the garden. My hand ached intolerably and I was still feeling a bit nauseous. I heard the sound of the door opening behind me but I didn't turn around. I knew it was her. I gulped a mouthful of my hot sweet tea. My mouth was parched and dry. She walked softly across the carpet towards me.

'Mark?' I was aware of the warmth of her body as she stood close behind me.

'Mark, why are you doing this to yourself?'

I stared out of the window, wondering why Uncle had such difficulty growing anything at this side of the house. Perhaps it had something to do with the problem of our football always landing in his prize petunias.

'Mark, don't ignore me. I'm not here to yell at you.'

Perhaps Uncle should try growing rhubarb. Fram's mother made wonderful rhubarb crumbles.

'Mark, are you listening to me?'

'Yes.'

'Then talk to me, please.'

I took a deep breath. 'They ... they ...' I hung my head, embarrassed.

'Yes?' She gently took my hand, the one without the bandage, and drew me towards the settee. We sat down.

It was strange how once I'd started talking about the kind of trouble I was getting into because of this so called 'crush' it became easier. She listened, but then she'd always listened to what I'd had to say. The only thing I left out was that the depth of my love for her was real and not some adolescent schoolboy crush. When I'd finished there was silence between us for a while. Then she said, 'Oh Mark, this has been blown up out of all proportion.' She hesitated before she said, 'You are my friend, Mark. My very good friend, and I care what happens to you. Tonight, when I saw that ... that scalpel ...' She shuddered. 'You gave me such a fright, Mark. Don't you know that?' She gently lifted my bandaged hand and as she stroked it there was a look of deep sadness in her eyes. 'Don't do anything like that again, will you?' she said sombrely. 'Promise me?'

I didn't answer her. Instead I clung to her hand while my heart bled with a deep and lasting love for her, my Lindsay.

Chapter 8

The following morning I was called back in to see Uncle and Aunty Andrews.

'Where did you get the scalpel from, Mark?' I could see Uncle was angry and Uncle didn't often get angry.

I swallowed hard and the sliver eased my dry and parched throat. 'I . . . I stole it . . . from school.'

'So! You've taken to thieving now?' Uncle shook his head. 'Thieving! Trouble making! Rebellion!' He pursed his lips. 'You have succeeded in creating an atmosphere in this home, the likes of which Aunty and I have never had to encounter in all our lives. You've caused disharmony amongst the staff and children and all because of this silly . . . infatuation . . .' – he spat the word out – '. . . infatuation with Aunty Lindsay! Hrrump!' He marched over to the window and looked out over his garden before he launched into another lecture on my obsession. I was actually glad to go to school, even though it was the CSE English exam that day.

By half past nine I was sitting in the assembly hall, emotionally traumatised, with the question paper face down, waiting for Mr Brooks, head of the English department, to give us the go ahead.

I liked Mr Brooks. He was a good English teacher. A serious, middle-aged man, he wasn't afraid to discipline his pupils if warranted, but he had plenty of time for those of us with learning difficulties. He had spent a lot of time helping me prepare for this exam.

'Right!' he called across the large hall. 'It's nine thirty a.m. You have two hours to complete the set questions. Please read each question carefully before answering it. You may turn your papers over . . . now! Good luck, everyone.'

There was rustling as each student anxiously turned his or her English paper over. In the studious silence that followed, I stared uncomprehendingly at the first question, my mind blank. All I could think about were the awful events of the previous evening and Uncle's comments: 'You've caused disharmony in this house because of this silly infatuation! *Infatuation!*'

I picked up my pen. I must concentrate! I thought of all the extra tuition Mr Brooks had given me. I could do it! Yes, I could get through this exam!

It wasn't so bad, once I'd got started. Thanks to Mr Brooks I was able to manage the first three questions quite successfully and thus encouraged confidently tackled the next one. In fact, I almost forgot the dull throbbing of my left hand. Almost, but not quite. It didn't take much to distract me. A sudden shaft of sunlight falling across my paper was all that did it. I lifted my head and stared out of the window into the summer sunshine.

Lindsay! Her name reverberated around my head. Focus on the exam, Mark! Focus! But the vision of Lindsay's warm sunny smile and the way her tawny hair bounced when she walked was far more pleasant to fantasise over than the reality of an English exam. But then the fantasy turned into the reality and the weeks of humiliation and pain of her rejection surfaced to the forefront. Stop it, Mark! Stop it! I gripped my pen firmly and fixed my eyes on the next question. Not many more to answer now. I wasn't doing too badly. I might even pass. Lindsay would be pleased if I passed. She'd spent hours helping me with the homework set by Mr Brooks. *Lindsay!*

My hand began to ache and I was suddenly conscious of the big thick bandage, which wouldn't be wrapped around my hand if I hadn't . . . hadn't . . . Tears prickled behind my eyelids. It wouldn't do to cry, not here. Not in the middle of the English exam with so many pupils around. An uncontrollable tear splashed on to the exam paper. I covered my eyes to hide the rest, which were gathering behind my eyelids, but it seemed as though once one had been released there was no stopping the rest of them. They began to run down my cheeks.

For twenty minutes or more I struggled to get back into the mode of a student in the middle of one of the most important exams of his life, but the concentrated effort wasn't there any more. Every last ounce of energy had been used up the night before and the small reserve I'd managed to muster up for this morning had dried up with the effort of answering the first few questions. What was the use of sitting here distressed and confused? I asked myself. I had to get out! Out!

My chair scraped across the wooden floor as I stood up. One or two students glanced casually at me but the majority were too engrossed in their work. As quietly as possible, I made my exit from the hall. I wasn't quite sure where I was going; I just knew I had to get out of that hall. I heard the door open behind me and Mr Brooks calling down the corridor.

'Edwards! Wait one moment. I'd like a word with you.'

I wiped my sleeve across my face in case there were any tear stains and waited for him to catch me up.

'Is something wrong, Edwards?' he asked, kindly. 'Why have you left the exam room?'

'I didn't feel too good,' I mumbled.

'If it would help you to know, I had Mr Andrews on the telephone this morning. He's told me all about the incident last night and informed me you might be a bit distressed. Can I help you?'

I almost told him about Lindsay. I wanted to. In fact, I would have done if he'd had the time, but he was in the middle of overseeing an exam, and I was also afraid I'd hear the same old thing. That it was abnormal falling in love with someone seven years my senior. That it was just infatuation, and that I'd get over it, so I just shook my head.

'Please, Sir, may I be excused? I don't feel well. My hand hurts.'

It didn't come as a complete surprise to discover that Uncle had asked to see Mr Trent, the social worker who'd taken over from Miss Vernon, and informed him of the scalpel incident. Mr Trent was a joke. He really was. It made me laugh just to look at his long, thin, miserable face – and believe me, there'd been precious little to laugh at over these last few months. He had brown, straggling, shoulder-length hair and a well-worn navy blue jumper that was far too big for him. He wasn't very old. Thirty-ish, perhaps, but he looked older. We sat alone in Uncle's study.

'Well, Mark,' he began and stared at me through a pair of thick black-rimmed spectacles. 'I'm sure by now you realise what a very silly thing it was that you did, huh? And I'm sure you won't do it again, will you? Huh?'

What a twit! And what a patronising manner! I shrugged. 'Can't say. I don't really know. Perhaps I will. Perhaps I won't!' The man wasn't bringing out the best in me.

He bit his fingernail and then examined the torn part. It was obviously more important than me. 'Look, Mark. I'm well aware you've got a crush on this houseparent, er . . . what's her name?' He looked down at his file.

'Lindsay.' It seemed as though the whole world knew about it.

'Yes, Lindsay. But that's no reason for trying to cut your wrists. I mean to say, most teenagers have a crush, it's part of growing up, but they don't all go around wanting to kill themselves. The world would be a very sorry place if they did, wouldn't it now?'

'If you say so.'

'Humph!' He dried up, obviously at a complete loss to know what to say to me. He shuffled his feet uncomfortably. 'You and I have not got to know each other very well, Mark. I'm afraid that's probably my fault. You know how it is. Work piles up and time just seems to fly by, doesn't it?'

I glanced at my watch. 'Yes, time sure does fly by when you're having fun.'

He shifted his eyes back to his torn fingernail. He had every right to feel embarrassed. We'd hardly seen him since Miss Vernon moved to Scotland. 'Right! Well, think about what I've said, Mark.'

Was that it? He hadn't said a *thing* worth listening to! 'And don't hesitate to contact me through the superintendent if you have any more problems. That's what I'm here for. I'll try to find time to call in to see you and Paul in a few weeks' time, and perhaps to discuss the possibility of you going to live with your older sister in Chester when you leave Ivy Cottage. Huh?'

'Whatever you say.'

I scowled after his car as he drove away. Fifteen minutes of his precious time was all he'd given me, but then I should be thankful for small mercies. At least it was five minutes more than the last time, whenever that was!

The breakfast gong the following morning woke me from a shallow, uneasy sleep. It had been an unbearably hot, sticky night and all the tossing and turning had made my hand throb. I rolled over and pushed my head under the pillow. What was the point of getting up? There was nothing to get up for. School exams were almost over and it was pretty difficult trying to raise any sort of enthusiasm for them anyway. In fact, life didn't seem to have much point at the moment.

'Mark! Get up!' Paul hurled one of his shoes at my bed and I winced as it bounced off my bandaged hand.

'Go away!'

'Come on! You'll have Aunty Gwen after you if you don't move it, and you'll miss breakfast.'

He pulled the covers off me and I groaned. I couldn't have cared less about breakfast. Over the last week or so I'd missed more meals than I cared to remember.

Dragging my weary body into a sitting position, I was alarmed to see the room tilt sideways. I blinked rapidly and remained perfectly still until it had righted itself.

'What's wrong?' Paul's anxious face appeared in front of me.

'Dunno.' Gingerly, I stood up, holding on to the chest of drawers at the side of my bed. The room swayed gently one way, then the other.

The bedroom door opened and Uncle marched in. 'How come you boys are always last down to breakfast? Hurry up!' he bellowed. Leaving the door wide open he banged on the next bedroom door. 'How come you boys are always last down to breakfast?' Hurry up!' The rest of the bedrooms were subjected to the same early morning routine. Slowly the room settled down.

'I think I must have got out of bed too quickly,' I said. I let go of the chest of drawers and as I made to cross the room the floor unexpectedly tilted towards me. I reached out to grab the corner of Brian's bed but lost my balance, toppled forwards and banged my head on the corner of it as I crashed to the floor. As everything turned black I could hear Paul shouting 'Uncle! Uncle!' in the distance, but a thick blanket of cotton wool had wrapped itself around me, giving everything a dream-like quality. I was vaguely aware of strong arms lifting me, then the security of being back in my own bed.

'Mark! Mark!' Uncle's deep Scottish voice penetrated through the cotton wool. I opened my eyes to see him bending over me. 'I don't feel well,' I whispered.

'I'm well aware of that, young man,' he said gently. 'I think you better stay put until till we find out what wrong with you, don't you?'

I was too weak to even nod.

I was kept in bed all that day and the next and, although I managed to drink plenty, the very sight of food turned my stomach. I was so weak I couldn't stand up. The doctor was called, Social Services too, and I was informed very firmly by Uncle and Aunty that in the opinion of the experts my problem at the moment appeared to be stress over exams, attention seeking from Lindsay and a bit of rebellion thrown in, and they were not going to play up to me.

One morning Lindsay walked in, smiling, carrying a tray with a glass of milk and two slices of toast on it.

I smiled back. I always felt good when she was around and it was a welcome relief from the boredom of being in bed.

'Mark, I want you to eat something,' she said firmly.

I screwed up my face. 'I can't. It makes me feel sick.'

Her smile vanished and her mouth developed that thin hard line that I recognised as her disciplining face. 'Don't you dare pull that face at me, young man. I've gone to a lot of trouble making this for you, so eat!'

'I can't,' I whined, and rolled over in my bed.

Next thing I knew she'd grabbed me by the shoulders and pulled me towards her. Our noses were almost touching.

'*You . . . will . . . eat!*' She was strong and forceful in the demand she made of me, and she was behaving just the way my heroine Lindsay Wagner would have done in one of my fantasies. I didn't have the courage to argue. I just nodded, not daring to look her in the eyes.

'Promise me you'll eat?' she demanded.

'I promise,' I whispered.

'Good. I'm going to my room to wash and change and I want to see that toast and milk gone when I return. Do we understand each other?'

I nodded sheepishly and without another word she turned on her heel and stormed out of my bedroom, slamming the door behind her. Pulling myself into a sitting position I reached over for a slice of toast. I was eating again. But only because she had shown how much she cared by being so forceful with me.

Within a week I was eating normally and Uncle allowed me to get up and go outside into the warm, sunny garden, which was quiet with all the children at school. Lindsay came and joined me as I swung gently to and fro on the swing.

'How are you feeling?' She sat on the grass a few yards from the swing, looking lovely in a low-cut yellow blouse and tight jeans.

I smiled down at her. 'Much better, thanks to your nagging.'

She laughed, and there was a comfortable silence between us. I closed my eyes, absorbing the warmth of the midday sun, and listening to the creaking of the swing as I swung backwards and forwards. A bird chirped somewhere overhead and for the first time in a long time I felt relaxed. I opened my eyes and watched an orange and red butterfly land on a nearby rose bush.

'Look at that butterfly.'

'Mmm? Where?'

'On the rose bush.' I skidded to a stop and moved slowly towards the bush. I heard Lindsay get to her feet. 'Keep still,' I whispered. 'You'll disturb it.'

I cupped my hands and was on the verge of imprisoning the creature when its wings quivered and it flew away. Endowed with a sudden surge of energy, I raced across the lawn after it. It seemed to hover near Uncle's flowerbed. I leapt up to capture it, missed my footing and sprawled ungainly in the middle of Uncle's Michaelmas daisies. The incident wasn't particularly funny, but I burst out laughing. The sudden release of tension was wonderful. I threw back my head and roared with laughter.

Lindsay came over and looked down at me, smiling. Then, reaching out her hand, she hauled me, still laughing, to my feet. Her hand was warm and soft and her lips were still parted with the smile. Something deep and sensual stirred in my body.

'You should do that more often, Mark.'

'What?'

'Laugh. It's a welcome change from seeing you so miserable.'

I laughed again and continued holding her hand. I wanted to press my lips firmly against hers and feel the warmth and tenderness of her body. She was looking at me with those big blue eyes. What was she thinking?

'Thanks,' I said, and on the spur of the moment reached out and pulled her towards me. For a split second I was able to revel in the sexual pleasure of wrapping my arms around the one person I truly loved, but as my ear brushed against the side of her face I saw, to my horror, Aunty Freda glaring angrily through the window at us. I released Lindsay as quickly as I'd pulled her towards me, noting her flushed face. But it gave me no pleasure. I felt as though someone had thrown a bucket of ice-cold water over the warmth of that lovely June afternoon.

A couple of days later, after the evening meal, I was packing my suitcase to go spend some time convalescing with my sister, Shene, and her husband, Graham, when Aunty Andrews came into the bedroom.

'Are you all packed, Mark?' she asked, sitting down on the bed.

'I think so.'

She paused, tapping her fingers nervously on top of my chest of drawers. 'Mark, we had to have a staff meeting concerning the problems you've been having with Aunty Lindsay.'

I sensed trouble and concentrated hard on pushing a pair of socks down the side of my battered brown suitcase.

'I don't think these feelings you have towards her are going to go away, are they?' she said gently.

I shook my head. At last! At long last they'd realised this was more than just a schoolboy crush!

'The trouble is, Mark, your moods, rebellion and hostility towards the other children have become a real problem and despite repeated warnings from Uncle and me you've made no attempt to change.' She watched me take a T-shirt from the drawer and lay it neatly on top of the pile of clothes in my case. I didn't dare trust myself to say anything. I was aware this was becoming more than just another lecture about my behaviour towards Lindsay.

'I understand you're spending ten days with your older sister, Shene, and her husband, Graham. Is that right?'

'Yes.'

She peered at me over the rim of her spectacles. She looked quite sad, really. 'We've given this matter a lot of consideration, Mark. We, er . . . we feel it may be better for you if you don't return to Ivy Cottage after your holiday.'

In the stunned silence that followed I could hear my heart thumping in my chest. I sat down slowly on the bed. 'Not come back?'

She reached out and squeezed my hand. The one without the bandage. 'We've spoken to Shene and Graham and explained the situation and they're quite prepared to give you a home straight away. You would have been going to live with them in three or four months anyway, until you found a job and place of your own, wouldn't you?'

I nodded, fighting down the waves of fear surging though my chest. At the age of sixteen it was the practice for us to leave the familiarity and security of Ivy Cottage to find lodgings or live in a hostel, but I was one of the luckier ones, having been offered a room with Shene and Graham for a few months.

Aunty continued talking, trying to reassure me everything would be all right, but I was so dazed by the news I could only sit on my bed pulling at the torn pieces of leather on my battered brown suitcase.

Leave! Leave the one and only place that had offered me security in the whole of my unsettled life? I wasn't ready to leave. Not yet. Perhaps by September or

Christmas, but not yet! This was my home. This was where my friends were. And what about Paul? How could I leave my brother! How could I leave . . . *Lindsay!* I put my head in my hands. Oh God! I'd never see Lindsay again! What had I done?

The following morning was a nightmare. One by one the children came in to say their goodbyes before going to school.

'Keep in touch,' Gary laughed awkwardly, and gave me an embarrassed thump on the arm.

'Ouch!'

'Sorry, I forgot about the injured, er . . .' He shuffled awkwardly from one foot to the other. It was the first time we'd ever been embarrassed in one another's company.

'Write, eh?'

'Yeah! I'll write?' Gary never wrote letters. How could I leave him and Fram? Fram! I hadn't even had a chance to tell my best mate about the change of plan!

Paul stood in front of me. His eyes filled with tears. What could I say? This was the first time we'd been apart in the whole of our lives. Even Social Services hadn't managed to part us. But this . . . this . . . !

Uncle placed a reassuring hand on Paul's shoulder. 'Come on, Paul. Mark's not going to the other end of the world, you know. You'll be seeing him at Shene and Graham's in a few weeks, so there'll be lots of news for you both to catch up on.' He ushered him towards the door, but suddenly my brother spun around. His eyes were wide and uncertain and he was grinding his teeth, something he hadn't done for some years.

'See you,' I said, trying to sound reassuring.

'Yeah!' His voice was husky. He was frightened without me. I could tell. 'See you in a few weeks, eh?'

'Yeah!'

The house was quiet once they'd all left. I wandered over to the window and watched the crocodile of children following Aunty Gwen out of Ivy Cottage. They'd be going down the road past the park to school. I'd been taking that same route for seven years now. It was as familiar to me as . . . as . . . I couldn't cry. There were no tears left to shed. I stood for a long time looking out of the window into the garden. Mental images of the years spent at Ivy Cottage flashed through my mind. The time we made a camp with Gary, Richard and Martyn in the branches of 'our' tree. The fun we'd had on the swing. The football team and the matches we'd had on the lawn. The laughter every time the ball landed on Uncle's flowerbed and we got into trouble – unless he was playing, that is. Good memories, happy memories.

Lindsay came into the room. I watched her walk over to the sewing table, wondering what to say to her. This was the person I loved more than anyone in the whole world and my punishment for loving her was to be sent away.

She smiled across at me. 'Don't forget to write to let us all know how you're getting on, Mark, will you?'

Write! Write! Was that all there was to be between me and the people who'd been my family for the past seven years? Just letters? Fram, Gary and Martyn, I could perhaps stand that, but Lindsay! Never to see her again! Hear her voice? Touch her? I suddenly let out a deep wail of anguish and flung myself into her arms, sobbing. There was so much I wanted to say, so many emotions I wanted to express, but I didn't know how, and even if I did they were so locked up inside me they wouldn't come out.

Lindsay held me tightly, just for a moment. I felt the warmth of her cheek pressed up against mine and the softness of her body as her arms embraced me, then somehow she turned it into a friendly hug before she firmly pushed me away.

'Mark,' she said gently. 'Remember all those evenings we attended church together?'

Numbly, I nodded, still sobbing. I couldn't trust myself to speak.

'They were special evenings for me because I enjoyed our discussions on the way home. Sometimes I enjoyed them even more than the sermon.' She drew me towards the settee and we sat down. 'You were learning about God, Mark. Learning about his love for people like you and me. Believe me, he does love you. He wants to be your friend and he wants to take care of you.'

I turned my head away. I didn't want to hear. If he wanted to be my friend, why was he taking the one thing I loved away from me?

She took my bandaged hand in hers. 'I want you to know something, Mark,' she said gently. 'I will always, always, be your friend. A good friend. Never forget that, will you? I mean it!' She nodded her head up and down as if to give weight to her words. 'But Mark, you must come to terms with the fact that a friend is all I will ever be to you. Nothing more, but nothing less. A friend! Do you understand what I'm saying to you?'

'Ye . . . yes.' My heart felt as though it were bleeding to death. All the life was going out of it. She squeezed my hand and held on to it. Her touch was firm and reassuring and enough to break the pent-up emotions. A stream of tears ran unhindered down my face. I reached out and clung to her, sobbing, knowing that when I released her it would be forever.

Uncle and Aunty bustled in. 'Come on, Mark.' Aunty Andrews rested her hands gently on my shoulders and pulled me away from Lindsay. 'We'll have to go if we want to be in time for that ten thirty train.'

I looked pleadingly into Lindsay's eyes and thought she had never looked more beautiful than at that very moment.

'Come on, Mark.' Uncle moved between us, breaking the magic.

Aunty Freda, Aunty Hazel, cook and the cleaners had congregated at the front door to wave me off. I dried my eyes and as if in a dream I received their kisses, well wishes and parting jokes – an attempt to cheer me up. Then I climbed into the back of Uncle's car. He started up the engine and moved slowly up the driveway.

Aunty Gwen rushed in through the gates of Ivy Cottage after having taken the children to school. 'Glad I caught you. Just wanted to say all the best, Mark.' She waved and blew kisses at me through the car window.

As we drove through the gates of Ivy Cottage I glanced behind, to the big red-brick building that had been my home for seven years, and I felt as though my heart was breaking. I remembered how frightening this place had appeared on our arrival and how we hadn't wanted to stay. Not now! This had become my home. The one place that had offered me and Paul security from our troubled childhood. I was being forced to leave it and the people I looked upon as my family. But worst of all, I had to leave my brother and my first love, Lindsay.

PART TWO

Chapter 9

Shene wasn't that many years older than me. She looked like me as well, with the same dark hair and big blue eyes, but she was plumper and had a gentle disposition, which was surprising considering she'd had a difficult childhood as well. Sometimes I would notice her eyes cloud over with sadness as some incident reminded her of our past and on one occasion I heard her telling Graham about those awful years. The arguments, the divorce, the responsibility of being the oldest with her twin, Jenny. The horror of Social Services knocking on the door to separate us and take us away to different foster homes. Then the uncertainty of life with one or the other of our parents until that parent couldn't cope with either life or us in general. And the pattern would start all over again.

Graham always listened sympathetically. I liked him. His raucous laugh would echo around the house and make Shene smile happily. He was a well-built, tall chap with thick wavy hair. 'Big Guy', his friends used to call him. He helped me find a job in a local menswear shop as a sales assistant so I could contribute to the family finances. He showed me how to use weights to build up my muscles. Then he would take me to his mum's house, where she'd fatten me up on cream cakes. Graham's mum was the sort of person a mum ought to be, and she was one of the few people who could lift this awful depression that seemed to hang over me.

During those first few months with Shene, Graham and their two children, I took to sneaking cans of alcohol up to my room, where I could lie on my bed and brood over the injustices done to me throughout the years. I developed a huge chip on my shoulder over the Social Services' system of fostering, which had pushed me and Paul from foster home to foster home when we were small, and had then, without warning, thrown us into a children's home. I was angry about the system of institutionalising children. I was angry with Uncle and Aunty for making me leave without my brother. I was angry with all the people who'd said my love for Lindsay was abnormal, and I would swing from hating my friends in the home who had taunted me over Lindsay to missing their constant companionship. The depression only lifted when Lindsay replied to my letters. She'd left Ivy Cottage a few months after me and had taken a teaching job in Sussex. I would read and re-read her letters until I knew them by heart, and each time I wrote back I wanted to tell her how deeply I loved her, but I couldn't seem to bring those feelings out into the open.

My seventeenth birthday passed uneventfully. As I moved towards my eighteenth birthday I found myself withdrawing even further from people and turning more angry and bitter about life and more dependent on alcohol. I became very conscious of taking up valuable space in Shene and Graham's overcrowded house and blamed everyone, including myself, for my increasing difficulty in adjusting to family life. I wondered if things would improve when Paul left the children's home. He was my one ray of hope. If we were both working perhaps we could afford a room together. It therefore came as a devastating blow when he told me he'd applied to join the Navy Cadets.

Bitterly disappointed, I went back to drinking, playing love songs, reading Lindsay's letters and grieving over a love that could never be. I could see Shene and Graham were at a complete loss to know what to do with me and that I was driving them both mad, hanging around the house with my Abba love songs droning on in the background. But I was on a downward spiral and refused to be manipulated into the role of a happy eighteen year old enjoying life to the full.

'For goodness' sake, Mark, go out and make a few friends!' Shene would admonish, but I would shake my head and wordlessly walk away in case she started nagging me again. What did I want with giggling eighteen year olds when I was in love with a mature woman? I hated them for sending me away. Hated them!

'Mark! Mark!' Shene's voice interrupted me as I sat miserably in my bedroom listening to love songs one Saturday. 'Come and give me a hand to bring this shopping into the kitchen. My arms are killing me and the kids . . . Oi! Leave those chocolate biscuits . . . Mark! Did you hear me?'

Angrily I switched off my record player, slammed down the lid and thudded down the stirs to find one nephew whinging and the other squawking and Shene in a fluster surrounded by groceries.

'Give me a hand with this lot, Mark, there's a love.'

It seemed to me she was managing remarkably well with two babies, a pushchair and half a dozen shopping carriers. I couldn't see what I could do. I stood in the doorway watching her, angry at being dragged away from my room for no apparent reason. Shene, even surrounded by all this chaos, seemed happy. Graham and the children were her life. They were a family. It was me that was the outsider.

Shene glanced up. 'Gone deaf all of a sudden, have you?'

Deaf? Yes, that was what I wanted to be. Deaf! Deaf to her and Graham nagging me to go out and enjoy myself. A packet of cornflakes fell to the floor. Shene sighed and ran her fingers through her hair.

'Are you going to help or what?' she demanded sharply.

I ceased holding up the doorframe and moved over to pick up the cornflakes, slamming the packet on the kitchen bench. Shene snatched up a child in each arm and deposited them in the living room. She glanced at my face as she came back into the kitchen.

'For goodness' sake, cheer up, Mark!' she snapped.

'Why?' I demanded. Shene was really getting on my nerves today.

'Because you're driving me crackers! You spend your entire life sitting in that . . . that bloody boxroom!'

'I thought you said it was mine and I could do what I like in it?'

'And you can, but all you do is moon over Lindsay. It's unhealthy. You've no friends, no hobbies. Nothing! Pull yourself together. An unhappy childhood doesn't give you the right to behave like a zombie for the rest of your life.'

I could feel my temper rising. 'Don't start nagging, Shene!'

'Don't start!' she snapped, ramming groceries into cupboards. 'Don't start! Somebody has to do something with you, Mark. You seem to have given up on life.'

I suddenly lost my temper. ' That's because every time I start being happy, something awful happens, so what's the point in trying in the first place?' I bellowed.

'You're an adult now, Mark. You've got to stop this drinking and get a grip on life.'

'Shut up, Shene! Just shut up!' I didn't want to hear I was an adult. I didn't feel like an adult. Anyway, what was the point of being an adult when the one person I wanted to spend my adult life with had rejected me? I stared at the pile of groceries in the middle of the floor.

'Mark! For goodness' sake!' Her voice ground on and on. Words! Pointless words that I'd heard countless times before. 'Go out . . . make friends . . . you're too withdrawn . . . too bitter . . . angry . . . drinking too much . . . dwelling on the past . . .'

'Did you hear me? I said shut up, Shene!' My head started spinning and waves of anger kept surfacing, but there was nowhere for them to go. I felt like a cork about to explode from a bottle top. I clenched my fists, struggling to keep my anger under control. I could hear my voice screaming 'Shut up! Shut up!', but it seemed to be at a distance. I banged my fists on the table and knocked something wooden, a handle. Subconsciously I must have grabbed it.

Shene had stopped shouting and a look of alarm crossed her face. Somewhere in my befuddled mind I asked myself why she was looking so alarmed.

'Mark, put that down.' She took a step back, looking quite frightened. 'Put the knife down, Mark.'

A knife? I looked down at the bread knife in my hand.

'Mark, don't . . .' Her voice was fading away. Why was her voice fading away? She was swaying backwards and forwards and . . . The last thing I saw before I collapsed and a welcome darkness descended upon me was the white of my knuckles around the bread knife handle.

'Mark! Mark!' Her voice was above me and more gentle now. Not so frightened. I tried to open my eyes but my eyelids were weighed down. Then I realised I was on the floor and finding it very difficult to breathe.

'Lie still, Mark. The doctor is on his way,' I heard her say before darkness descended again.

'A fit', the doctor said. Probably brought on by emotional stress.

'Stress!' I overheard Graham echo as I lay upstairs in my bed. 'Stress! He doesn't do anything to get stressed up about!'

I couldn't quite hear what the doctor said, but Graham was obviously very upset.

'We've tried everything we know, doctor. He just shuts himself up in his bedroom and won't attempt to go out or make friends.' Then someone shut the door downstairs and I drifted into an uneasy sleep.

I woke a few hours later, exhausted by what had happened. The thought of having had some sort of fit frightened me, but as I lay in my bed thinking, the thing that concerned me most of all was having threatened Shene with a knife. I wasn't a violent person and the thought of being capable of such uncontrollable fury was mortifying.

Shakily I got out of bed and made my way downstairs, fully expecting Graham to be furious with me and tell me to pack my bags and leave, but he didn't.

'Perhaps if we could arrange for you to talk to someone about your feelings, Mark, it might help. Someone professional. What do you think?' he asked kindly. I nodded. I didn't dare say no. I'd caused enough trouble in his house and I was scared by what had happened.

I seemed to live in a heavy cloud of despair for the next couple of days. I went into work, against the doctor's orders, because I couldn't bear staying cooped up in my little boxroom. It was too depressing, and I knew Shene would complain if I was under her feet all day, but I would return from work in the evening absolutely exhausted.

Pans were steaming and children were screaming when I arrived home on the second night.

'Busy day?' Shene called from the kitchen. Strangely enough neither her nor Graham had mentioned me threatening her with a knife. Shene had just given me a hug after the doctor had left and said, 'I think we better get you sorted out, Mark, don't you? We don't want another day like today, do we?'

I poked my head around the kitchen door. 'Yes. Pretty busy. Dinner smells nice.'

'So it should. Cost me a pretty penny, this meat, I'll tell you!' she retorted. She drained a pan full of vegetables in the sink. 'By the way, there's a letter for you.'

As it turned out there were two letters. One was from Fram. I would recognise his scrawl anywhere. I glanced at the postmark on the other one. It was from Sussex. Lindsay! I took the stairs two at a time to seek the privacy of my bedroom. From downstairs Shene called, 'Dinner in two minutes!'

I closed the door and switched on my record player. The haunting melody of a sad ballad filled my small boxroom. I grabbed a can of beer then flung myself on the bed and ripped open Lindsay's letter.

The first page was filled with news of her job in Sussex. I turned over and my heart missed a beat.

. . . his name is Geoff and last week we became engaged. We hope to get married sometime next spring . . .

Married! Lindsay married? I took a couple of long swigs from the beer can.

. . . I met him a few months ago when we . . .

Lindsay with someone else! For some stupid, stupid reason I'd never envisaged Lindsay being married to anyone!

The words of the ballad droned on in the background. *What's another year to someone who's lost everything* . . . I took another swig of beer. Oh God! How could she?

'Dinner, Mark!' Shene called from downstairs.

Married early next year, she said. Married! I stood up. There was a heavy weight across my chest making it difficult for me to breathe.

'Hurry up, Mark. It's on the table!'

I staggered across the room to the door like a drunkard. How could she! How could she! I let out a deep wail of anguish. I couldn't take this continual rejection in my life any more!

And why should you?

The thought was almost an audible whisper.

I shouldn't, should I? I shouldn't have to take rejection after rejection. I opened the boxroom door and the narrow landing seemed to close in on me.

You could end this pain.

No I couldn't. How can you end pain? It just keeps coming in waves.

I clung on to the banister at the top of the stairs, fighting to get a deep breath. Oh God! I didn't want another one of those nasty turns again!

Go on! End the pain! Finish it!

Hatred for Lindsay, for Geoff, for everyone, seemed to spread its long ugly fingers across my heavy body until it reached the button marked 'self-destruct'. Suddenly I was out of control. With a sudden surge of emotional frenzy I let go of the banister and propelled myself forwards, down the stairs.

I lay at the bottom in a half-conscious surreal world of physical and mental agony. I heard voices, anxious and worried. They thought I'd slipped and fallen because I'd drunk too much too quickly and on an empty stomach, and by the time I'd regained a bit of self-control I was too afraid to tell them the truth. But next time ...

You'll know what to do next time, won't you?

Yes. I'd know what to do next time.

I began to find this surreal world into which I constantly drifted a protection against the painful reality of my life and my mind started reaching out for its numbing comfort. I became less talkative because the sound of my own voice brought me back to reality, and I was avoiding reality.

I didn't reply to Lindsay's letter. How could I? What was there to say? I'd never been able to tell her of the depth of my love in the past, so what was the point in doing so now? She'd find out soon enough.

I didn't exactly plan to cut my wrists, but I think the idea had been there ever since the episode with the scalpel. You get tired of living at the bottom of a muddy pit where you can't see or think straight and the future appears bleak and empty. The only escape is into an unreal world, but then that unreal world can be filled with thoughts of destruction, which can be equally as frightening.

The house was quiet and empty. They'd all gone out. The razor blades were in the bathroom cabinet. They were sharp. I held them carefully between my fingers.

You were almost successful with the scalpel.

Yes, I was, wasn't I?

You were younger then. A boy. Couldn't do things properly. You're a man now.

Yes, I was.

Go on! You know how to do it.

Was this what I wanted?

Yes, it is.

I sat on the edge of the bath and pressed the blade against the vein in my wrist. It was a familiar gesture. I'd done this before, but then I'd been a boy. Just a boy. I closed my eyes, pressed hard against my wrist, then wildly slashed the blade across the vein, cutting deeply as I did so. There was a searing pain.

The other wrist! Go on! Do it now!

Shakily I pressed the bloody blade against my other wrist, then pulled it sharply over my vein. More pain. Red! Red blood! It was pouring down the sides of the bath, over my trousers, on to the carpet. Slowly what strength I possessed started ebbing from my body.

Not long. Not long now!

As I slumped to the floor, writhing in agony, some force, not totally unknown to me, made a last desperate attempt to regain life. It surged through my body and in a deep heartfelt cry I reached out for help to the One who knew the pain and agony of approaching death.

'God! Oh God! Don't leave me! Don't let me die!'

Chapter 10

They came back early, Shene, Graham and the children, and found me. I don't remember that. The first thing I recall, through a semi-conscious haze, was the wail of a siren and the gentle swaying movement of the ambulance as I was rushed into hospital. Then it became a blur of starched white caps and fevered attention from doctors and nurses and, after two hours, I decided being unconscious had been by far the more pleasant experience. But it was the agonising pain across my slashed wrists that gradually brought me back into the painful world I'd tried to leave. As I surfaced back into consciousness, I was aware of Shene standing over my bed, crying.

It seemed that any future plans I might have had for a repeat performance of my attempted suicide were now going to be dealt with very firmly by the medical system in which I found myself. I couldn't even go to the toilet without having to ask permission! Shene kept on crying. She had been put into the awful position of having to sign the papers committing me to a psychiatric hospital. And God? Well, I forgot all about calling on him in my desperate hour of need!

I spent a week on the medical ward of the local hospital being treated and assessed, and then they came and told me that as soon as I was well enough I was going to be admitted to a psychiatric hospital for treatment. I was horrified, but I didn't have an option. It was obvious, even to me, that Shene and Graham couldn't cope with me the way I was.

It therefore came as a pleasant surprise to find that the psychiatric hospital, situated in the country on the other side of the town, had spacious, well-kept gardens, where patients were taking a stroll or sitting under the shade of the trees. The building itself wouldn't have won any architectural awards, but it was pleasant enough, with ivy growing up the walls. The nurse who came out to greet my ambulance laughed when I asked if I'd be allowed to take a stroll in the garden.

'It's not a prison, you know,' she said, taking my battered brown suitcase. 'You're here to get well, and that includes fresh air and exercise. Some of the patients walk into the village or even into town. It all depends on the doctor's recommendations, your medication and on how you're feeling.'

The inside was dark and depressing. The iron bars obscuring the windows were a constant reminder of why I was here and were a miserable blight across the colourful view of flowers and shrubs and activities going on outside. Even when the sun shone through the windows, iron bars were reflected on the walls.

A small and attractive blonde nurse of about twenty-six or twenty-seven came to introduce herself. Alison, they called her. She had warm brown eyes and a mannerism of running her hand through her hair that attracted me to her straight away. The familiar gesture reminded me a bit of Lindsay. Yes, I liked Alison.

'Don't worry, Mark. You'll soon settle down.' She smiled reassuringly as she took me to a lounge with half a dozen small bedrooms leading off it, small being the operative word. My room had purely the basic necessities, including the customary bars at the windows. Alison dropped my suitcase on the bed.

'I'll leave you to unpack, then I'll introduce you to everyone,' she said.

I discovered my four new companions to be a mixed bag of characters. There was Annie, a large, buxom woman in her early forties. She'd suffered from severe depression ever since her children were born. One minute she'd be laughing heartily with us, her enormous bosoms heaving under lacy home-knitted jumpers, and the next minute she'd hide herself away in a corner, swathed in a cloud of deep depression and unable to communicate with anyone. I soon learned when she wanted to be sociable and when she didn't.

Then there was Sally, tall and skinny, with hazel eyes peering warily at me through a fringe of long mousy brown hair. She was about my age. She gave a curt 'hello', then backed away sharply.

'Don't fret, hen,' Annie said, patting my arm consolingly. 'She'll come around. It takes a bit for our Sally to get to trust men-folk.' She pulled me closer to her enormous bosoms. 'Rape!' she whispered in my ear. 'It sent her . . . you know?'

Then there was George. With the slow, gentle movements of a large, overweight man in his early thirties, he ambled across the room in my direction and with a shy smile held out his hand in greeting. 'Hope you'll soon settle down with us, Mark.' He had a deep, mellow voice. I shook his hand and smiled back. I liked George.

Jake I didn't like. He had a long, wiry body and the shifty eyes of a weasel, and he smelt like one as well! Something about the slimy way he shook my hand gave me the creeps. Jake the weasel. It suited him!

I had a feeling I wasn't going to like this place and my first appointment with the psychiatrist proved me right. He asked me intimate questions about my mother, my father and my sexual fantasies. It was one of the most humiliating interviews of my entire life.

However, having always lived in a community of people helped me settle into the psychiatric hospital better than I thought I would. Certainly the moods and antics of the characters around me helped pass the time. Then, of course, there was Alison, the nurse. She would breeze into our ward and with a bright smile briskly order us to 'Get off the bed!' or 'Go and get your pills – *now!*' and because she was so nice we set about following her instructions like lapdogs.

The only other humiliating experience was having a bath under supervision. I'd been through this detestable ordeal before, in the children's home. I'd hated it then, but I hated it even more now, especially when I had to stand naked in front of a couple of young female nurses who were definitely no older than me. My self-respect was at pretty low ebb anyway, but suffering the indignities of being treated like a child again just about finished it off!

I'd been in the psychiatric hospital for less than three weeks when, in one of my sessions with the doctor, I happened to mention how difficult I found it expressing my feelings. I was thinking of Lindsay at the time and the desperate need I'd always had to tell her how much I loved her. He sat thoughtfully, stroking his chin, all three of them, peering at me through large prism-lens spectacles. I think he was from India. He seemed to know what he was doing and was easy enough to talk to, but I had considerable difficulty making out what he was saying to me at times. Still, as I was the one doing most of the talking, it didn't seem to matter too much.

'Have you ever thought of keeping a diary?' he asked.

I shook my head. I hadn't, but it was an interesting suggestion.

I mentioned it to Shene and Graham on one of their visits and the next time they came they arrived with beaming smiles and an old heap of a typewriter.

'Mind, it's not expensive,' Shene warned. 'We couldn't afford a good one.' Knowing the state of their finances and the upset I'd brought into their home, I was extremely touched that they'd bothered buying it for me in the first place.

I found a home for it on top of the small table at the side of my bed and as soon as they'd left I set about playing with my new toy.

Write down my feelings, the doctor had said. It occurred to me that what I ought to do was write a letter to Lindsay expressing the depths of my love for her. I needn't post it; just pretend I was going to. The idea seemed so obvious: I didn't know why I hadn't thought of it before. Annie, Sally, George and Jake left me alone when they heard the clatter of my typewriter. They knew I hated being disturbed.

Two days later I came to a decision. I would post my precious letter to Lindsay. Precious, because in it I had been able to express my devotion to her over the last two and a half years, my grief in leaving her and the bitterness towards those who'd misunderstood me and separated us. As I licked the envelope, sealed it and handed it to Alison to post, I was in tears.

For the next couple of days I couldn't concentrate on anything. I spent some time down in the gym, but as my wrists were still very painful I was limited as to how much exercise I could take. Kevin, the gym coach, was very good. He could see I needed to work something off, so he let me work out as long as I didn't put any weight on my wrists. It was amazing how working up a good sweat made me feel better. I chatted to Kevin about it and he suggested we could work on a weights programme after I'd had a word with the doctor. It sounded like a good idea. At least it would help fill in the time. I went for a shower, then returned to my room and stared, glassy eyed, at the calendar. All I had to do now was wait for Lindsay to reply. For days now I'd been fully occupied typing and re-typing my letter, and now it was posted I was lost for something to do. What had the doctor said about writing everything down? I suppose it wouldn't be a bad idea to keep a diary. After all, there was precious little else to do around here. I ran a sheet of paper through the roller of the typewriter.

Sunday June 30th
Sent my letter to Lindsay but I've been worried sick every since. I don't know how she'll take it when she reads that I've loved her for the last two years. I told the doctor, the one with the chins, that I'm angry with everyone who's rejected me, not loved me and misunderstood me. I told him I found it difficult to trust people as I've been let down and hurt so often. He listened to me. At least that's something good about this place. They listen to you. But then they don't have much option; they're paid to!

Alison poked her head around my door. 'You've a visitor in the lounge, Mark.' My only visitors were Shene and Graham, and today wasn't their normal day. Puzzled, I hurried downstairs.

The last time I'd seen Lee he'd hurled abuse at me. The time before that I'd boxed his ears and the time before that he'd slammed the toilet door in my face at the children's home, so he was the last person on earth I'd expect a visit from. But there he was, large as life. He'd grown taller and broadened out quite considerably since

I'd last seen him, but then I suppose that was only to be expected. We were both, after all, nearly nineteen.

'Hi, Mark. I heard you hadn't been . . . well, so I thought I'd call and see you.' He was obviously embarrassed, and I'm not surprised. We'd never been able to stand the sight of each other. 'How are you?'

'I'm not too bad,' I said, equally embarrassed.

'Actually, I asked the nurse if it was possible for you to come out for a spin in my car. I thought you might like a . . . a change of scenery. What do you think?'

What did I think? I was completely taken aback by the idea of leaving the security of the hospital with the very boy who'd spent the majority of his childhood as my sworn enemy. 'Well, I, er . . . I'd better just check with the nurse.'

Ten minutes later I found myself speeding through the countryside in a very old and clapped-out Beetle, being given the full spiel on how many miles per hour and how many miles to the gallon it did, and strangely enough I was responding with interest. It seemed a long time since I'd enjoyed the company of a lad my own age.

We found a quaint little cafe in one of the villages nearby and over sandwiches and cream cakes he brought me up to date with the affairs of the children's home. Lee had found a job with a company who were giving him day release to study at college so he could become an engineer. He'd also managed to find two other lads to share a flat with. Everything seemed to be working out for Lee. I felt an acute stab of envy as we sat chatting in the cafe. His long, lithe body was sprawled, relaxed, across the chair, his smiling face bronzed and happy. He'd lost that smirk that used to irritate the heck out of me and he genuinely seemed to want to spend time in my company. Why?

He dropped me back at the hospital just before six o'clock. 'Fancy a run out next Sunday?' he asked as I slammed the car door.

'Er . . . Yes . . . Yes, that'd be great. Thanks a lot.'

His tyres squealed as he pulled away. I gave him a cheery wave and made my way back across the grounds to the ward, still puzzling over his visit. I couldn't deny we'd had a great afternoon, and it had been interesting catching up with all the news from the children's home. It had also done me good to have a taste of the outside world, but what were Lee's motives in visiting me? Genuine friendship? No. Not Lee!

Sally was standing in the corridor waiting for me as I made my way through the front door. There was a worried furrow across her brow.

'Mark, I must talk to you. It's Annie.' She jerked her head indicating I follow her and a few minutes later we were sitting at an empty table in the corner of the canteen.

'What's wrong with Annie?' I kept my voice low.

'I can't find her. George and I have looked everywhere.'

'Perhaps she's just gone out for a walk.'

Sally fidgeted with a Kit-Kat wrapper someone had left on the table. 'You know how she's been talking about going home all week? Well, apparently she mentioned it to the doctor this morning and he strongly advised against it.' Sally turned her hazel eyes pleadingly upon me. 'Mark, come and help me find her. I think she might have gone down to the canal and . . . and I'm scared she's done something silly.'

'Don't worry.' I patted her hand reassuringly and noticed with some pleasure that she didn't withdraw it. 'How long has she been missing?'

'Since about dinner time. She saw the doctor while you were in the gym and when she came back into the ward she was terribly depressed.'

I sensed my first pang of unease. 'Did she say anything?'

Sally shook her head. 'Not much. She just kept crying and saying she was sick of people telling her she was too ill to go home and what a waste her life was and she might as well be at the bottom of the canal for all anybody cared. Then she said she wanted to be left alone, so that's what I did. Left her alone. Half an hour later I took my book outside to read and saw her going out of the grounds. I thought about stopping her, but . . .'

'But?'

The Kit-Kat paper disintegrated. 'Last time Annie left the grounds in a depressed state it took several of the nurses to bring her back. She's such a large lady and she created mayhem, so when I saw her go this time I just let her go. Oh Mark! Please help me find her!'

'I will. Only what makes you think she's gone down to the canal?'

'That's where she usually walks.'

'Trouble is,' I said, glancing at my watch, 'it's after six. The gates will be closed.'

'I know.'

I didn't like the sound of where this conversation was leading. All patients had to be in by six unless relatives or a nurse accompanied them. 'What does George say?'

'He's been right through the hospital and grounds in case she came back and we didn't see her. He thinks if we tell the nurse and then find Annie is all right, she'll be furious with us.'

'I can imagine,' I said soberly. Facing the temperamental emotions of this very large lady wasn't an issue to be taken lightly. We sat quietly for a while wondering

what to do. To be honest, I was a bit nervous over Sally's
expectation of me. It hadn't been too bad leaving the
hospital grounds with Lee for a quiet afternoon
excursion, but the very thought of having to sneak out
after hours in search of the troublesome Annie was pretty
stressful.

I glanced up as a shadow fell across our table. It was
George. He hovered over us in his bright yellow sweater,
but the expression on his face certainly wasn't one of
sunshine. Tears were streaming down his face. 'It . . . it's
Annie!'

I pushed a chair toward him. 'Sit down, George.' He sat
down heavily between Sally and me. I was scared to ask
what had happened, but I did.

'They've found . . . An . . . Annie. She . . . she's dead!'
He sank his round, tearful face into his large hands and
sobbed like a child. The shock registered on Sally's pale
white face and I tried to surface through the horror that
was slowly dawning upon me. I rested my hand on
George's shoulder. 'How? What happened?'

His big fat jowls shook with uncontrollable sobs. 'They
found her . . . in the canal. They don't know for certain
whether she fell or . . . or . . . jumped. The police have just left
Sister Miriam.' George grasped my hand, desperately
seeking some form of comfort. I had none to offer. I
had my own problem to work through with regard to Annie.

'It's my fault.' Sally buried her face in her hands
whispering more to herself than to George and me. 'I
should have stopped her.'

'No, Sally, no! You could never have stopped Annie.'

'I should've guessed what she was going to do,' she
persisted. 'After all, haven't we all in our ward tried
to . . . to kill ourselves?' It was an effort to even say the
words. With my free hand I grasped hers and squeezed it
tightly.

'Stop blaming yourself, Sally. Annie is lucky to have had a friend like you to care about her. Isn't that right, George?'

Poor George. All he could manage was a nod through his sobbing, but then he would have agreed to anything, he was so upset.

We walked back to the ward together, the three of us, each with our own private thoughts of Annie and drawn closer together by the tragedy. Alison asked us if we'd like to talk about it, but we said we just wanted to be left alone. How sad that it had taken the death of one of our little group to make Sally take a step of trust towards a member of the opposite sex. I should have felt flattered it was me, but I had a problem to work through.

I sat down on my bed and stared numbly at my typewriter.

Sunday June 30th (continued from this morning . . .)

Annie died today. She fell – or jumped – into the canal. We all feel guilty about her death – except Jake. He didn't say anything when we told him, but George can't stop crying and Sally blames herself for not stopping Annie leaving the grounds. I daren't tell them I'm really the one to blame.

On my way back from the gym I spotted Annie crying. 'What's up?' I'd asked.

'I want to go home but the doctor said my family couldn't cope with me.' Annie had wiped her large red face with a small lacy handkerchief. 'But I think I'll go anyway. Once I'm there they'll see I'm much better. Don't you think so?'

'No, Annie, I don't. You're sick. Going home will just make things worse. You need the right medication and things.'

I'd stood for over twenty minutes trying to talk her out of it but then I became exasperated with her and said, 'Oh please yourself, Annie! It's your bloody life!' and stomped away for my shower.

I think I may have been the last one to talk to her and now I'm torn with pangs of guilt about the things I said and the things I should have said but didn't. I'm so confused and depressed. This is a terrible, terrible place!

Oh God! Get me out of here. And Lindsay! Write soon! Write quickly!

Chapter 11

Tuesday July 16th

This incident with Annie has made the nurses stricter. I even had a nurse escort me to the local shop this afternoon and that annoyed me. Still no word from Lindsay. I told Alison all about her. She said to give Lindsay time to reply – after all, it took me two years to write the letter and it will be just as hard for her to write back.

Monday July 22nd

I saw the doctor this morning. I told him I was still very depressed and tense and that since I'd had my breakdown I couldn't stand a lot of noise. He just said 'Mmmm?' and that was it! It was a complete waste of time.

I decided to go to the OT [occupational therapy] room. The only other occupants were George and Mrs Ellerby. She's a hard, unsympathetic person with legs like tree stumps. I don't like her. She was doing her dragon imitation – huffing and puffing and blasting flames all over poor George, who was valiantly struggling to sand down some obscure wooden object. I found a fairly decent piece of wood and decided to make a duck.

Sally has been very quiet since Annie's death and last night she told me she couldn't get Annie out of her mind and was starting to feel suicidal herself. That scared me. I don't want anyone else pouring his or her heart out to me then jumping into a canal! I tell you, it's more stressful living here than in the outside world!! I am worried about Sally, though. I wish I could think of something to say to help her. Last night I suggested a trip to the canteen for a game of cards. I wish I hadn't bothered. It was a disaster!

Most of the really mentally sick patients hang out there. We sat watching them for ages. Their long, dreary faces expressed a sense of hopelessness. These are people who have given up on life. Their only incentive appeared to be staggering from one vacant chair to another where they would sit, depressed and lifeless, passing the time away. Where is God for people like that? It's really hard to believe in him in a place like this, where depression, anger and hopelessness surround me. Perhaps all those stories of him healing the sick folk were a fairytale, anyway? There's certainly no evidence of him healing any sick folk in here! Sally and I returned to our ward more depressed than when we'd left it!

Thursday July 25th

The new 'inmate', Deliah, who's taken Annie's room, is a queer one. She comes from Miami and she paid her own private 'quack' to admit her to this hospital – or so she says! She's only in her twenties but behaves like an old woman.

I asked her if she liked Abba and she thought it was something to eat. Idiot! This morning after breakfast she pointed her finger accusingly at us and screamed, 'Someone's taken my watch!' We glanced at each other suspiciously and I felt guilty. Goodness only knows why. I'd done nothing wrong. Then she began searching our belongings.

'Right!' she snapped. 'I'm giving you all till two p.m. Friday to return my watch, otherwise I'll call the police!'

Sally looked alarmed. She could do without this sort of hassle, the way she's feeling at the moment. George looked worried and Jake just snorted in disgust and turned away. He can't be bothered with any of us.

In the afternoon we played musical chairs, pass the parcel and juggle the balloon. They must think we're round the twist, playing childish games. Jake enjoyed it though.

Friday July 26th

There was a right racket going on in our ward when I got back from the gym. Jake was ranting and raving at the top of his voice, waving his arms in the air, and occasionally prodding George in the stomach. Poor George just stood there looking scared stiff. His jowls drooped and his face was red with embarrassment.

'What are you getting at him for?' I demanded.

Jake turned and glared at me. 'Shut up, squirt!' He turned back to George and gave the poor fellow a shove.

'I don't want no trouble, Jake,' he said, raising his hands as he backed away. He could do with a bomb under him at times, George could.

'Leave him alone, Jake,' I said. He ignored me. I hate being ignored. People have ignored me and my needs all my life. It makes me very angry. 'The trouble with you, Jake, is you're nothing but a bullying . . . !'

I knew I shouldn't have interfered, but the sight of poor old George being abused like that, and finding myself ignored . . . Next thing I knew I was right in the middle of a full-scale row and hurling a few home truths at Jake. Unfortunately once I'd started I didn't seem to know how to stop. I wish I could control these sudden outbursts of anger that keep coming over me.

Deliah's new deadline for her watch to be returned has changed. It's now eight p.m. this evening. She's nuts!

Saturday July 27th

Today is Saturday and I'm really depressed. I still haven't heard from Lindsay. I'm convinced that if I go on like this much longer my heart will literally break! Why doesn't she write? Perhaps the letter got lost in the post? I wonder if I should write again? Perhaps I ought to talk to Alison about it. She's one of the best nurses on the ward. She understands me better than anyone else, just as Lindsay did.

Jake still continues to ignore me. I swear I'll swing for him one of these days!

Lee rang to ask if I'd like a run out in his car. I said yes, because I enjoyed myself last time, but I'm still suspicious. I'm not very good at trusting people.

Deliah found her watch!!!! Stupid bitch! It was under her pillow all the time. But she swears blind one of us stole it then got scared by her threats to call the police and anonymously returned it.

Friday August 3rd

'You've got a visitor,' Alison informed me. 'It's your sister.'

I was a bit surprised, because Friday isn't Shene's day for visiting. I hurried downstairs, hoping nothing was wrong, but on entering the visitors' lounge I was amazed to find Maxine, one of my other sisters, waiting. She'd travelled over sixty miles just to visit me.

We sat and talked for ages then went for a walk through the grounds until dinner time. We reminisced over the mischief Paul and I got into when she'd taken us out of the children's home to visit her during one of the school holidays. Then we talked about our life at home, such as it was, and shared our disastrous childhood memories. I don't know where the time went. I don't, really. I was horrified when she looked at her watch and announced it was time to leave to catch the train back home. I didn't want her to go because I'd suddenly found myself drawn close to this sister who could share the same sort of pain as me and I felt so much better for her visit.

After she'd gone I actually experienced the emotion of happiness. Real happiness, for the first time in ages.

Going to relaxation classes in a minute. I enjoy them. Not because they make me relax, but because seeing all the old dears lying on their beds with their arms and legs flaying all over as they attempt to follow nurse's instructions and keep time to the music is the most hysterical sight I've ever seen. One day I might even manage following the instructions myself instead of rolling around the floor in hysterics.

It was Maxine's visit followed by the laughter in the relaxation classes that induced my amiable frame of mind. Amiable, that is, until I bumped into Jake.

'Hi Jake,' I said cheerfully. I was everyone's friend today.

He gave me the sort of look that would normally have reduced me to mincemeat – but not today. The next thing I knew he'd swung round and without warning punched me full in the face. I staggered back, stunned by the sudden aggression. Gingerly I touched my nose. It was warm, sticky and excruciatingly painful. I looked at my fingers. They were wet with the blood that was running down my nose to my upper lip. How dare he go for me like that! I was only trying to be friendly. A sudden surge of anger swept through me.

'So help me, God! If I had a knife I'd stick it in you, Jake! I swear I would!'

His lip curled in a sneer. 'You? Squirt? You wouldn't dare!'

A knife! If only I had a knife. But the only sharp object I had on me was a blue biro. Whipping it out of my pocket I thrust it against his stomach. 'If this was a knife ...'

It was a stupid thing to do. The next thing I knew another searing pain shot across my cheekbone as his fist lashed out at my face. I staggered back and landed on the floor. Jake turned his back on me and walked casually out of the ward without giving me a second glance.

I didn't allow myself to cry. I *wouldn't* allow myself to cry, although I desperately wanted to. I made my way back into the ward and slumped into the nearest chair. George stared at my face, horrified. 'What on earth happened to you?' He was out of his chair and by my side quite quickly for an overweight man, and then he pulled my chair towards the basin and began bathing my nose. Deliah sat in the corner reading, totally ignoring us.

'It was Jake, he . . . Ouch!' As he dabbed my rapidly swelling face I told him what had happened.

'You'll have to report him, Mark. Violence shouldn't be allowed in here.' He peered at my face and grimaced. 'There. That's stopped the bleeding. Can't do much about the swelling though. What a mess!'

'I can't report him, George. There'll be an awful fuss.'

Deliah looked up from her corner. 'If you ask me, I think you provoked him.'

I snorted in disgust and instantly regretted it. My nose started bleeding again. 'Mind your own business, Deliah!' I grabbed the flannel and held it to my nose.

'You shouldn't have interfered when he was having a go at George. You've only yourself to blame.'

'Shut up!'

'If you ask me . . .'

You can't argue with a nutcase, and Deliah was certainly a nutcase! Furious, I stormed out of the ward and into my bedroom, leaving her to rant and rave about the rights and wrongs of the situation.

I told the nurses I'd fallen in the gym. I think they were suspicious, but they didn't make an issue of it.

The following morning George and I went to the shops to buy Sally some flowers to cheer her up. She'd been depressed for days. Thanks to my friend Lee taking me out for a weekly jaunt in his car I was beginning to feel more confident walking to the local village shops.

When we got back, Sally's bedroom door was open, and she was lying on her bed staring into space.

'Hi! Can we come in?'

Reluctantly she sat up. 'What do you want?' Her voice was almost a whisper. George handed her the large bunch of colourful flowers, flushing with embarrassment, and Sally's eyes widened in surprise. Slowly she took them from him, cradling them in her arms. She stared at them for ages and when she looked up her eyes were full of tears. 'You really do care, don't you?' she said softly.

George's face turned scarlet, but he nodded his head before he turned and fled out of her bedroom. I sat on the edge of her bed.

'It's funny,' I said thoughtfully. 'I never imagined myself worrying over someone else, but I do worry over you.' I smiled at her. 'Yes, Sally, I really do care about you.' The realisation surprised me.

A smile slowly and shyly crept across her face and her eyes warmed to mine and suddenly I felt incredibly happy. After a few minutes I left her room and made my way back into our ward, and for once I was even nice to Deliah!

Monday August 26th

A quiet day today. Did some weight training with Kevin. Jake continues to ignore me. I'm wary but not so scared of him now.

Shene came to see me but for some stupid reason I was horrible to her, lost my temper and told her to clear out of my bedroom. I don't know what I'll do when I have to leave here. I couldn't possibly impose on her and Graham again.

Thursday September 5th

These mood swings I have are awful. Perhaps it's all the medication. I couldn't seem to face the day today so I slept on my bed until I was rudely awakened by a nurse who told me to get up and mix with the others, as sleeping wasn't part of my treatment. I ignored her and went back to sleep.

Blinking nurses! The night staff are the worst. They won't sit and talk like the day staff. If you're depressed or can't sleep they just threaten you with an injection or a padded room to shut you up! And they get paid more! One male nurse, a big ugly Irish guy, told me to go away and not to bother him with my silly little problems. I've a good mind to tell his boss that he's moonlighting. He comes on duty at eight p.m., signs in, then goes out driving a taxi till gone midnight. The rest of the night staff do very little else but sleep. One of them stays awake in case the supervisor comes around. They'd all get the sack if they were caught.

Perhaps there'll be a letter from Lindsay tomorrow.

Friday September 6th

These pills the doctor has given me don't seem to be doing any good. I've felt dreadful all day and through the night I've had horrible dreams. The first half of the night I was reliving the time I was dragged away from my mother, kicking and screaming, by the social worker. It was very upsetting. Then just before dawn a frightening incident Paul and I had had with one of the foster parents when we were quite small started surfacing. I could see this foster parent so clearly. She was a tall, gaunt lady, and she had a stick. I can't remember what happened because for years I've managed to push those awful memories to the back of my mind, but now, thanks to those damn pills, they're struggling to rear their ugly heads again.

I decided to go for a walk into the village before tea. I wanted to see if I could lift this heavy weight of depression that had been hanging over me all day.

Normally it's a lovely walk from the gates of the hospital into the village. Today the trees lining the quiet country road were looking tired from the long hot drought we'd had that summer, and the first tinges of yellow and brown were showing through their branches. I tried to enjoy the walk, I really did, but all I could think about was Lindsay. She'd sounded so sincere the day I left the children's home. 'I will always be your friend. Always!' she'd said, and I'd really believed her. So why hadn't she written? The sense of rejection that crept over me as I walked towards the village was awful. I found myself venomously spitting out the names of all the people who should have been or who had promised to be there for me in the past but who had ended up betraying and rejecting me. Hatred for each one seemed to rise up in one huge, frightening wave, intent on suffocating me.

I came to the railway bridge quicker than I expected. I usually liked to stop at this spot. It was quiet and there was a lovely view up the railway line towards the station in the village, but today I saw neither the lovely view nor soaked in the peaceful environs. An awful deep depression was settling over me, blotting out my surroundings. I leant on the wall of the railway bridge and stared, glassy eyed, at the long thin railway lines below me.

Go on! Do it! Jump!

The crazy thoughts leapt unexpectedly into my head.

Go on. You can do it! Jump . . . jump . . . jump!

The word reverberated around and around, spinning, whirling, sending me dizzy with their persistence.

'Shut up!' I slapped my hands over my ears and shut my eyes tightly. I don't remember how long I stood like that, struggling and fighting, drifting in and out of battle with the crazy mixed-up thoughts inside me, but eventually, weary and numb, I opened my eyes. It should have been a shock to find myself standing, balancing precariously, on the stone wall of the bridge, but it wasn't, even though I had no recollection of having climbed up there. My eyes travelled slowly down to the railway track below me. It swam backwards and forwards as I swayed. It was a long way down. Somewhere in the distance came the sound of slamming doors and chunter of carriages as a train left the railway station.

The approaching train could end your pain.

Yes, it could. It dawned on me that I wanted to jump. Oh, how I wanted to jump, to end this awful life! The railway line swam in front of me and my body swayed uncontrollably forward . . . forward . . . All of a sudden my legs gave way from under me and I found myself sprawling across the wall with my legs dangling over the bridge. The unexpected jolt against the rough stonework broke the wave of depression. I felt myself slipping. 'Oh, God, No! No!' The stonework tore at my fingers as I struggled to gain a firmer grip. Waves of terror swam over me. I heard the rumble of the train drawing closer. I didn't want to die!

'God! Dear God! I don't want to die! Help me!'

My fingers grasped a firm hold and, hauling myself up from the edge of the bridge, I rolled over, landing in a crumpled heap on the ground. I lay for a while until my body had stopped shaking, then crawled on all fours to the grassy bank at the side of the road and sat with my head in my hands, taking deep breaths and trying to regain some feeling of normality.

For the first time in my life it hit me how easily I could have killed myself because I wasn't fully in control. What was happening to me? I had doctors to talk to, pills to take. Why weren't they working?

I was so frightened by what had happened I couldn't get back to the safety of the hospital quick enough. Even though I knew the life I was returning to was empty and futile, the psychiatric hospital was my only means of refuge. By the time I ran through the hospital gates I was nauseous with shock. I staggered into the ward just in time to see a strange young girl taking *my* Abba record off *my* record player.

'What do you think you're doing?' I screamed. 'That's *my* record! How dare you touch my things!'

'Now, Mark, calm down.' Alison hurried into the ward at the sound of my screaming. 'This is Sharon. She's a new patient, so we're trying to help her understand the running of the ward.' She noticed the perspiration on my brow and her tone changed to one of concern. 'What's wrong, Mark?'

'I've . . . I've just . . . nearly thrown myself off the damn railway bridge!'

A look of alarm crossed Alison's face, but she didn't say anything. She just took my hand and led me into my bedroom.

'Now then,' she said, sitting beside me on the bed. 'Tell me what happened.' Her fingers were warm and comforting as she stroked my hand reassuringly. 'What happened, Mark?'

I told her as best I knew how and she listened intently. Then I went on to tell her how it had all happened because I was depressed I hadn't had a reply to my letter to Lindsay, and how scared I was she'd rejected me and wouldn't want anything to do with me now she was married. All the pain and anguish came pouring out through a fresh flow of tears and she kept on stroking my hand. I wanted to snuggle into her and be comforted. I wanted to have someone stand in the centre of my emotional dungheap and shovel it away for me. I knew I was starting to depend on Alison and on the love she was offering, just as I had with Lindsay. I knew I shouldn't, but I couldn't help myself.

Wednesday September 11th – ten a.m.

Any minute now the nurse will be shouting for us to go for our tablets and we'll have to wait in a great long queue for them. It's those old people. They stand around asking questions for hours and discussing how they never slept a wink and I'm left hanging around waiting impatiently for my pills.

I wrote to Lindsay again. This time I posted the letter myself. You can't trust the nurses. I'm sure they only bother with us because they're paid to.

George gave me some disturbing news. He said Alison might be moving to Scotland. Why did she confide in him? I hope she doesn't go. I couldn't stand not having her around.

The new girl, Sharon, is very nice. She's the same age as Sally and me. She's small and dainty with curly auburn hair and a soft Irish accent.

Sally and I went for a walk in the afternoon. It was the first time I'd been out since the incident at the railway bridge, so I was quite nervous.

We ambled along the same country road to the village, with the same yellow and brown leaves gently falling from the trees. There was dampness in the air, making the thin carpet of leaves under our feet slippery. The sun struggled to bring a bit of warmth through the mist, but failed miserably.

As we walked Sally began to talk a little bit about herself. Hesitantly at first, then gradually more comfortably, she told me about being raped and how she'd tried to kill herself afterwards by putting a plastic bag over her head. Then she told me about her parents, their lack of understanding and how eventually they had thrown her out. As we walked over the railway bridge it vaguely crossed my mind that I should be feeling scared or ashamed or something because I was crossing the very spot where, a few days ago, I'd almost committed suicide. But I was so engrossed in what Sally was saying I was over the bridge before I realised it.

Sally gave me a sidelong glance. 'How did you feel about going over that bridge, Mark?'

I shrugged. 'Not too bad, I suppose.'

She turned and smiled at me. 'I find it very difficult to trust people,' she said, 'especially men, but you're . . . you're different.'

I chuckled. 'I can assure you I'm all male, Sally.'

She laughed and gave me a friendly shove. 'You know what I mean. It's just, you seem genuinely concerned for me and for George and . . . well, I'd hate you not to be there to talk to. So don't do anything silly. OK?'

Thursday September 19th

A whole eight days have passed and still no reply to my second letter to Lindsay. If she writes and says she doesn't want anything to do with me, I'll find the courage to end it all from somewhere. God help me, I will! And I won't call out for God to come and rescue me this time! I don't want his damn interference! It's my life and I can do what the hell I like with it!

Norman from the next ward was upset during group discussions as tomorrow will be a year since he lost his son. I feel really sorry for him and hate this sense of helplessness to do anything for him. Poor Norman. I know I cry a lot, but Norman is a full-grown man, and he cries his eyes out all the time.

Then we started talking about death, and one of the patients said, 'I think we should make the best of this world and thank God we're still alive!' God again! Why the hell should I thank God for being alive? Living sucks! Someone then said that it doesn't matter if you're discharged from a mental hospital, because the people outside still think you're mental, and the religious nut from the next ward agreed wholeheartedly and said the smell in the hospital was awful and he was going outside to breathe in God's clean fresh air. Group discussions ended at eleven a.m. – thank God! At least that's something I can thank him for. I tell you, these group sessions are getting dafter every minute!

Tuesday September 24th

My future is bleak. I cannot see from one day to the next. I thought my eighteenth birthday was bad, but my nineteenth in a couple of weeks' time will be worse. I'm dreading it! I wish I could go to sleep and never wake up! I slept most of this morning, then after dinner I decided to re-read some of Lindsay's old letters and found she'd given me her mother's address. With a sudden wave of inspiration I decided to telephone her.

She sounded nice, Lindsay's mum. I didn't have much money, so it wasn't a long call, but I think I managed to get over to her how important it was for Lindsay to contact me and she seemed genuinely sympathetic and promised to tell Lindsay I'd rung. It gave me hope.

Woke up in the middle of the night– saw a man standing at the bottom of my bed. This place is driving me mad! MAD!

Saturday September 28th
Went to the gym, then for a swim, then spent a frustrating time in the OT room trying to unstick the head of my duck, which I'd accidentally stuck on backwards when I was depressed. It's now almost nine p.m.

George, his face red with the exertion of running, burst in through the door. 'I've been looking everywhere for you, Mark. Have you seen Sally?'

'No. Why?'

He sat down beside me and his bottom lip trembled. 'Sharon said she was in a dreadful state this afternoon, then Jake said he saw her running towards the hospital gates after tea.'

'What? He's lying. You know what he's like.'

George shook his head. 'Not this time. They've told the nurses, but we're frightened she might . . . might . . .'

The frightened expression on George's face sent alarm bells ringing in my head. It was dusk. The hospital gates were closed. The nurses wouldn't have a clue where to look. 'Come on.' I grabbed George by the sleeve of his jumper and hurried him along the corridors towards the nurses' room. I burst straight in through the door. 'I've come about Sally.'

Alison looked up from her desk. 'We know, Mark. We're looking for her.' She inclined her head. 'Do you know where she might be?'

I hesitated. 'I've an idea, but Alison, please, Alison, open the hospital gates and let me go and find her.'

She shook her head. 'No way! Tell us where you think she might be. One of us will go.'

'No, Alison. Please. It's important to her that she comes back of her own accord. If one of you finds her and forces her back she'll see it as a defeat.'

Alison thoughtfully chewed her pen. 'Well,' she said hesitantly, 'I shouldn't, but if you think you know where she is then . . . OK. But one of the male nurses will have to go with you.'

It was dark by the time Harry, the male nurse, and I reached the badly lit road leading to the village.

'Come on!' I urged, but Harry wasn't one for hurrying. He was overweight and the pace I set soon had him out of breath. He stopped, holding his sides and panting, looking like a beached whale. I walked back to where he stood. 'Look, Harry, I'm heading for the railway bridge. I can make it much faster on my own. Can I go?'

Still holding his sides, he gave me a wave of dismissal. I didn't need a second bidding. Taking to my heels, I raced along the dark road as fast as I could. It wasn't easy. I kept landing in a pothole or slipping on the leaves and as I ran I found myself praying, 'Oh God! Don't let her die! Suicide isn't what you want for, Sally, I know it! Please keep her from hurting herself! Hold on to her till I get there!'

Then I saw her. A solitary, slender figure leaning over the wall of the bridge, looking down towards the railway line. I suddenly realised how desperate she much be feeling to have embarked on this long walk, in the dark and all alone.

I didn't want to alarm her, so I called softly, 'Sally! It's me, Mark.'

She turned her head as I came up to her. Her face was wet with tears, her eyes wide and frightened. I put my arm around her shoulders and drew her away from the edge of that awful bridge. 'They're looking for you, Sally. Harry's just behind me.'

She let out a groan of despair. 'They'll never let me out after this. They'll think . . .' She buried her face in her hands. 'They've told me I'll be sent to a secure unit if I keep trying to . . .'

I gave her shoulders a squeeze. 'Come on. We'll start walking back along the road. We can say you took ill or fainted or something.'

'Mark, I'm scared, I . . . I . . .' Her body shook with sobs and it seemed the most natural thing in the world to wrap my arms around her, pull her towards me and let her cry on my shoulder. After a few minutes she seemed to calm down. Her body was still now, but she made no attempt to move, so we stood together in the middle of that awful bridge that seemed to draw us when we were at our lowest ebb.

'Come on,' I said. 'Here's Harry. We'll be getting into trouble for taking late-night walks.' Gently taking her face in my hands, I kissed her on the forehead in a brotherly fashion. Then we walked hand in hand down the road to meet Harry.

Sally took a big step forward that night when she turned to me and allowed me to hold her, reassure her and comfort her. She was taking the road back to recovery by learning not to be afraid of men, and I, Mark Edwards, with all my problems, had been part of that healing process. I felt good about that, but I did wonder whether God had played a part in answering my prayer, keeping her safe until I arrived on the scene.

Chapter 12

Sunday September 29th – six thirty p.m.
Very depressed today. Perhaps it was the strain of yesterday with Sally, or Lee ringing up to say he had flu and couldn't take me for a spin in his car.

Saw the doc this morning. He's not concerned with my progress. The only thing he's good at is increasing my tablets. Why is no one helping me?

Still no letter from Lindsay. I rang her mum again. She told me Lindsay is going to have a baby! A BABY! I hate that Geoff! I asked Lindsay's mum to hurry up and get her to write to me, then my money ran out.

Walked into the village with George in the afternoon and because I was still upset I bought 100 tablets at the chemist. I'm sick of everything in my life!

Reaching into the bedside drawer I extracted the neatly wrapped pile of letters from Lindsay. I knew each one of them by heart.

'I will *always* be your friend, Mark. Always!' I'd trusted her commitment to our friendship. Really trusted her. So why was she ignoring my cries for help now? Perhaps she didn't want to know me any more because I'd been nothing but trouble to her and now that she had Geoff, and there was a baby on the way, I was to be pushed to the back of her mind. That was it! That could be the only reason for her silence. If she wouldn't write to me then I didn't want anything more to do with her! So much for promises of friendship! Angrily I ripped up her letters and hurled them across the floor, and then, snatching the bottle of pills from my bedside drawer, I stormed out of the bedroom and made my way down to the kitchen. The sudden explosion of anger had made my head ache again.

There was no one in the kitchen, but the tap was running. More of a dribble than a run, really. I didn't increase the flow, but stood dreamily, watching it slowly fill my glass with water.

You need a full glass – for all those pills.

The thoughts were familiar, almost like old friends. Yes, I would need a lot of water to wash down those pills. The glass was almost full now. I opened the bottle and stood motionless, staring at the tablets.

Go on! It's easy. Swallow them!

I didn't argue. My actions moved with the flow of the words. I threw my head back and shook about half a dozen pills into my mouth. Then I chewed. They were dry and gritty. I lifted the glass and gulped down the water, washing the dry grittiness away.

There! That wasn't so bad, was it?

No. It wasn't. I threw back my head and shook the bottle again, chewing and gulping down water. Shaking the bottle, chewing and gulping down water. It shouldn't be long before they took effect. Not long. The bottle was almost empty now. I threw back my head once more and shook the bottle.

'Mark! Mark! Oh God!' Sally's strangled cry startled me. As if waking from a bad dream, I turned and stared first at her shocked face and then down at the bottle of pills in my hand. Sally was trembling when she took them from me. 'How many have you taken, Mark? How many?'

'I . . . I don't know. The bottle . . . the bottle was full.' The full impact of what I'd tried to do suddenly hit me. I grabbed her wrist. 'Oh God, Sally. What have I done?'

Her face was deathly white as she pushed me on to the kitchen stool, but she didn't panic. 'Wait here, Mark,' she said urgently. 'Do you hear me? Wait here!' Then she ran out of the kitchen and I heard her calling frantically for help.

Within minutes there were nurses everywhere.

'How many pills have you taken, Mark?'

'Was the bottle full?'

Question followed question, but my mind was starting to drift into a world of its own. I couldn't seem to concentrate on finding answers to their questions and my legs were growing weaker as they walked me up and down the kitchen and as the pills took effect. In the background I heard a siren. My eyes began to mist over as the ambulance men wheeled me out on a trolley. I tried to say I could walk, but my lips were numb and I was slurring my words. I was vaguely aware of feeling scared. What had I done? As the ambulance raced towards the town centre and I drifted into unconsciousness, I vaguely wondered if I would see my nineteenth birthday –tomorrow!

Something kept dragging me back into consciousness. I was choking! Suffocating! I struggled to sit up, fighting with the long thick tube stuck down my throat, but hands held me down firmly. I tried to scream, but vomited instead. Oh God! I was dying!

Monday September 30th – two thirty p.m.
I'm not dead!

Woke up early this morning on the general word of the hospital. Today of all days is my nineteenth birthday! Oh God! Why did you let my mother give birth to me in the first place if you knew it would be like this?

My throat is very sore and no wonder! You should have seen the size of the tube they rammed down my gullet to pump my stomach out.

The nurses are very kind, but they will keep asking me why a lad of my age, with his whole future ahead of him, should want to commit suicide. They told me I'd be going back to the psychiatric hospital tomorrow.

Don't feel well. Think I'll go to sleep now.

Tuesday October 1st

As soon as I arrived back in the psychiatric hospital I was given a pep talk from Sister Miriam, then another from Alison, then another from Shene when I rang her. Eventually I couldn't take any more and stormed off to the OT room for some peace and quiet.

It was quite therapeutic, chiselling out the wings on my duck. Mrs Ellerby was there and asked me what I was doing. I told her I was chiselling out the wings on my duck (as if she couldn't see that for herself) but she said she didn't think it was a good idea for me to have any sharp instruments at the moment. I'll never get this damn duck finished!

Wednesday October 2nd

Talked to Shene about Lindsay this afternoon. I begged her to write to ask Lindsay to contact me. She said she'd write as soon as she got home.

I decided to telephone Lindsay's mum again. I said, 'Sorry to bother you, but ...' and before I had time to say anything else she replied, 'Yes, you really must not ring me any more!'

My heart sank and I was quiet and depressed for the rest of the evening.

Friday October 4th

It's three fifteen in the morning. Just come back from the toilets and to my surprise there's no nurse on the ward. None asleep in the chairs either. Wonder where they've gone? With a bit of luck some extraterrestrial being has absconded with them!

Sunday October 6th

Lee came as usual. Good old Lee, always comes on a Sunday, although for the life of me I still don't know why he bothers. Went to the pub for a drink. I'm only drinking shandy. I've gone teetotal since my breakdown.

Wrote to Lindsay apologising for bothering her mother.

Friday October 11th

I don't think I'll ever try to kill myself again, even though I still suffer from days of depression. Perhaps these damn pills are starting to work?

Sunday October 13th

Lee took me out for a run. Watched a football match in one of the villages.

Friday October 18th

Queued up for the happy pills this morning, but became so fed up with listening to everyone complaining that I decided 'To hell with the tablets' and went for a walk with Jake. As I anticipated, there was a long lecture on 'You must not miss your pills' from one of the nurses later that day.

I saw the doctor in the afternoon and he talked about discharging me. Surely that can't be right? It wasn't my idea to be put in here in the first place, but now I am here I would like some sort of help! All they've done is dig up and expose my emotional state of mind, then give me pills to suppress it all again! The doctor said he was going to work out some form of domestic training programme for me so that when I left the psychiatric hospital I would be able to cope with cleaning, cooking, shopping, etc. He asked me if I would like to live in a hostel. 'No way!' I told him vehemently. 'I've had enough of living in institutions with their rules and regulations!'

It is rather worrying, what's going to happen to me, though. I can hardly go back to Shene and Graham, after all I've put them through. I'm scared! Is this all they can do for me?

Disturbing news! Alison is moving to Scotland in a few days. How can I stand this place without her!

Tuesday October 22nd

Still no word from Lindsay!

It's cold, wet and miserable outside today and the nights are drawing in.

Sharon and I walked into the village despite the weather. I like her and I think she likes me.

Wednesday October 23rd

Sharon kissed me tonight. Nineteen! And the first time I've been kissed!

Thursday October 24th

Unsettling news! I'm being discharged when I find somewhere to live. The doctor told me, but he made it sound as though he was throwing me out. He said there was nothing more they could do for me and they needed my bed. I don't know how I'm going to be able to cope with life, but the doctor says I'm fit enough. After he'd finished with me I was so depressed and frightened that I rang the Samaritans.

Monday October 28th

I spent the day looking for somewhere to live. There was a bedsit not far from the menswear shop where I work. It was a right dosshouse with two old drunks living on the floor below. I lay awake worrying till midnight.

Tuesday October 29th

This morning I cooked an apple pie and a few scones in the OT room. I was quite pleased with the way they turned out. In the afternoon I decided to visit the menswear shop to inform them of my return. After an absence of three months it felt strange walking in through the doors. I don't know how I'll cope once I'm back at work full-time.

The people I'd worked with for over two years used to treat me so coldly, as if I was mad or something. How will they cope with me when I return? Still, it was good of the manager to keep my job open all this time, and it certainly takes the pressure off looking for another job.

There's a chance Sally will be discharged in a few weeks. Like me, she's terrified, but her unmarried sister has suggested they find a flat together, so that's reassured her a bit. I hope it works out for her. I really do. We've said we'll keep in touch; we've been such good friends.

'Mark?'

I turned and was surprised to see Shene standing at my bedroom door.

'Hi!' I said, closing my diary. 'Didn't expect you till this afternoon.' My stomach gave a lurch as I spotted the envelope in her hand.

'It's a letter from Lindsay,' she said quietly.

I couldn't move. I'd been waiting for this moment for three whole months and all I could do was sit and stare at the small pink envelope in Shene's hand.

'I couldn't wait till this afternoon to give it to you,' she said, holding it out. 'Here. Aren't you going to read it?' I took the envelope. 'Tell you what,' she said, 'why don't I leave you in peace to read it and afterwards you can come and join me for coffee in the canteen, eh?'

I nodded, but I didn't look at her. I couldn't take my eyes off the envelope and as soon as she'd closed the door

I tore it open. *I knew you wouldn't let me down Lindsay! I knew it!*

Dear Mark [I read],

How nice to hear from you. I'm so sorry you've been so poorly . . . etc. . . . . etc. . . . Geoff and I are really excited about the new baby coming. We've been . . . etc. and so forth . . . My mother hasn't been too well lately . . . etc. . . . . etc.

Hope you will be feeling better soon.

Love,
Lindsay

That was it? I'd spent hours! days! weeks! finding courage to compose and expose my heartfelt emotions in my letters to her and she'd ignored them completely. Almost as though my feelings never existed! I couldn't believe it! Angry, I read and re-read the letter. Perhaps if she'd written to me via Shene, then Shene might just have a letter as well. Perhaps there was more in hers. I hurried downstairs to the canteen to join my sister.

'I hear Alison, your favourite nurse, has left today?' Shene greeted me as I sat down beside her at a corner table with a cup of coffee.

'Alison? Oh yes. Shene, did Lindsay . . . ?'

'You'll miss her. You used to like to talk to her best of all, didn't you?' Shene sipped her coffee, watching the comings and goings of visitors and patients. She was obviously avoiding the subject of Lindsay.

'You received a letter from Lindsay, didn't you Shene?' I challenged.

She had the grace to look sheepish. 'I was hoping you wouldn't ask.'

'Can I read it?'

'You could, but I, er . . . left it at home.'

'Deliberately, I bet!'

'No, it wasn't, Mark. You can read it when I bring it in. All she said was . . .'

Shene sipped her coffee and stared into space, deliberately avoiding eye contact with me.

'Yes?'

Shene sighed. 'Apparently when she received your letter she was so disturbed to hear you were in a psychiatric hospital that she rang the hospital and she was told it wouldn't be in your best interests for her to speak to you.'

I stared at my sister, horrified. 'They said what?'

'Mark.' Shene grasped my wrist firmly. 'Now, Mark, promise me you won't cause trouble over this?'

I pulled my arm away angrily. I was wound up like a time bomb ready to explode. 'How could they, Shene? How could they! What right have they to do that to me? Who took the call?'

'I've no idea, Mark. This was some weeks ago, after she received your first letter.'

We sat quietly for a long time after that. Sheen looking decidedly worried while I fumed at an institutional system that could take away the rights of individuals. Then suddenly my taunt muscles flopped and I slumped in my seat, exhausted by the emotions of hate and revenge. How can you fight against a system? It wins every time.

'You won't make a fuss over this will you, Mark?'

I shook my head. What was the point? 'I'd like to find out who took that call' was all I said, but I knew it would be like trying to find a needle in a haystack. I thought of all those anxious days of waiting and watching for the post every morning, the despair when nothing came, the sleepless nights and the attempted suicide, and all this time Lindsay had been trying to contact me. My head sunk into my hands. I hated the whole set-up of the psychiatric hospital with such intensity that I felt physically sick.

Shene shook my shoulder. 'Let's talk about something pleasanter, eh, Mark? Tell me about the bedsit you looked at the other day.'

I tried to focus on her question. 'Oh, the bedsit. It was drastic. I won't be taking it. I'm sure I can find something better than that.' There was an ominous silence and I noticed she was avoiding eye contact with me again. 'What? What's wrong now?'

She sighed. 'I suppose you might as well know. You'll find out soon enough anyway.'

'Find out what?' She was frightening me.

'Mr Carpenter rang.' Mr Carpenter was the manager of the menswear shop where I worked. 'He says he's very sorry, but he's unable to keep your post open any longer.'

I was horrified. 'You're kidding! But I'll be out in a few days!'

'I know, Mark, I told him, but he thinks you might not be up to the job any more.'

'But . . . what'll I do?'

Shene smiled kindly at me. 'I know you want to find a place of your own, Mark, but let's be realistic. You've no money and no job. So how about coming back to us, just for a while, till you get yourself settled?'

Back with Shene and Graham, to their overcrowded house, the noise of the children and that tiny boxroom again? No way! But what was the alternative? I was homeless, jobless and penniless.

Two weeks later I was discharged from the psychiatric hospital on the grounds that, in their opinion, I was well enough to cope on my own. That night I sat alone in my familiar small bedroom in my sister and brother-in-law's home. It was quiet and I was lonely without the nurses, Sally, George and Sharon. Even Deliah and Jake would have been welcome company. I read and re-read Lindsay's letter because there was little else to do. There was a tap on the door.

'Are you all right?' Shene came in carrying a steaming cup of cocoa.

I nodded. She placed the cocoa on the bedside table and sat down on the bed beside me. She didn't say anything, she just wrapped her arms around me and held me close. I buried my head into her shoulder and allowed the tears to flow.

'What's the point of going on, Shene?'

'Sshh, now. Sshh.'

'I feel as if my whole world has caved in.'

She stroked my head.

'I've no job, no money, and what have those months in hospital achieved? Nothing! All they've done is release a whole load of awful memories and hurt and pain, and then given me pills to suppress them again. Now they've thrown me back into the world *they* removed me from, and why? I'm no further forward. What was the point of it all? And Lindsay . . . Lindsay . . .' I broke into sobs of anguish and Shene held me closer.

'I just want to feel special to someone, Shene,' I whispered through my tears. It crossed my mind that at one time, when I was a boy, I might have felt I could be special to Jesus because I identified with so much of his suffering. But not now. That childish phase had passed and I wasn't special to him . . . or to Lindsay. Her letter fell, unnoticed, to the floor.

Chapter 13

'Soup?'

'Pardon?' I stared, horrified, at the young girl offering me a bowl of soup across the trestle table.

'I said would you like some soup?'

I shuffled uncomfortably. 'Well, er . . . I think you've made a mistake. I'm not, er . . . one of your homeless visitors, at least not yet. I was told to come down to the Mission House to help serve soup to them. I'm the new volunteer.'

'Oh! I'm sorry.' She blushed, and very attractively too. 'Well, in that case you'd better come round to this side of the table in case someone else makes the same mistake.' Brown eyes twinkled mischievously as they gave me the once-over, but there was nothing unkind in them, and I had to admit it had been an easy mistake to make. I hardly cut a dashing figure in my faded blue jeans and washed-out jumper with shrunken sleeves. 'My name's Lesley, by the way. Here. You need bowls.'

'Thanks.' I joined her behind the long trestle table and began ladling bowls of hot soup out to the queue of homeless men and women gathered in the church hall.

'What's your name?' she asked.

'Mark.'

'Hi, Mark. Are you at the university as well?'

'No. I'm, er . . . not . . . exactly. I'm . . . between jobs at the moment. I take it you're a student.' It was a statement rather than a question, but it helped take the focus off me.

'Yes. Doing a degree in history and English.' She pulled a face. 'Or trying to.'

I glanced fleetingly at her between ladles of soup. She was dressed like a student, with a baggy blue sweater hanging loosely over her small, shapely body. The short brown curly hair was rumpled, as though she'd just run her hand through it, and her pert, heart-shaped face was flushed with the heat from the kitchen stoves. She stopped serving soup to stir the pan and bring the thicker vegetables to the surface.

'So who was it suggested you come to give us a hand?' she asked me.

'A friend of mine. Lee.' I handed a young man a bowl of hot soup from another pan, ignoring his obscene mutterings. 'He's a member of the Gospel Hall Mission and heard the pastor asking for volunteers.' This revelation from Lee that he went to church and had been a practicing Christian for the past year had come as a bit of a shock. We'd been meeting regularly every Sunday for months, and never once during our little jaunts out had he mentioned he was a Christian. In fact, most of our conversations revolved around cars, football, work, girls or news from Ivy Cottage. Perhaps his being a Christian explained why I'd found him so changed from the Lee I'd fought with when we were younger?

Lesley served a bowl of soup to a young girl who looked half starved. Her hands shook when she took it from her. 'Yes, I know Lee. I go to the Gospel Hall Mission as well.' She smiled warmly at me. 'Welcome aboard, Mark.' She turned her attention to the old man in front of her. 'Did you try that address Pastor Coombs gave you, Sam?'

Vacant, lifeless eyes stared back at her before being lowered. Then Sam shook his head, shakily picked up his bowl and shuffled over to the nearest table.

Lesley sighed. 'Poor Sam' was all she said, but I was drawn by the genuine concern in her voice. These Christians from the Mission Hall seemed to care enough to get involved practically, a bit like the ones who sent all those toys to the children's home.

There wasn't a chance for further conversation as an influx of people kept us busy for the next half hour. There were some forty to fifty people with bowls of soup, bread buns and mugs of tea seated around the tables in the large church hall. Some of them, Lesley informed me later, were mentally ill patients who had been discharged from psychiatric care and didn't have suitable accommodation, but I didn't need to be told that. I recognised the vacant, lifeless eyes filled with that same sense of hopelessness I'd come across in the psychiatric hospital. I was quite surprised to see how many homeless young people there were. Some of them looked even younger than me. Probably runaways, sleeping rough. Others were older, probably drifters who'd simply lost their way in life. I observed them all closely and with a degree of understanding and couldn't help but reflect how close I'd come to being in a similar situation. In fact, it was only because of the generosity of Shene and Graham that I had a home at all. After losing my job in the menswear shop I'd discovered no one, but no one, it seemed, wanted an orphan on the dole who'd been discharged from a psychiatric hospital. And who could blame them? The last few months had been extremely frustrating, very humiliating and had left me with an even greater chip on my shoulder. That was why it was like a breath of fresh air when Lee introduced me to a young group of Christians doing more than just talking about love and going to church on a Sunday.

'Whew!' Lesley wiped her hand across her brow. The hall was hot from the cookers. 'So what do you do at the moment, Mark?'

I leant over one of the big pans to give it a stir and myself a moment to think. I was embarrassed at having to reveal I had neither practical work nor academic qualifications to show in my life. 'I'm a volunteer in the local hospital at the moment,' I said.

'That sounds interesting,' she encouraged, and because she sounded genuinely interested I continued.

'Yes, it is. I work with geriatric and stroke patients in the gym. I help feed and bath them and make their beds. I enjoy it.' I smiled to myself because it was true. I did enjoy working there. It was thanks to Lee, who'd encouraged me to expand my voluntary work while I was still unemployed, that I hadn't slid down into that pit of despair again but had found something worthwhile to do.

It was inevitable that at some point he would invite me to one of his Christian meetings. They weren't the sort of thing that appealed to me, but I was always drawn to the fact that there must be something worthwhile about believing in God, because people I respected – like Uncle, Aunty and Lindsay, the Taits, the church people who sent us all those gifts at Christmas, Lee – all believed in him. I still maintained that when all was said and done God hadn't done very much for me, so why would I want to spend time in one of his churches?, but because Lee had been so kind I went along.

The service wasn't what I expected at all. I actually found I enjoyed being squashed like a sardine between Lee and his girlfriend, Karen, in a crowded church hall with dozens of other young people. They sang, clapped and waved their hands in the air in time to the choruses and seemed to be thoroughly enjoying themselves. It was a far cry from the formal church service I'd been used to. The only disappointment was the speaker. He talked about God as a consistent, loving Father, and about how we're all special to him. Never having experienced a consistent, loving father as a child, or known the joys of being special to anyone, this was something I couldn't really relate to and came to the conclusion he was probably seeing this idealistic God of his through rose-coloured spectacles. However, I can't deny I enjoyed being amongst so many young people and tucking in to the enormous supper afterwards.

'Ah! So you're Mark?' A lightly built, elderly man with thick-rimmed glasses and a bald head came up and shook my hand vigorously. 'I'm Pastor Coombs. Lee has told me all about you.' I think it was the way he said it that made me feel completely naked before him, but somehow I didn't mind. There was something about this little man that I liked instantly. When he smiled he fairly beamed and as our conversation progressed he seemed genuinely interested in my voluntary work and the difficulties of finding a job after coming out of a psychiatric hospital. I hadn't intended telling him all that, it just seemed a natural progression of our conversation.

'You seem to have led a very stress-filled life for one so young,' he observed.

'You can say that again!' I said ruefully.

He smiled. 'If ever you want to talk more fully about it, when we don't have to shout over the noisy babble of my young people, I'd like to hear your story.'

'You would?' I was surprised by his interest, but he seemed to mean what he'd said. 'Yes, I'd like that,' I found myself responding.

He wandered off to talk to someone else, but I wasn't left alone for very long. To my delight, Lesley came over. 'Hi. I see you've met our Pastor Coombs.'

'Yes. He seems nice. Very attentive.'

She managed to nod her head and drink hot coffee from a plastic cup at the same time. 'That's why he's so popular. He simply loves people and makes time for them. What did you think of the speaker, by the way?'

I screwed up my face. 'Interesting, but I'm not sure he did much for me.' I hoped my comment hadn't upset her, but she appeared unperturbed by my lack of enthusiasm.

'Come on,' she said. 'I'll introduce you to the rest of the crowd.'

Lesley seemed quite contented to stay in my company for the remainder of the evening, and who was I to complain! It was almost eleven fifteen p.m. by the time we left the hall. I opened the door for Lesley and as she brushed passed me I caught a whiff of perfume. Smiling with pleasure, I followed her tight blue jeans out into the cool evening air and decided a night at church wasn't such a bad thing after all!

I crept back into the house just before midnight. Shene, Graham and the children were in bed, but there was a letter propped up against the telephone addressed to me. I debated whether to open it or not. It had been such a good evening that I didn't want it spoilt by yet another job rejection. Curiosity got the better of me. Picking up the letter, I tiptoed it into the kitchen, poured myself a glass of milk, sat down at the kitchen table and ripped it open.

Dear Mr Edwards,

Further to your claim for compensation for wrongful dismissal from . . . menswear shop, I now have pleasure in enclosing a cheque for £800.

We wish you well in looking for further employment.

Yours sincerely . . .

I stared in amazement at the cheque: £800! I'd never had so much money in all my life! I hadn't really expected to get anywhere when Shene and Graham had encouraged me to start proceedings against the menswear shop for wrongful dismissal. After all, nothing good ever seemed to come my way, but being compensated for a wrong that had been done to me gave me a good feeling. There was still some sort of justice left in this world after all! As I drifted off to sleep that night I was aware of a spirit of optimism hovering over me. The first I'd experienced in a long, long time.

That little bit of success seemed to go to my head. I wouldn't normally have had the courage to ask Lesley out, but she did seem to seek me out at church and at the soup kitchen, so perhaps she quite liked me. Plucking up my courage, I asked her if she'd like to go for a walk in the park and have an ice cream.

It's strange how two people can meet and be instantly comfortable in each other's company. It was like that with Lesley and me. I didn't feel I needed to explain myself to her, she just accepted me the way I was, and if ever my past was referred to it just seemed to come up in casual conversation and she was never shocked by my admission of attempted suicide. It was very pleasant having such an easy-going person to go out with.

A couple of weeks later Lesley, who normally lived in halls at the university, invited me to spend the weekend at her home so I could meet her parents and sister. I was horrified. My confidence with my little bit of success hadn't grown that much!

'It'll be OK, Mark. They're nice people and I really would like them to meet you,' Lesley pleaded, and because I wanted so much to please her I reluctantly agreed.

I discovered Lesley's parents' – Mr and Mrs John's – bungalow to be in a pleasant, leafy, well-sought-after area of Selby. We walked up a long garden path with neatly trimmed bushes, colourful flowers and not a weed in sight. The front door was flung open by an older version of Lesley, who beamed at me as she looked me up and down. 'Hi! I'm Lesley's sister, Alison. Nice to meet you, Mark.' She gestured to Lesley with her head. 'Dad's in the living room, Les.'

My first impression as I entered the house was that I was well out of my league in this comfortable, middle-class home. My feet sank into thick beige carpets as Lesley led me into the living room. A long plush settee and designer leather chair waited elegantly for guests, but I could hardly see myself sitting in one of them. Wide patio windows, partly covered by rich cream velvet curtains, looked out on to a large lawn and colourful garden. Silver-framed family photographs stood neatly on a grand piano and an array of ornaments decorated a brick fireplace.

'Hi, Dad.' Lesley threw her arms around a tall thin gentleman seated at his desk in the corner of the room. He looked remarkably like Sir Anthony Eden, a previous Prime Minister. He stood up and gave his daughter an affectionate hug, then, untangling himself, stretched out his hand. 'Hello, Mark. I'm Elfed, Lesley's father.'

'Hello, Sir.'

We eyed each other warily. I heard Lesley's sister pounding up the stairs, whispering hoarsely, 'He's here!'

A moment later Lesley's mother, Jennette, appeared. She was an attractive lady with short brown curly hair,

not unlike Lesley's, but more controlled. A brightly
flowered apron covered a plain but elegant olive-green
dress. Her pleasant smile put me at ease. 'Hello,
Mark. Nice to meet you. Lesley has told us so much about
you.'

'Oh?' Why didn't I feel as comfortable with that
remark as when Pastor Coombs had made it? I hoped
Lesley hadn't told them too much.

'Would you like me to show you to your room?'

'Yes, that would be very nice, thank you.'

If only I hadn't glanced towards the full-length mirror
in the hall I might have retained some vague air of
dignity, but as I glimpsed the scruffy tramp with long
dark shoulder-length hair, my remaining puddle of
confidence drained away. With a sinking heart I stared at
the jumper with more darns in the sleeves than sleeves
themselves, the frayed shirt collar and faded, shrunken
jeans. With some strange idea of creating an image for
myself, I'd grown a moustache, but the only image
staring back at me through the hall mirror was that of a
rather unkempt walrus. Some image! Self-consciously I
carried my shabby brown suitcase, the one I'd humped
around foster homes, children's homes and hospitals all
my life, and followed Lesley and her mum up the stairs.
What on earth was I doing becoming romantically
involved with an intelligent, classy girl like Lesley!

The bedroom they gave me was the sort I would have
given the earth for as a child. Cosy, colourful matching
curtains and bedspreads, fitted carpets, pictures on
the walls, teddy bears and dolls crowded together on a
chair in the corner and a long bookcase cluttered
with books and games. Lesley's mum had even placed a
vase of flowers on the windowsill for me. I couldn't
believe children could have a bedroom like this all to
themselves.

Somehow or other I managed to get through the evening meal, although the conversation did become rather awkward at one point.

'Lesley tells me you've been working as a volunteer at the hospital?' Lesley's mum said, handing me a serving dish filled with roast potatoes.

'Yes. But I'm expecting to get a job in a couple of weeks.'

'Oh? Doing what?' she asked politely.

'I've, er . . . I've been offered a post as a . . . a domestic assistant.'

There was an awkward silence. Had they surmised this was the posh title for a cleaner?

I was glad when I could escape to my comfortable bedroom and wallow in the pleasure of having such a lovely spacious room all to myself for the night. I couldn't resist wandering around examining the toys, cupboards and wardrobes as I leisurely undressed for bed. I'd never slept in anything like this in my entire life!

Before switching off the light, I stood at the window overlooking the garden. There seemed to be acres of garden: it was almost as spacious as the one in the children's home, but seventeen of us used to share that. I moved the pretty pink vase containing the fresh flowers to one side, then reached up to close the curtains. The left-hand curtain pulled along the rail quite easily, but the one on the right refused to budge. I tugged, then tugged a bit harder, then gave it a sharp yank. Suddenly the rail shot off the wall, clattered on to the windowsill and dragged the curtains over the pink vase and flowers. It smashed to the ground. I didn't see any more after that because I was draped in pink flowered curtains, and before I could untangle myself footsteps were thudding along the landing and my bedroom door was flung open.

'Mark! Mark, are you all right?'

'What on earth . . .'

I disentangled myself to find Lesley, her mum, dad and sister all standing the doorway in their dressing gowns, staring in disbelief at the havoc I'd created in their beautiful bedroom.

'The curtains . . . fell,' I stammered. I wanted to curl up and die.

'Oh dear. You've knocked the vase off the windowsill,' Lesley's mum said. 'I'd better clear it up before you move. I wouldn't want you to cut your feet.'

'I'm sorry,' I said. I handed her the curtains, still attached to the rail, and watched her struggle helplessly with them until her daughters came to her aid, then I made a vague attempt to gather up the soggy fresh flowers strewn around my feet. I handed them to Lesley's dad. I couldn't think of anything else to do with them.

Lesley giggled. 'Don't worry, Mark. Dad'll fix it in the morning, won't you, Dad?'

'Harrumph!' He didn't sound too happy with that idea.

Despite my growing love for Lesley and the new crowd of friends I'd made, Lindsay still remained hovering at the forefront of my mind. I'd heard from her once since I'd moved back with Shene and Graham, and that was to tell me she'd given birth to a little girl. I'd sent a card and formal letter of congratulations to her and Geoff, but I was still hurt that she'd never replied to my deep, heart-rending admission of loving her.

One evening a few weeks later Lee's girlfriend, Karen, a bright, cheerful nurse who worked at the hospital where I was a volunteer, was driving me at breakneck speed from the hospital to the Mission Hall for a service. It was quite amazing, the number of services I'd been to over the past few weeks, although I must admit the main attraction was far from being the need to worship. We were late – as usual. As Karen screamed around yet another corner, narrowly missing a cyclist, I couldn't help but reflect, with a spate of black humour, what an asset she'd have been when I'd been trying to commit suicide!

The Mission Hall was already filled to capacity when we screeched to a halt outside. The doors and windows were open, but the warmth of the July evening did nothing to dispense the sticky heat. The sound of thunder rumbled in the distance. We made our way towards the seats Lesley and Lee had saved for us. I sat down, glanced at Lesley, who looked hot but very beautiful, and gave her hand a squeeze. As she responded by squeezing my fingers and moving closer I felt a deep glow of happiness wash all over me. Falling in love and actually being loved back was a very pleasant experience and well worth sitting through yet another sermon for.

That night was different. Pastor Coombs spoke about how we let each other down, hurt each other, even abuse each other. Sometimes it is done accidentally, sometimes deliberately, but the damage and hurt that causes to our emotions could be carried around with us for years. Then he went on to emphasise how God was a God of love. Steadfast and reliable. He would never let us down and he wanted to heal those damaged emotions and make us whole.

'It's only when a person feels worthless, unloved and has no hope that he or she considers suicide,' Pastor Coombs continued.

Suicide!! I listened intently.

'*You* are special to God,' the pastor thundered from the pulpit. 'God wants to make *you* whole, to love *you*, and to heal *you* . . . *you* . . . *you* . . . *you* . . .'

I ran my finger around my shirt collar. The prickly heat in the hall was making me perspire.

'Making him part of your life doesn't just include looking to the future. It includes looking at the past. Asking him to heal the emotional traumas you've suffered and that have affected the way you respond to people and situations today. Responses that could be ungodly, hurtful to others and ourselves and prevent the ongoing work of Christ in your life. When we respond to Christ we're saying "yes" to a *perfect* love. A love that never abuses, hurts, rejects or lets you down, but which heals, affirms and gives you hope for your future.'

No one had ever given me hope for my future. No one had ever loved me with that type of love before. People had claimed to love me, but they had always let me down, hurt me and abused me. Was it possible that it was different with God? That he could love me despite the fact I wasn't worth very much? Could he?

The quiet, gentle presence that moved in to make itself known to me at that moment made no demands and spoke no words, but the unconditional love that steadily grew within me was something I'd never experienced in the whole of my life. It seemed to stretch throughout the whole of the sermon, but it must only have lasted a few short moments. I was blissfully lost in the experience when it suddenly flashed across my mind how often I'd been let down in the past. Frightened, I mentally slammed down the shutters. Nothing but *nothing* was allowed to filter through my brick wall! And yet . . . and yet . . . I had experienced something too wonderful for words. Once again I was confused, upset, frightened. I didn't want to go down that road of confusion again. I wouldn't go down that road again! A sob of anguish rose to the surface. I leapt to my feet and, struggling to the end of the aisle, trampling on toes as I did so, fled out of the hot and stuffy Mission Hall and into the small garden surrounding the church.

The first drops of rain were beginning to fall as I stumbled to the wooden bench round the back of the church. Still shaking from the experience, I sat down. I knew I'd caused a scene, rushing out of the church like that, and that Lesley would be worried, but there was nothing I could do about it. I had been completely and absolutely caught up in the message of a God who could love a person like me, *me!* A God who would be willing to take away *my* pain and heal *my* memories. Even now, alone in the tiny garden with the traffic thundering past, I was still aware of that flow of love I'd received from him, but I was scared that if I responded he would find me worthless and withdraw his love the way so many people had in the past.

'There you are, Mark. We were worried about you.' Lee and Karen joined me on the bench.

'Do you want to talk, Mark?' Karen rested her hand comfortingly on my shoulder.

I shook my head. I didn't, but somehow I found myself pouring out my confusion and fear over this God others claimed could love me, give me hope, find me worth something and heal my painful memories.

'But he can,' Karen insisted. 'Why don't you give him a chance, Mark?'

'No! No!' Fear held me in its grasp. 'He'll let me down. Whenever someone claims to love you they always let you down. They never really mean it.'

'God means it.'

It seemed like forever that we sat outside talking, quite oblivious to the rain soaking through our clothes, pinning our hair to our heads. They opened their bibles and quoted scripture at me, pleading with me to give God a chance with my life. Everything they said seemed to make sense, but I was scared of being let down again. Even in the midst of my confusion the old Abba song

'Take a Chance on Me' – *I'll never let you down* – reverberated through my head.

Take a chance on him? Dare I? After all the times I'd been let down in the past, dare I take a chance that the love that was reaching out to me this evening would stay faithful?

It occurred to me that as a child I had been able to identify with Jesus. He'd lived in a community, like me. Not in a children's home, but with a mixed bunch of brothers and sisters, like mine. He ate, slept and worked with them. Like me, he knew betrayal and rejection from them and from others. Even God, his own Father, had let him down, and Jesus had cried out to him on the cross, 'My God! My God! Why have you forsaken me?' Yes, he knew all about being let down by a parent, so he should be able to understand my reluctance to take a chance on him.

I hesitated, for into my mind came the scripture reading the Bible study group had brought up two weeks ago. We'd explored the many times Jesus had left his disciples, the crowds and his ministry so that he could spend time in prayer to his Father. His Father was someone whom he obviously held in the highest esteem. Had I perhaps misunderstood the relationship between them?

Perhaps I did have a lot of questions and uncertainties about God being a Father to me because I didn't rate father figures very highly. In fact, I was downright suspicious of them. But Jesus seemed to trust his Father and he came to tell us what his Father was really like. He came to get rid of all those misconceptions, so perhaps . . .

'Therefore, if anyone is in Christ, he is a new creation; the old has gone, the new has come!' (2 Corinthians 5:17). That really appealed to me. To be a new person, a new creation. Someone with hope, a future, a person worth something to someone else. I wanted that! I wanted to be healed of the painful memories of my past life and if Jesus Christ, who knew what brokenness was, could, according to Pastor Coombs, heal me and make a person like me into a new creation, then . . .

It was quite simple, how it happened, really. There were no flashing lights or voices from the heavens, just a simple prayer said by Karen for Christ to come into my life and love me. I didn't say anything; I just watched the rain splash on my trousers and nodded my head in agreement, hoping that would be enough to be taken as an act of commitment.

When they'd finished praying they left me and went back into the hall, soaked to the skin. I needed time to be on my own, I said.

The town hall clock struck ten and a pigeon flew into the darkened sky, alarmed by the noise. I sat very still, totally unaware of the noise of the traffic around me, the heavy dark skies, the rain soaking through my clothes and the singing taking place inside the church. And in that stillness I knew, without any doubt whatsoever, that today, July 27th at ten p.m., in a torrential thunderstorm, I had given Jesus Christ my life to heal and to do something with, and now . . . now I was beginning something new!

Chapter 14

I waited patiently for God to start showing he really did love me by healing me of the awful memories from childhood, but it seemed this was going to take longer than I imagined. I dread to think what would have become of me if it hadn't been for Pastor Coombs. He was my guide, my mentor and the first father figure to give me that most precious of commodities: time. Sometimes, when the memories were too painful to talk about and all I could do was sob uncontrollably, he would gently wrap his arms around me; then, when I'd calmed down, he would quietly pray for God to heal me. There were many occasions over that two-year period when he would sit with me until well into the night and I began to feel through this action of love that God was less of an austere figure and less remote.

Pastor Coombs didn't always pander to my emotional outbursts, either. He was a hard taskmaster, and after one of my particularly stormy disruptions during a church service he gave me a very stern reprimand. That was the day I completely lost my temper with him, storming around the manse living room in a state of frenzy.

'How do you know what it's like to have such a hellish life?' I bellowed.

'This sounds very like self-pity I'm listening to, Mark,' he said calmly. 'I think you need to learn more in the way of self-control. Perhaps you should go home now. You may return when you've calmed down.' He pointed firmly to the door.

I saw red! Whatever remained of my self-control disappeared in an outburst of obscenities, while my hands grasped the first object to hand, which happened to be a dining room chair. With uncanny strength I hurled it across the room towards him. He automatically raised his hands to shield himself from the inevitable blow. Fear and shock registered on his face. Fortunately, my aim wasn't too accurate, but nevertheless he landed a nasty bruise on his arm and side. I was thoroughly ashamed of myself over that little fiasco.

He didn't spend all his time listening to me, either. He continually encouraged me to become more actively involved in the plight of homeless people, and coming across destitute men and women, many of them my own age, sleeping rough, sometimes from psychiatric hospitals and nearly all with an air of hopelessness about them, helped me put my own situation in perspective.

Some of the first painful memories that surfaced were those of continually being dumped into foster homes by my parents. I remembered my cries of anguish – 'Mummy! Mummy!' – as I struggled to get away from the social worker. I never thought I would be able to forgive my parents for doing that to me! However, over those months of talking to Pastor Coombs, I was able to gain a little understanding of the problems in their lives. Gradually I realised that despite all they had put me through my bitterness towards them was not as deep as it had been, although I still hurt from the pain of their rejection.

Another memory to surface was the time Miss Vernon and Mrs Robins physically dragged Paul and me away from Mr and Mrs Tait's secure home. As the tears flooded down my cheeks, so did the bitterness of knowing that, once again, someone I trusted had let me down. What was so terrible about me that I should continually be rejected and abandoned? I'd always blamed myself as I'd searched for the answer, but all I'd done was drag my self-esteem even lower. Pastor Coombs talked and prayed this issue through with me until the time came when I recognised the fault lay with the system of fostering in social work, not with Miss Vernon, and that I was a victim of that system. Only then was I able to release my angry and hurt feelings in prayer to God and recall once more my affection for the social worker who had tried to do her best for us.

The more time Pastor Coombs gave me the more I selfishly demanded. Even Lesley found it necessary to gently rebuke me when we went for a walk in the park one evening.

'He has other people to pastor as well as you, Mark.'

'I know Lesley, but he listens. He's the first person who has ever really sat down and listened to me because he wants to.'

I couldn't fail to see the look of hurt cross her face. 'I'll listen, Mark.'

'I know you will, love.' I hesitated, partly to think and partly to make sure we were out of earshot of passers-by. 'You're someone I've fallen in love with, Lesley. I don't want to spoil the happiness we've found by burdening you with my past. Besides which, you have given me something much more precious. Do you know that?'

'Oh?'

I nodded and pulled her closer towards me. 'Hope,' I said. 'For the first time in my life I have a hope. Admittedly, I'm still unemployed, but I have a positive outlook for the future. I also trust you more than I've trusted anyone in the whole of my life.'

She snuggled closer to me with pleasure. 'And you love me?'

I smiled and hugged her. 'Yes, I love you,' I whispered in her ear.

Becoming a Christian had made me want to tell everyone what had happened to me, so I was more than delighted when I received a letter from Paul on HMS Something-or-Other to say he'd be home for a few weeks' leave and would be crashing out in my tiny boxroom for a couple of days. I think Shene and Graham viewed his visit with mixed feelings. Much as they loved him, their home was already overcrowded.

He arrived home, bronzed, beaming from ear to ear and looking very smart in his Navy uniform. With a whoop of joy he hurled his bag across the lawn, raced up the path and with cries of delight we slapped each other on the back and danced wildly around Shene's tiny garden, trampling her precious pansies underfoot.

'Mad as hatters, the pair of you,' she admonished, laughing. 'Ow! Give over, Paul!' she shrieked as he grabbed her around the waist and swung her around.

It was lovely to be a family together again and Paul had so much to tell us about his life in the Navy, but it wasn't until Shene, Graham and the children had gone to bed that I was able to tell him of Lesley, my conversion, Pastor Coombs and the church. He lay stretched out on the settee with his eyes half closed and was quiet for so long I thought he'd gone to sleep. Eventually he stirred. 'So you've gone and got religion?' was all he said.

'Yeah.'

'And you think you've found the solution to getting over a bad childhood, do you?'

'I think I have.'

There was silence for a while. Then he said, 'So have I.'

I stared at him in amazement. 'You're a Christian?' I was thrilled.

'Well, not exactly,' he grinned shamefacedly. 'The Navy. I don't need to look at the past when I'm hundreds of miles away from it.'

'That's escapism.'

'So is religion.'

'No it's not.'

Yes it is. You tell your problems to God. I tell the petty officer – and end up scrubbing decks! Believe me, the pain in the arms, wrists and knees that gives you soon makes you forget the pain of the past!' He let out a roar of laughter, highly amused at his own wit.

Paul wasn't interested. In fact, it seemed as though his coming home and seeing me, Shene and Graham and visiting Jenny and Maxine, our other two sisters, brought back too many bad memories for him, and he appeared only too pleased when his leave was up and he could sail as far away as possible from everything that reminded him of his childhood. I watched him go with a heavy heart.

Pastor Coombs didn't allow me to mope over Paul for very long.

'How did that job interview go, Mark?' he asked as we walked from church one cold November evening.

My heart sank into my boots, which it always did at the mention of finding a permanent job. 'Same as usual,' I muttered.

'No luck, eh?'

'It's always the same story. They take one look at my atrocious academic record, then discover I've been in a psychiatric hospital, and show me the door. It's so ... degrading!'

'It's just a thought,' Pastor Coombs mused, 'but while you're still unemployed, how do you fancy studying for better grades, perhaps with a view to going into some form of community work? After all, you've had plenty practical experience with me, and that should stand you in good stead.' He hesitated. 'Or . . . or you could consider going to Bible college. How does that appeal to you?'

I thought I'd misheard him. 'Study? Bible college? Are you mad?'

He chuckled. 'Possibly, lad. Nevertheless, you have a real compassion and understanding for folk in trouble and you have a firm grasp of the Bible. And to be honest with you, Mark,' he added, 'I'm not as young as I was and recently I've been finding some of the work pretty heavy going. It dawned on me I might have to look towards retirement myself soon and I'd like to see you settled in a good job before then.'

I gave him a sidelong glance. I'd never really thought of Pastor Coombs as being old. I'd never taken any notice of the telling wrinkles across his forehead or his stooped shoulders before. With a pang of guilt I hoped I hadn't been responsible for ageing him. I had been quite a handful.

Almost as though he was reading my mind he said, 'You've worked through a lot of problems in the last couple of years, Mark, but we can't be spending *all* our time concentrating on your past. We have to think of the future. Qualifications, and a job. You're not stupid or ignorant, but you have been unfortunate in your schooling. Perhaps studying will help you to be worthy of that young lady of yours.'

I raised my eyebrows questioningly at him. 'What do you mean?'

'You need a goal in life, a career, an income if you're thinking of marrying Lesley.'

'Who says I'm going to marry Lesley?'

'Ah! But she loves you,' he said simply. 'And I'd like to marry the pair of you before God calls me home.'

I didn't need to think very hard about whether I wanted to marry Lesley. She was the best thing that had ever happened to me. She was attractive, intelligent and humorous, yet I wondered, and not for the first time, what she saw in me.

The following day was one of those cold, crisp November afternoons when the sun shines but nothing looks as if it will ever grow again. The trees were lifeless and bare and the ground hard and colourless. As Lesley and I walked through the park I took the opportunity of telling her about Pastor Coombs' suggestion that I study for higher grades and think about Bible college or community work.

I laughed nervously. 'He even suggested we should get married before he gets his calling cards home.'

She tilted her head thoughtfully, cradling my arm in hers as we took a short cut across the grass. 'That sounds like a pretty sensible suggestion.'

I glanced at her suspiciously. 'You mean you'd actually, er . . .'

'Marry you? Yes.'

'You would?'

'I've just said so.'

'But . . . I've no money.'

'Neither have I.' She giggled and squeezed my arm. 'At least you'll never be able to say I married you for your money.'

'I didn't . . . didn't think you'd consider . . .'

Her warm body pressed comfortably against mine. 'Idiot!' she whispered, kissing my ear. 'Why do you think I've been going out with you all this time? I love you, Mark. I don't care that we haven't any money.'

'I haven't any qualifications either,' I said ruefully.

'So? We'll work at getting you qualified in something.'

'That's what Pastor Coombs said, but . . .'

'But what?'

'Do you really think I've got it in me to study?'

She gazed at me, loving me with her eyes. 'Yes, I do, and I'll help you. We've our whole lives in front of us, Mark. There's so much we can do together.'

I had a sudden fleeting glimpse of myself standing in Shene and Graham's bathroom with the life flow ebbing away from my body as my wrists poured with blood. I shuddered. How close I had come to losing all this. I untangled Lesley's arm and threw mine around her shoulders. 'So you will marry me?'

'Yes please.'

'And what will we live on?'

She grimaced. 'We'll manage. There's your dole money and I'll be bringing in a small wage from the Mission House.' She groaned. 'I still have to tell my parents I've chosen to work there for a while instead of becoming a teacher. They're going to get an awful shock.'

I didn't say anything. They were going to get an even bigger shock when she told them she was marrying me!

I never expected the wedding preparations to run smoothly. After all, why should they? My life had never run smoothly in the past. So it was a shock to the system when Lesley's parents, although obviously concerned about their daughter's marriage to an unstable, unemployed, penniless individual, showed genuine pleasure at receiving me into their family and began plying us with gifts for our 'bottom drawer'. As neither of us could think of any good reason why we should wait before we tied the knot, we planned an April wedding. Even a one-room bedsit turned up. Poor I might be, but I was proud of this one small room with its bed-settee, two-ringed stove and shared bathroom facilities across the landing, because it was mine, all mine – albeit rented. We were given a proper wedding as well, not a cheap penny-pinching affair. Lesley's parents did us proud. Vibrant pink and white carnations, their sweet fragrance filling the church, decorated the aisles and altar. They were a present from the congregation.

My spiritual mentor, Pastor Coombs, was beaming all over his face as he moved towards the centre dais. The little man looked so happy you'd think it was him getting married! He leant forward as I came within earshot. 'This is one of the happiest days of my life.' His voice trembled. 'I shall remember it always Mark. Always!'

As if in a dream, I saw Lesley walking towards me on her father's arm, smiling and beautiful, her cheeks flushed with excitement, her eyes sparkling, but even at this most precious moment in my life, as the woman I loved walked towards me, I was unable to suppress the cry in my head – *Lindsay! This should be Lindsay!* For a split second the obsessive love I carried for this other woman soared to the surface. But then Lesley reached my side and was squeezing my hand and I found myself responding in like manner and taking this sweet person to be my lawful wedded wife.

Two nights in a hotel was all we could afford, and even then we knew we were being extravagant. Then it was back to our new one-room bedsit. We opened the door, dropped our suitcases in the middle of the floor and gazed around us in amazement.

Pink, white and red carnations decorated our new home. Lesley wandered over to one of the vases and picked up a card.

'Oh, Mark, how lovely. They're a "welcome home" from the people at the church.'

A large box of groceries stood on the table. A gift from Karen, Lee and a few other friends. Everyone had been so kind it was almost embarrassing.

We stood in the middle of the room and wrapped our arms around each other.

'Happy?' Lesley whispered, lifting her face to mine.

I smiled. 'I've never been this happy in my entire life.'

'And we'll keep on being happy.' She slowly unbuttoned my shirt.

'I know.' I kissed her nose and eyelashes.

'Our first night in our own home.'

'It's not night, and it's only rented,' I whispered, but I didn't care what time of day it was. We were still on our honeymoon and she was warm and soft and I was losing myself in this most precious of moments when the doorbell rang.

'Hell!'

Between giggles she helped me quickly button up my shirt and after checking I'd tucked it back into my trousers she opened the door.

'Karen! Lee! What a lovely surprise. Come on in. We've just arrived back What's wrong?'

I knew there was something wrong the moment they walked in. Karen was white and tense and Lee's expression of solemnity warned me of bad news. Lesley and I exchanged anxious glances.

'What's happened?' I asked quietly.

Karen pulled out her handkerchief. 'Mark, oh Mark. I'm so sorry.' She looked pleadingly at Lee, who cleared his throat before saying, 'It's Pastor Coombs, Mark. He died yesterday morning.'

There was a gasp from Lesley, and then my heart began a dull pounding in my ears. I was vaguely aware Lesley had slipped her fingers through mine.

'Dead?' I repeated. 'There must be some mistake.' But the haunted expressions on the faces of my friends told me not.

'What happened?' Lesley asked quietly, and I thought, *Why does everyone speak quietly when there's death around?*

'Heart attack.' Karen matched Lesley's sombre whispers. 'We didn't contact you straight away, we thought . . .' She blew her nose noisily.

'No, no you're wrong. He couldn't . . . couldn't . . .' I heard myself blabbering like a fool while I tried to control the pounding in my chest, which was making it difficult for me to breathe.

'Mark!' Lesley rested her hand on my shoulder reassuringly, but the touch that had stirred my senses earlier now left me cold and empty.

'He can't be . . . dead! He can't!' My voice shook. 'No! No!' A blinding rage that I hadn't experienced in almost two years now exploded and gave expression as I hurled my old brown suitcase, still standing in the middle of the floor, across the room. It smashed against the box of groceries on the table sending tins and packets crashing to the floor. A vase smashed, flowers fell, water spilt, but I was past caring. Flinging open the door I raced out of the room, vaguely aware of voices in the background calling, 'Mark! Come back! Don't do this, Mark!' I ignored them. I needed space to be alone with this awful thing that had happened.

I headed towards the park. It was midday, but the grey clouds that had been hovering around all morning had now turned into a fine drizzle, sending folks scurrying back to their homes. I'd left home without a coat, but I was hardly aware of the dampness soaking through my cotton shirt, chilling me to the bone. All I could think about was this man I had grown to love above all others. My father figure, mentor and friend, Pastor David

Coombs. Time seemed insignificant as I walked through the half-empty streets, trying to come to terms with the awful shock. At one point I was vaguely aware that the streetlights had come on and the rush hour traffic was building up, but then the scenery around me became less familiar and there were more fields and trees than houses and buildings. Then the cold, dark, friendless night set in and some inner instinct drew me back towards the lights of the city, where I continued wandering the streets, tired, cold and wet, like the homeless and destitute people I'd been working with for the past three years.

'Why God? Why?!' My explosion of anger turned towards God but there was no answer to my pain-filled cry.

I found shelter in the tunnel under the bridge down by the canal. It was draughty, but afforded some refuge from the driving rain. Shivering with cold, I curled up in the corner of one of the buttresses.

'*You* took him!' I silently accused God. '*You* took him when you knew how much he meant to me. *You* took him, and I hate you for that!' It was the same story repeating itself. People I loved were always being taken from me, or I was taken from them. My parents, the Taits, Miss Vernon, the children's home . . . Lindsay . . . *Lindsay!*

A great sob of anguish rose into my chest. Once again I was a lost, empty and frightened child, abandoned by someone he needed, and as the accumulated pain from all these losses broke free I screamed out, 'I HATE YOU, GOD! Do you hear me? I HATE YOU!'

PART THREE

PART THREE

Chapter 15

I took the long way home from the doctor's, through the leafy suburban housing estate with its well-set-out flower gardens, then through the big iron gates that led into the park. I sauntered past children playing on the swings and couples lazing on the grass enjoying the warm summer sunshine. I needed the exercise and I needed time to think.

This was one of the most contented periods of my entire life. It was nearly five years since my marriage to Lesley and our love seemed to have grown stronger with each passing year. Admittedly, it had been a difficult start in that tiny bedsit. Money had been almost non-existent and the untimely death of Pastor Coombs had hit me severely. It had taken me a long time to stop being angry with God and come to terms with the fact that I'd lost not only a friend but also a father figure who really cared and would no longer be there for me when I needed counselling and prayer. In fact, I don't know what I would have done if it hadn't been for Lesley. Her loving support flatly refused to let me sink into a pit of depression, but brought me through the deep time of mourning and encouraged me to look to the future.

It was almost like a dream when, a few months after Pastor Coombs' death, we moved to Dorset so I could study for a two-year diploma in theology at the Moorlands Bible College, the college Pastor Coombs had thought would suit my needs best. I never believed they would accept someone like me. I felt neither qualified as a person nor a Christian, but I worked hard over those two years, gaining experience in an open Brethren Assembly, running activities and leading Bible studies with a boys' group. Then two years later I was accepted as a pastoral assistant and lay worker at a large Baptist church in Lancashire. Admittedly, it was poorly paid, but I didn't mind because I was ambitious enough to believe that, if I worked hard enough, in a couple of years I could be an accredited pastor.

As soon as the pastor of the Baptist church discovered my background, I was called upon to work in the wider community: talking to people who had attempted suicide; working in a drug rehabilitation centre; discovering a niche for myself in the local children's home. Because I shared the unhappy childhood experiences of many of these children, I was accepted as one of them. Pastor Coombs had been right. Drawing alongside people whose pain I understood was something I was good at.

I came out at the far side of the park and stopped for a moment to watch the up-and-coming tennis players, freshly enthused by the exciting Wimbledon finals, then headed towards the row of terraced houses where we lived. As I opened the front door there was a smell of liver and onions, talcum powder and fresh laundry.

'Daddy! Daddy!' The bundle of arms, legs and noise that hurled itself at my knees had made me the proudest man on earth and had only added to my determination to make something of my life. I threw my son into the air and proceeded to blow raspberries into his neck. He squealed with delight.

'You encourage his noise,' Lesley complained, but her smile was one of contentment as she sat feeding our baby daughter some indistinguishable pea-green gunge from a bowl. 'Let Daddy sit down, Jonathan, and you can finish drawing that picture for Grandma.'

My son planted a sticky kiss on my cheek then toddled off to continue his masterpiece. I loved being a father. Jonathan and Fiona were the most precious things in my life.

'How did you get on?' Lesley asked.

I removed a pile of clean nappies and building blocks from the chair. 'You know what doctors are like.'

'That doesn't answer my question,' Lesley chided gently. 'I asked how you got on?'

She was too sharp for her own good, my wife.

'He thinks it could be trauma from a disturbed past that's causing these stomach problems,' I reluctantly told her. 'He wants me to see a psychiatrist.' I pulled off my shoes and stretched out. 'The very thought of having to go and see a . . . a . . .' I couldn't even finish the sentence. Lesley knew how much I hated reminders of my time in the psychiatric hospital.

'You know . . .' Lesley began, but was interrupted by Fiona spitting out her food. I wasn't surprised. It looked revolting! 'You could go and have a word with that Anglican vicar who supposedly has a healing ministry in his church. What do you think?'

'Mmm' seemed a pretty safe, non-committal reply. Our previous church had not encouraged such things as healing services and I was a little sceptical. From what we'd heard, some of them could be too much of an emotional drama, and I'd had enough emotion and drama in my life without encouraging more.

'It can't do any harm. Can it?' Lesley persisted. 'At least it's better than having to see a psychiatrist.'

She had a point. After all, being counselled by Pastor Coombs had done more for me in the way of healing than the psychiatric hospital with all its drugs and qualified psychiatrists.

'I'll think about it,' I said cautiously.

So, over the following week, while I thought, Lesley set about making an appointment for me to talk to the Reverend Peter Haywood.

I found him to be a small, bald-headed, very ordinary sort of vicar who didn't bamboozle you with long words and deep theological insights.

'I'm on a diet,' he informed me, laughing, as his wife, Jane, brought a pot of tea and three very large cream cakes into his shambles of a study. He patted his paunch and shook his head as though it was all her fault for bringing the cream cakes. While we ate them I told them my story. Occasionally one of them would interrupt to clarify a point, but it took me most of the session to relate all that had happened to me. Then there was silence. I wasn't too sure whether they were praying or thinking, but either way I was exhausted with all the talking, so I sat back against the large flowered cushions on my chair and closed my eyes. There was a smell of coffee, pipe tobacco and musty books in the room and a steady hum from an electric fire throwing warm air in my direction. Somewhere in the distance I could hear the sound of the washing machine in the kitchen doing a late-night stint, the cars on the main road busily going about their own business, but over and beyond what I couldn't smell, see or hear was an unmistakable sense of there being a reverend peace in that tiny study. A bit like a church. Here was a place of quiet and prayer, a place of thought and meditation. My body and mind were relaxed and at ease when suddenly and without warning I was seized with one of those excruciating stomach pains I'd been having recently. I shuffled in discomfort, my first thoughts being, 'It's that damn cream cake.' Peter Haywood turned to look at me but didn't say anything. Suddenly I knew my condition had nothing to do with cream cakes but was the forceful surfacing of one of those long-suppressed memories. *Lindsay!* I sat waiting for the pain to ease, then slowly sat up and leant back against the cushions and put my head in my hands.

Jane Haywood rested her hand on my shoulder. 'Do you want to talk some more, Mark?'

I did. But I was very tired, so we decided to fix up another appointment.

Lesley was curled up on the settee watching television when I arrived home.

'How did it go?' She switched the television off with the remote control.

'It was fine.' I sat down opposite her, pulling off my shoes, playing for time to work out how I was going to tell her that Lindsay was still an issue in my life.

'And?'

'And it seems the doctor is probably right. The pain of the past wants to be out.'

She waited for me to continue. When I didn't she gave me a prompt. 'So?'

'So I'm going to go back to see Peter and Jane Haywood.'

'Uh-huh. What aren't you telling me, Mark?'

I groaned inwardly. 'What I'm not telling you, Lesley is . . . is . . .' I found one of Jonathan's building bricks behind the cushion and turned it over in my hands, carefully examining the colourful pictures on all sides, avoiding her eyes. ' . . . is that . . . one of the emotions to surface was the love I . . . I carried for Lindsay. I'm not going to tell you about that because I love you, Lesley, and I don't want to hurt you.'

I wanted to reach out and touch the pain I knew I'd created in her when I'd said that. I wanted to take her in my arms and reassure her, but I needed to see how far along this road she would go with me to resolving my awful past before it affected us both. I put down the building block and faced her squarely. She was still curled up, staring at the empty television screen, her face expressionless; her hair, now long and curly, hung in a loose tangle around her shoulders. Her figure, slightly fuller after having had two children, was still curvy in all the right places. I loved her dearly and hated myself for doing this to her.

'Do you still . . .' Her voice was almost a whisper. 'Do you still think of her . . . often?'

I knew I had to be truthful. My marriage depended on it. 'Yes.'

She digested my answer, then asked, 'Do you still . . . love her?'

I took a deep breath. 'I thought I was over her, but I realise I've always loved her. I wish I didn't, because it's a love that got all screwed up and wrong.'

Her face had turned pale and her lovely brown eyes were brimming with tears. 'And me? Do you still love . . . me?'

I couldn't bear not to hold her in my arms a moment longer. I pulled her towards me.

'Love you?' I whispered as she curled up beside me. 'No, I don't love you any more, funny face. That's why I've been so contented these last few years. Hadn't you noticed?'

She smiled at me through her tears and I held her tightly. 'Lesley.' I wrapped a strand of her hair around my finger. 'Lesley, you and the children mean more to me than anything in the whole wide world. You need to know that, because I need you to stand by me while I deal with this . . . screwed-up love I have for Lindsay and all the other bits and pieces that have got screwed up along the way. I'd thought being so happily married to you, having the children and doing a job I love would put the past behind me once and for all. But, as I keep being reminded, these things always catch up with you somewhere along the line because something happens that triggers off a past memory.' I kissed her gently on the forehead. 'I want rid of it all, Lesley. I want to be free of the past so I can concentrate on us and our future together, and I need to know where you'll be standing in all this?'

She lay with her head resting on my shoulder and was quiet for so long I was beginning to get anxious. When she spoke it was barely above a whisper.

'Tell me about Lindsay,' she said.

'Are you sure?'

She lifted her head. 'I want rid of your past too, Mark. I won't have what we've got threatened by a . . . a ghost.'

'She's hardly a ghost.'

'I know.'

Lesley was right. Lindsay wasn't a ghost. She and I corresponded about twice a year. My letters were long, non-threatening, newsy letters, enclosing birthday or Christmas cards, and hers were along the same friendly vein. She and Geoff were happily married with two children and had written expressing their delight when I went to Bible college and later became a pastor's assistant in the Baptist church.

'So, tell me about her.'

I don't think I have ever loved my wife more than that evening when, despite how threatened she must have been feeling, she reached out to take my hand as a gesture she would walk this journey with me.

The months that followed weren't easy ones for Lesley or for me. It seemed as though the Reverend Peter Haywood and those involved with the healing ministry at the Anglican church began picking up where Pastor Coombs had left off, although their techniques were very different.

Peter Haywood explained to me that, because I hadn't been able to cope with my feelings in the past, I had in effect built a brick wall around me for protection, and the pain I was now experiencing was God breaking through the wall. It was a good analogy, as I could distinctly remember sitting on the swing by the big brick wall surrounding the children's home and deciding quite emphatically that in order to protect myself from being hurt any more I needed a big brick wall around me.

One incident to arise was the particularly horrible memory of the time I was abused in the bathroom in the children's home. The well-meaning advice I had been given was 'Put it behind you. Forget about it.' So I had. I'd built a brick wall around the whole experience and all the feelings that experience contained.

'God doesn't want experiences that cause damage to his children to be bricked up in a corner of their lives and to reappear like gremlins when some future incident sparks them off,' Peter Haywood explained. 'He wants them and the strongholds that protect those feelings out of your life altogether. He wants wholeness.'

The trouble was, to heal the memories of that abuse meant re-examining the whole incident all over again. It meant identifying the fear and shame I'd experienced. It was an exhausting and extremely painful process, and at the end of each session Peter would say a short prayer. I didn't experience any immediate difference, either through the counselling or the prayers, but as the weeks and months progressed I was aware of my general health improving.

We looked at other issues, such as the difficulty I still had in forgiving my parents for abandoning me to Social Services, but gradually I discovered a greater acceptance of my state at that time, which was one of being a victim of circumstances beyond my control. The releasing taking place within me was what drugs and psychiatry should have effected, but hadn't.

At one session I found myself sobbing over the injustice at having been sacked from the menswear shop and the frustration of knowing no one was willing to give me a chance to work. I was 'psychologically disturbed', they said. I'd 'never hold down a job'. I'd 'always be in and out of psychiatric care'. These were the negative responses I'd taken on board in the psychiatric hospital and out of it. Negative thoughts that had taken root, and these thought patterns needed changing.

The only area where there seemed to be no movement was in my obsessive love for Lindsay. Time and time again I thought it was dealt with, only to find it all flooding back some days later. Healing was not only difficult to understand, but was obviously going to take some considerable time.

I didn't spend all my time focused on the past. Encouraged by the local Baptist superintendent, I applied to the Baptist church with a view to becoming a full-time pastor. Lesley and I really believed this was a calling from God. It therefore came as a devastating blow when, after my interviews, I returned home one evening to find a letter of rejection.

'Here I am, rapidly heading for my thirties and looking to advance my career by being accredited as a pastor, and once again I'm thrown on to the rubbish heap!' I stormed to Lesley.

'You can't blame them for raising the question of your lack of education and whether you could cope with the stress of the job,' she consoled. 'All we can do now is accept their decision and continue to trust God with our future.'

'What future?' I snapped. 'It's back to the same old pattern again! All I need is a chance to prove myself, Lesley. Just one chance!' Devastated, I threw the letter on to the table. I would not stay where I was not wanted, not even in the role of pastoral assistant. Was it too much to ask to earn a liveable wage for my family? I stormed out of the house. I needed time to think.

'You heal me with one hand and slap me across the face with the other!' I reproached God angrily as I slammed the door behind me.

The air was damp from the fine mist that had hung around all day and the streetlights trying to penetrate through it cast an eerie glow across the grey, leaden sky. I slowed my pace, as the fallen leaves of late autumn were wet and slippery underfoot. Normally I would have enjoyed an early evening walk, but tonight I couldn't concentrate on anything but my letter of rejection.

'I've no option but to resign my post after this!' I muttered. 'How can I stay when it is been made impossible for me to advance my career?' But what else could I do? I must have walked for miles with my mind churning over a confused jumble of thoughts.

Suddenly a loud toot jolted me out of my brooding. With a start, I jumped back, narrowly missing the wing mirror of a car. Slightly shaken, I stood unsteadily on the edge of the pavement, taking a few deep breaths to calm my nerves. I'd been so wound up over my future I'd almost solved my own problem by making sure I didn't have a future to worry about.

For the first time I became conscious of the scenery around me. There was a smell of smoke from the chimneys of the old stone cottages nearby and through the lit windows of the houses I caught a glimpse of families watching television, having their evening meal or engrossed in some other home activity. That was where I should be – at home with Lesley, Jonathan and Fiona. Slowly and thoughtfully I retraced my steps. The leaves were so slippery underfoot that more than once I almost landed on my rear.

With one of those sudden flashes of insight that you've done this sort of thing before, my mind flashed back to the evening I'd run along the slippery country lane from the psychiatric hospital to find Sally. It had been late autumn then, and Sally had been suicidal. We'd stood in the middle of that awful bridge that always seemed to draw us when we were at our lowest ebb and Sally had allowed me to hold her, comfort her and kiss her on the forehead. It hadn't been easy for her, but I had been part of that healing process. Healing her fear of men. Then, hand in hand, we had walked away from the bridge.

I crossed the road leading to my home, where Lesley, Jonathan and Fiona were waiting. There were others holding my hand now, enabling me to face the terrifying memories behind my brick wall. I took the keys out of my pocket and fumbled with the latch. But before I turned the key, I turned to God.

'I *will* walk away from my past and make something of this life you've given me!' I prayed vehemently. 'I don't know how, but . . . but, by God, You've given me my life back and I'll take every ounce of strength and power You can give me and go through every door You open for me and . . . and God help me, I'll make my life worth something!'

It was Peter Haywood who suggested I contact the DDO (Diocesan Director of Ordinands) for the Anglican church with a view to applying for full-time ministry. A few weeks later I was requested to attend a series of interviews.

'The real problem is, you've had no previous connection with the Anglican church,' I was informed. 'However, after due consideration, we feel that if you can see your way clear to resigning from your present position with the Baptist church and becoming a member of the Anglican church, then it would be a step in the right direction.'

'But what would I live on? I have a wife and two pre-school children to support.'

The DDO smiled as one might when about to present a surprise package. 'As it happens, I've a proposal to put to you which has come from the Reverend Peter Haywood.'

'Oh?'

'Reverend Haywood would be willing to take you on a pastoral assistant in his church for a year. That arrangement would provide you with valuable experience within the Anglican church.' The DDO's expression changed somewhat, showing bad news was following the good. 'Unfortunately, on a practical level, this post can't be made available for some months, so you'd be unemployed for a while, and £40 per week plus state benefits isn't much for you and your family to live on.' He shrugged his shoulders as he watched my reaction to his proposal and I realised my sense of vocation was being severely tested. I'd not only have to give up my livelihood with the Baptist church but the house that went with the job. I was in a real dilemma. We were poor enough without me putting my family through more hardships. I left, promising a reply by the end of the week.

It didn't take Lesley and me long to make our decision. We had to do it. After all, we'd never had much money anyway, so living on very little was nothing new to us. So we took the drop in living standards. But my heart bled when the worried furrow appeared on Lesley's brow whenever the children needed new shoes or when Christmas or birthdays came around or when a bill that we couldn't pay came. 'Money isn't everything!' she kept saying, but those were the times I tried hard not to remember the plush-carpeted, velvet-curtained home of her parents and the level of poverty I'd dragged her down to. If it wasn't for the practical support of the Anglican and Baptist congregations we would never have kept our heads above water. Odd donations would appear through the letterbox or a bundle of clothes would be given to us for the children. But perhaps the greatest gift was the Baptist church allowing us to keep our home until my transfer into the Anglican church.

My counselling was put on hold during those months of unemployment and when, eventually, the Anglican church took me on as a key worker there was never any time for delving into my past, as I had to prove my worth by throwing myself wholeheartedly into the work of pastoring others.

Eventually the decision reached was that I could go forward for training as an Anglican priest, but only after a two-year pre-ordination course, which I needed because of my lack of Anglicanism. This decision placed me in an impossible situation. I could hardly impose on the Baptist church to let me live in the manse for a further two years, and even if we could afford to rent somewhere we had hardly any furniture of our own.

Peter and I talked this situation through a number of times and I tried very hard to keep faith in God, but with a background of failures and rejections like mine, it wasn't easy. The problem seemed to loom over us like a big black cloud with no solution forthcoming. The breakthrough fell upon us so suddenly it almost took our breath away. In an unusual occurrence, an Anglican bishop, hearing of our situation, overruled the recommendation that I should do the two-year pre-ordination course and informed us that, if the college accepted me, I could start my training in a few weeks.

I'd never been so scared in all my life, but when the interviews were over I was informed there was a place for me – and a house! *A house!* We were ecstatic! It turned out to be a three-bedroom, semi-detached house situated in a cul-de-sac on a pleasant leafy housing estate with gardens front and rear, and only a five-minute bus ride from the college.

So I began my training for the Anglican priesthood at Cranmer Hall, Durham University. The academic side of college life proceeded without a hitch; I actually found I enjoyed the mental stimulation, and my grades and tutorial reports were surprisingly good, considering I'd had such bad school reports. My only difficulty lay in adjusting to the college discipline of Daily Office and formal weekly Eucharist. I missed the informal worship of my previous church, but otherwise those first eight or nine months of settling in were happy ones. There was nothing to stop us now! At last, I was on my way! Or was I? Once again an incident occurred to trigger off the uncontrollable love I had carried for Lindsay all these years. *Lindsay!* Would I never be free of her?

Chapter 16

In September a number of us students spent a week in a rural parish, followed by a retreat in Rydal Hall, a grandiose Edwardian mansion in the Lake District. The idea was to address those deeper personal issues of our self-assessment assignment within a group and with our course tutor. It was a beautiful place, surrounded by hills and trees. A waterfall cascaded gently into a shallow rocky pool close by the chapel in the mansion grounds, and the grounds themselves were ablaze with summer roses. The rooms were comfortable but sparse, and mine had a magnificent view across the lake and countryside.

I threw my battered brown suitcase on to the bed and myself after it. I was exhausted from the hard work of the past few weeks and extremely stressed at having to write about unresolved areas of pain in my assignments. That was probably why I was stupid enough to choose to share one of the smallest bedrooms in the house with one of the biggest guys in the college. Andy Hudson. I didn't really mind. I got on well with Andy, so when he and two other students, Paul Holly (often referred to as 'Holly') and Nigel Sinclair, suggested relaxing for the evening by taking a walk to a pub in Ambleside for a drink and a game of pool, I was all for it.

The warm, balmy air, the remnants of a glorious Indian summer, encouraged us to leave jumpers and jackets behind, and the four of us ambled along the deserted unlit road by the lake towards the village. It was very quiet, except for the gentle tinkling of the rigging on a few yachts berthed at the side of the lake, the lapping of water on the shore and our footsteps echoing on the country road. I gazed across the lake, watching the full moon quivering brightly on the calm waters, and allowed the mental tensions of the week to unfold.

'Anyone fancy a swim?' Andy broke our silence.

'What? In the lake? Are you serious?'

He laughed. 'It certainly looks inviting,' was all he said.

None of us took the conversation seriously: that is, until we'd had a few drinks. For me it was my first alcoholic drink in over twelve years. I suppose weaning me off alcohol was one good thing that the psychiatric hospital achieved.

I remember our game of pool being absolutely hilarious. Andy broke the leg of the table when he decided to straddle across it for a 'perfect' shot. Then some of the locals insisted we make up a team for a game of darts and insisted, even more profusely, on buying the losers a drink. We lost!

We toned our hysterical laughter down somewhat as we sneaked back into Rydal Hall at some ridiculous hour that night. It wouldn't do for the course tutors to catch four slightly intoxicated theological students, but as we crept passed the little chapel Andy caught me by the scruff of my neck.

'Let's go skinny-dipping,' he whispered hoarsely.

Nigel snorted. He'd had more to drink than any of us. 'In that?' We stood giggling at the pool a few yards from the chapel.

Holly hiccupped. 'It would be more sensible to swim in a shallow pool when you're ineb . . . when you're ineb . . . when you're drunk.'

'That is a shallow pool.'

'I know. That's what I'm saying. It's more sensible to swim in a shallow pool than . . . than . . . Shounds a very sensible idea to me. Shaves having to bath. Helps shober . . .'

'Shut up, Holly. Come on!' Andy's face shone in the dark like that of a little boy who knows he's about to do something he shouldn't but can't resist the temptation.

A few minutes later we were streaking naked across the lawn towards the pool with our towels. It suddenly reminded me of the fun we used to have in the children's home. With a whoop of sheer abandonment I leapt into the pool, gasping as the icy water sent shock waves through my body. Holly, Andy and Nigel came hurdling in after me. We splashed and pushed each other under the waterfall and turned into the rowdiest theological students Rydal Hall had ever witnessed, but I didn't care. It had been a great evening and I hadn't realised how much I'd needed the simple pleasure of a relaxing time with the lads.

I worked my way across to the far side of the pool and lay down, panting, on one of the cold, hard rocks while Andy, who appeared to have gone stark raving mad, continued splashing the others. As I lay listening to the rowdy behaviour of my friends I suddenly remembered I had my camera with me. I grinned and, under cover of darkness, climbed out of the pool and sneaked back across the lawn to where we'd left our clothes. Rummaging through my belongings I found my flash camera and made my way back to the pool.

I stood for a moment, positioning the viewfinder to get the best shot before I called, 'Smile, please.'

Three wet, astonished students stopped splashing and looked up. The horror of what I was about to do showed clearly on their faces and as of one accord they dived for the towels on the side of the pool. Too late! The camera flashed.

'Here, let me take one.' Holly climbed out of the pool and, grabbing a towel, I jumped in and turned to face the camera. This time, with towels draped modestly in all the right places, we turned beaming smiles upon him as the camera flashed away, recording one of the happiest moments of my life. Then, shivering with the cold, we dried ourselves and, thoroughly sober, sneaked into the mansion.

After breakfast – ugh! breakfast! – the following morning, we had a briefing session on our presentations. I won't record what I felt like physically. Anyone with half an imagination could guess. I only hoped I didn't look as bad as the others!

Sleepily I opened my folder containing my self-assessment. The photograph I'd enclosed of Lindsay and the children at the home stared back at me. I didn't expect to have such an emotional reaction on seeing her again; after all, I knew it was there. I'd put it in the folder in the first place. My head began to spin as her beautiful face stirred up memories from the past. I remembered the way she'd sat close to me when she'd helped me with my homework, her warm body occasionally brushing against mine, her perfume reeling my senses. I remembered her reassurance that she would *always* be my friend and the strength in her body as she'd wrestled with me to prevent me cutting my wrists. As memories of Lindsay surfaced the muscles in my body grew tense and my breathing became heavy and laboured to such an extent I started having palpitations. I struggled to stay in control. What was causing this? Perhaps it was having an alcoholic drink after an abstinence of twelve years? Perhaps I'd caught a chill from my midnight skinny-dipping with the lads? Whatever was causing it, I was alarmed. I hadn't had a turn like this since I was in the psychiatric hospital, and I certainly didn't want one now. Not in front of the whole class!

'Which group would you like to join, Mark?' John Pritchard, the tutor, was looking in my direction. I stared at him blankly. Group? What was he talking about? I was conscious every eye was riveted in my direction. My breathing became more laboured. What was happening to me? It was hopeless! I had to get out of that room!

Totally ignoring the fact that everyone was waiting for me to respond, I rose slowly from my chair and with as much dignity as I could muster headed for the door. Somewhere in the background I heard John saying we could discuss it later when I was feeling better, but my only response was to shrug my shoulders at him. At that moment I couldn't have cared less what group I was in.

I hurried along the corridor to my bedroom, grabbed my jacket and headed towards the lake, my mind in turmoil. I must be more mentally exhausted than I'd imagined to lose control over the sight of Lindsay's photograph and to march out of the classroom like that. What must they all be thinking?

I can't remember where I walked, but it must have been for some miles. Occasionally I was aware of the squeal of brakes as a car negotiated the sharp bends on the quiet country road or that I was following a well-worn path across a field. Then my feet were crunching on pebbles at the side of the lake. At last I was forced to come to a halt as a ramshackle fence blocked my path ahead. Weary, I rested my arms on an old gate which made up part of the fence and looked out across the deep blue lake with thick green forest and hills on the far side and made a conscious effort to listen to the tranquil sounds around me rather than the ones going around in my head. The call of one bird to another, the bleat of one sheep to another. The lap of water against the shingle. It was quiet out here, away from people. I liked that. I stretched my arms above my head, trying to ease the tension in my shoulders, and lifted my face to the warm sunshine.

I don't know how long I stood leaning against that gate, forcing myself not to think about much at all. I was only drawn back to reality by the sound of footsteps on the shingle, heading in my direction. It was John.

The Reverend John Pritchard was a tall, slim man in his late forties, with thin greying hair and large round spectacles, the sort that befit a tutor in theology. He was a quiet, pleasant man with a ready smile that made him easy to talk to, and talk was what he obviously wanted to do. He rested his arms on the gate alongside mine.

'I've been halfway to Ambleside looking for you,' he said.

I didn't know what to say to that. 'Oh?' seemed a pretty safe bet.

'Do you want to talk?' The genuine warmth in his voice reminded me of the little man who had meant so much to me: Pastor Coombs. He always asked me if I wanted to talk. The memory of Pastor Coombs filled me with emotion and I was close to tears when I nodded my head.

I didn't tell him anything he didn't already know. After all, I'd expressed a lot of my story in my self-assessment assignment. He was quiet for a long time after I'd finished speaking and I was grateful for that. It was always exhausting talking about the past.

Then he said, 'After I'd read your assignment, Mark, I had a talk with one of your other tutors, Reverend

Nicholas. We wondered if perhaps, while you're at college, you could not only address this issue of Lindsay, but also perhaps come to terms with some of the other traumas of your childhood. How does that sound to you?'

I didn't answer straight away but stood watching a speedboat skim over the surface of the lake. It was travelling so fast that at times it seemed to be out of control. Then I nodded my head. I'd already come so far, firstly with Pastor Coombs, then with Peter Haywood. 'I think you're probably right,' I said. 'I have to see this thing through to the end.'

He smiled at me, obviously pleased by my response. 'Good!' There was a slight hesitation, as though there was more to come. 'We also wondered how you would feel about meeting Lindsay and talking to her again. What do you think?'

'I . . . don't know,' I said uncertainly. 'Do you think it will help?'

'I have no idea,' John said. 'But you've had the guts to come this far and, judging from your story, I believe it would be a wise move to go the rest of the way.'

'I do as well, but I'm scared.'

'I know,' he said quietly. 'I can see that.'

Slowly we retraced our steps back to the mansion for dinner.

That night, while everyone was at the pub, I took a stroll out into the garden. Heavy black clouds overcast the moon that had shone so brightly the night before, so the only light came from the mansion windows, and they cast a dim and eerie glow across the lawn. I shivered. The first hint of autumn.

I crossed the lawn and headed towards the pool and waterfall where we'd had so much fun last night, then I turned sharply by the pool and followed the steep woodland path by the side of the waterfall, but I didn't really see any of it. My mind was on Lindsay and John's suggestion that I should see her again. How would she react to that? What would I say to her if I did meet her? She'd think I was a fool and overreacting, wouldn't she? After all, our final parting at the children's home had been nearly fifteen years ago. Fifteen years! Yet still the physical pain of loving her could overwhelm me.

Brambles cut through my trousers and stung my legs, and the darkness hindered my progress, but I didn't care. Some inner instinct called me to climb. 'Oh God! Show me what to do.' A hot tear ran down my face. It was a long time since I'd cried for Lindsay. I wiped it away, but they kept on coming, and I kept on climbing, desperately trying not to lose control of my emotions, but the more I thought of Lindsay, the more my body was consumed with longing for her.

How could this be happening again? How could the floodgates have been opened by a simple assignment? How? Perhaps I was just mentally exhausted with the academic work and tired from a night of drinking and skinny-dipping in the pool? I heard myself groaning with each steep step I took, almost as if there was a physical burden on my back that had been weighing me down for years.

Eventually I found myself standing on a wooden bridge leading across the gorge. A bridge! It had to be a bridge! Whenever I was at my lowest ebb I headed for a bridge! I rested my hands lightly on the rail and stood, numb and silent, watching the water cascading over the cliff face. I listened to its thunderous roar and felt its spray soaking my face. Leaning over the rail, I looked below into a pitch-black abyss. Far below me lay the rocky pool where we'd gone skinny-dipping.

'Anything, God! I will do anything, *anything* to be free of this . . . this . . .' A great sob welled up in my chest and in the silence and darkness of the night I screamed her name. *'LINDSAY!'* It echoed across the lake and around the hills before fading into the distance and allowing the silence of the night to descend upon me again. Gripping the rail on the bridge, I slumped down and wept uncontrollably for this woman I had loved all my life.

When my sobs were finally exhausted I lay on the rough, damp and rather precarious wooden bridge, physically and mentally drained, devoid of all feeling and oblivious to time. Not even God was in this timeless, arid desert where I found myself. The loneliness was unbearable and seemed to drag on into eternity. It was almost an effort to whisper 'Where are you, God?' – an inner cry for him to fill the emptiness rather than a searching prayer.

Rejected! Rejected! Rejected! The answer hammered back at me. I banged my fist furiously on the wooden planks of the bridge as the first angry emotion swept through me. I would *not* be rejected again! I wouldn't! I stood up. My legs were sore from the needle-sharp brambles, but I was oblivious to physical pain as anger at God soared to the surface. It was years since I'd been this angry.

Why should I give my life up to be a priest if this God I professed to serve could ignore me when I needed him most?

'I might as well be serving the . . . the devil for all *You* care!' I screamed.

'Devil! Devil! Devil, Care! Care! Care!' My voice echoed into the distance.

Yes! You might as well be serving the devil for all he cares.

It was a long time since such strong thoughts had entered my head, but when they did I recognised them immediately.

Look at you! You're not up to priesthood!

No I wasn't, was I? Not in this condition.

You might as well give up. Why go through all these memories again? No one can help you. You know that. No one! No one! You're all alone. Rejected! Rejected!

That was true. Even this God I had professed to be serving had left me. Rejected me.

Why go through this pain again?

It was also a long time since suicidal thoughts had entered my head, but they did so now, and I found myself moving to the edge of the bridge, my eyes drawn to the cascading waterfall.

Go on! Do it! Jump!

I clung to the rail on the bridge, my mind in turmoil as a spiritual battle raged on inside me, tearing me apart. 'I . . . I . . . I . . . God! *My God!*'

I suddenly sensed an awesome power of protection around me. I didn't hear any words, but some deep inner voice seemed to penetrate the whole of my existence. 'Don't listen to any other voice but *Mine*. I am with you. I will bring you safely through. Go on back down to the house.' Then a wave of indescribable peace flowed over and through me. Very slowly, I released my grip on the rail, and took a step back.

I must have stood on the bridge for over an hour, staring into the darkness. My face and clothes were wet with spray, chilling me off, but I didn't want to move, not just yet. Occasionally my eyes would fall on the lights of a passing car or wander towards the nearby village where some of the students were having a night out. People! I needed people! Eventually, much calmer and in control, I retraced my steps down the hill, slithering and sliding when the track got rough. Soon I could see the lights of the house welcoming me back through the trees. I hurried towards them with a sense of relief.

Chapter 17

I suppose I should have sensed Lesley and I were heading for some form of confrontation when I returned home, as she remained decidedly cool to my gestures of affection, but as I was still feeling emotionally drained after my own stressful fortnight, I missed all the obvious signs. It came to a head after our evening meal.

'I knew you would be like this,' she snapped, vigorously brushing Fiona's long hair.

I didn't say anything. Disagreements with Lesley in front of the children were something I avoided, as rows between my own parents had left some nasty childhood memories, but the moment Fiona and Jonathan were in bed I tackled her.

'What did you mean, you "knew it would be like this"?'

'Just what I said.' She snatched the children's dirty clothes off the floor in a distracted attempt at tidying up. 'Every time something reminds you of . . . of Lindsay, you go all moody. I'm sick of it, Mark. I really am! When you rang to tell me how depressed you were after writing about Lindsay in your self-assessment, I . . . well, to be honest, I just dreaded you coming home and having to go through this all over again!'

She sat down abruptly on the chair and abstractly folded the dirty washing into neat piles. I turned my back on her and stood at the window, staring out into the garden. I could have done without this type of hassle right now!

'Well? Have you nothing to say?'

Nothing to say? No, I hadn't anything to say. I wanted to scream at her.

'Mark! Speak to me!'

'You've no idea, have you?' I snapped, rounding on her. 'I'd have given anything, anything, for a childhood like yours, a home like yours . . .'

She sighed. 'I knew you'd take that line.'

' . . . and I've give anything not to be constantly reminded of Lindsay.'

'Lindsay! It's always back to bloody Lindsay!' Lesley jumped to her feet and hurled the pile of neatly folded dirty washing at me. 'I'm sick to death of hearing about her!'

I fended off the onslaught, then furiously snatched it up and hurled it back at her again. 'You've always known about Lindsay!' I bellowed. 'You assured me you'd stand by me until this problem with her was resolved! Now is not the time . . . !'

'*Now* is *exactly* the time!' she yelled, kicking a pile of toys across the floor. '*Now* is the time when I've problems of my own and could do with a bit of *your* support!'

I stared at her, aghast. 'That's wonderful! Just wonderful timing, Lesley!'

'It's all very well for you. You've got friends at college, but what about me? Didn't it occur to you that I might be lonely?'

'Of all the stupid times to . . .' Suddenly we were screaming hysterically at each other, pointing fingers, blaming, hurting with condemning words that could never be taken back and which would always be regretted.

'I'm leaving, Lesley!' I shouted, storming towards the door. I tripped over one of the toys on my way. 'I don't know where I'm going, but I can't cope with this aggravation at the moment!' I slammed the living room door behind me and ran up the stairs, hunting for my shoes on the way. I found one on the bedroom floor and shoved my foot in it, then thumped along the upstairs hall searching for the other. From the top of the stairs I overheard Lesley crying down the telephone.

'He's furious, Andy. He's gone completely berserk and threatened to leave us.'

My blood rose to boiling point when I realised Lesley was pouring her heart out to Andy. Spotting my other shoe on the landing, I hurled it down the stairs at her.

'Bloody right I'm furious!' I bellowed. 'And I'm even more bloody furious that you're blabbing our affairs to every Tom, Dick and . . . and Andy!'

She let out a cry of alarm and ducked, and the offending object narrowly missed her. Then, slamming down the telephone, she fled into the living room, but not before I'd had the chance to pull off my other shoe and hurl that after her. It thudded against the slammed living room door. I raced down the stairs after it and threw my full weight against the door. For all I was a lightweight, Lesley was even lighter, and the door she had her weight against gave way easily. She staggered back into the room, her eyes wide and frightened. Three paces across the floor, and I was beside her, gabbing her by the shoulders and shaking her. Her face contorted with pain but I didn't let up. What self-control we'd maintained was lost in a barrage of screaming abuse at each other until she struggled free and ran from me, crying. Her feet thudded up the stairs and the bedroom door slammed behind her. Angrily, I kicked Jonathan's half-inflated beach ball against the wall, then flopped down, exhausted, in a chair.

The room was a shambles! Dirty washing was strewn everywhere, even across the dirty dishes that still lay on the dining room table. One of the coffee mugs had spilt on the hearth and there was a sock hanging off the light shade. Toys, which normally filled the toy box when the children went to bed, littered the floor, and the evening newspaper lay crumpled on the settee.

It's always at such times that there is a knock on the door. Visitors! That was the last thing I wanted. I made my way into the hall, reluctantly, and was relieved to see a large, familiar figure looming through the frosted glass of the front door.

'Hi, Mark! It's me. Andy.'

I ran my fingers through my hair, embarrassed not only that Andy had been dragged into our domestic quarrel but by the upheaval in our house.

'Right! I'm coming!' I took a deep breath and opened the door. As I said before, Andy is a big guy. Not the sort you'd want to tangle with on a dark night, but at times he's like a gentle giant. This was one of those times.

We sat on the stairs, quietly talking about the stresses Lesley had faced while I was unemployed, her uncertainties about the future and the continual threat of Lindsay to her marriage. As I sat listening to Andy talking, I realised this man had a deeper insight into the pressures my wife was having to face than I had.

Sometime during our talk I heard the bedroom door open and sensed Lesley standing behind us at the top of the stairs. I felt too ashamed to turn around. Andy did it for me.

'No more battering rams?' he enquired quizzically, smiling and reaching out his hand to Lesley. 'You'll talk this thing through rationally?' He gave Lesley's hand a squeeze as he sat her on the stairs beside me.

'Yes.'

'Good. Then I'll leave you to it.'

The house seemed strangely quiet after he'd gone. By some miraculous means, the children, whether they'd heard us or not, were now fast asleep. Lesley and I didn't talk. We'd spent the best part of the evening talking and shouting cruel, bitter words at each other. More words were the last thing we wanted to hear. We just wanted to be friends again, and besides, we had a far better way of making up.

It was a good hour later, almost ten o'clock, when we were jolted back from our peaceful snoozing by the telephone. Leaping out of bed, I pulled on my pyjama bottoms and hurried down the stairs.

'It's probably Andy checking up to see whether we've killed each other yet,'

Lesley called after me.

I chuckled and picked up the receiver. 'Hi!' I said.'Mark? John Pritchard here.''Oh? Er . . . Yes.' He was the last person I had expected to hear from so late in the evening.

'Sorry to telephone so late, but I wondered if I could pop around to have a quick word with you?'

'Now?'

'Only if it's convenient. I've been speaking to Lindsay in Scotland.'

Lindsay? I was stunned. He'd actually been talking to Lindsay? My Lindsay? Somewhere in the distance I heard my name being called and realised I had dropped the telephone by my side. 'Sorry about that, John. Yes . . . yes, you're quite welcome to come round now. We'd love to see you.'

There was a squeal from upstairs as Lesley leapt out of bed.

'Fine,' came the voice from the other end of the telephone. 'I'm leaving the college now, so I should be with you in . . . ten minutes?'

I replaced the receiver without replying, vaguely aware of Lesley charging around the living room, screaming at me to snap out of it and help tidy up, then suddenly the screaming stopped and I felt her fingers resting on my arm.

'Are you all right?' she asked quietly.

I turned and looked down at my wife. Her tousled hair fell across her concerned face and she'd pulled her nightdress on inside out. I tried to speak, but I had no voice. I swallowed, and tears began to run down my cheeks. Lesley wrapped her arms around me and held me close for a moment before she said, 'Come on, Mark. We better get dressed. John'll be here in a moment.'

Somehow or other Lesley worked a miracle in the living room, prepared coffee on a tray and even managed to pull a jumper and jeans on, as though the sort of evening we'd just been through was normal.

'I thought I better catch you before you went to bed,' John said, settling himself in the big chair in the corner. The chair behind which Lesley had thrown the children's toys, the dirty washing, the evening newspaper and . . . I'm not quite sure what she'd done with the dirty dishes.

'Coffee?' Lesley came in, looking as cool as a cucumber, carrying a tray with a pot of coffee and plate of biscuits. After doing her 'hostess' bit, she left us alone.

'So you rang Lindsay?' I prompted, trying to sound as though it was a matter of indifference to me whether he'd contacted her or not.

'Mmm.' He spooned an even measure of sugar into his mug, then helped himself to a chocolate biscuit. 'I introduced myself, then brought her up to date with what had been happening.'

'Was she surprised?'

'Difficult to say,' he said. 'I told her you had a good marriage and that Lesley understood the attachment you have towards her and supported you in your desire to put the past behind you.' He stopped talking and sat back in his chair while he ate his biscuit and drank his coffee. 'Anyway,' he continued after a while. 'It was suggested that October 31st would be a good day for you and me to travel to Scotland to see her. We can make it there and back in a day. How does that sound to you?'

'That sounds fine.' I was amazed at how calm I sounded compared to the turmoil going on inside me. 'Although I must confess I'm a little anxious about seeing her again after all these years and for the life of me I don't know what I'll say to her. How do you tell someone that for the past thirteen years or so you've been in love with them? Especially an older, married woman with a family of their own.' I shook my head. The idea of visiting Lindsay suddenly seemed outrageous. 'Did she mention the letter I wrote while I was in the psychiatric hospital?'

'No, but I did, and her comment was that she can't remember having received it. Her only recollection is hearing from your sister, ringing the hospital and being informed it wouldn't be in your best interests for her to speak to you.' John shrugged. 'Nothing you can do about that one, Mark. It sounds as though there was a few crossed wires at the hospital.'

John stayed for a while longer, reassuring me as he left that we would get through this and that tomorrow morning he would ring Lindsay and confirm October 31st for our visit. I closed the door after him but remained behind it with my head on the doorknob. What a night! My head was spinning and my stomach was churning. Lesley had gone to bed, but despite my recent late nights I knew I would never sleep.

On the spur of the moment I decided to sit up and write in my diary.

Monday September 28th

I suppose one good thing to have come out of my time in the psychiatric hospital was being encouraged to keep a diary of how I feel during events of great significance. The event of significance in this case is my forthcoming visit to see Lindsay. Lindsay! I can hardly believe I'll be seeing the houseparent I've loved all these years. I'm sick with worry over what it will do to Lesley and me, but I have to confess there's a tinge of sweet anticipation as well. I'm in distress again and it will never go until the problem with Lindsay is resolved – once and for all!

Wednesday September 30th

Fiona and Jonathan woke me by bouncing up and down on the bed waving plastic bags in the air and wishing me a happy birthday. Bless them. They'd bought me chocolate out of their pocket money.

Lesley came into the bedroom carrying a tray with my breakfast and her present of two lovely stylish sweatshirts. My family were so loving and all I wanted to do was sleep. I felt a real heel!

In the afternoon I sat watching Manchester United losing to a Russian football team in a penalty shoot out.

I was surprised to find the children were eating at a friend's house. When I asked Lesley why, she just smiled sweetly and said she had planned a surprise birthday meal out. I told her she was wonderful, but I didn't really feel like going out. However, when we met up with Andy, Holly and their wives at the restaurant I found I quite enjoyed myself, even though I was physically sick. It had nothing to do with the food. That was great. It's just I don't seem to have been able to keep anything down for the last few days.

Sunday October 4th

I lay on the bed all morning staring at the group photograph of me standing next to Lindsay at Ivy Cottage. I realise I've been living in a fantasy world that is about to come to an end, and I'm scared! I don't know how I'm going to live without my love for this woman, despite the pain it causes me. I'm grieving over my impending loss.

Tuesday October 6th

I went to talk to John about it. No matter how busy he is he always makes time for me. I'm very grateful to him. He suggested I see Rebecca, the university psychotherapist. I surprised myself by agreeing.

Wednesday October 14th

Marks for my New Testament essay? 56%. My tutors comments? 'An unplanned essay! No real understanding of Judaism! Poor sentence construction and far too many spelling mistakes!' I have to agree with him, but at least 56% makes a pass mark.

The psychotherapist, Rebecca, is patient and understanding. She talked about me being in some form of time warp as far as my relationship with Lindsay is concerned. Apparently I'm still in adolescence, seeking that special figure in my life to love, someone who will discipline me and show me I'm worth something. My childhood never had that, so there's part of me that's never really developed.

Saturday October 17th

I was rudely awoken this morning by shrieks of laughter from downstairs. I couldn't imagine what the cause of such hilarity could be; then to my horror I remembered Andy's wife, Tracy, had offered to collect the skinny-dipping photographs from the chemist!

Panic-stricken, I leapt out of bed and rushed downstairs to be greeted by photographs strews across the coffee table and Lesley and Tracy rolling around the settee, convulsed with laughter.

I grabbed the photos and to my horror discovered that in one particular shot my towel hadn't quite covered my 'embarrassment'. There was also a good rear view of Nigel and a horrendous shot of Holly squatting like a bird in the water, stark naked.

I censored the one of my 'embarrassment' with a felt-tip pen!

Sunday October 18th
Andy called with a bottle of non-alcoholic wine to see the skinny-dippingphotographs.

Thursday October 22nd
Nigel called to see the skinny-dipping photographs!
I'm still not sleeping. Everything I do seems unreal, as if the only real issue will take place in nine days' time, October 31st.

Saturday October 24th
Holly called to see the skinny dipping photographs!

Monday October 26th
At six thirty p.m. I went into the common room for tea. A young girl was standing near the window and as she turned my heart leapt. She was the image of Lindsay. I'm seeing her everywhere, and it hurts just being reminded of her. John is right. If I don't get this thing sorted out while I'm at university there will always be that risk of someone reminding me of her and causing untold problems in my marriage or my parish.

Tuesday October 27th
I thought Holly was joking when he told me he'd put the skinny-dipping photographs on the notice board, but when I went to check it out I discovered he had also stuck a caption underneath which read: 'If you recognise anyone in these photos, please contact the Revd J. Pritchard.' *I was about to unpin them when who should walk through the door but the Reverend J. Pritchard himself. He looked at me, then at the photographs.*
'I see,' *he said, without a flicker of amusement.*
I suppose a priest and theological tutor could hardly give his approval to a photograph of four of his students standing half-naked in a pool.
'Nothing to do with me,' *I said, mortified.*
Naturally, he didn't believe me. What a rogue that Holly is!

I was in a happier frame of mind when I went to bed and relived a few of the happier moments at the children's home with Lindsay.

Friday October 30th
In the middle of watching a Blackadder *video, the telephone rang. Some instinct told me it was bad news the moment I answered it. It was my sister Jenny. 'Mark . . . Oh Mark!' The uncontrollable sobs on the other end of the telephone turned my mouth dry with fear.*

'What's happened?'

She took a little while to calm down. 'It's Paul. Oh Mark, he tried to commit suicide last night. He's alive, but . . .but . . .' There was a fresh outbreak of sobbing. I calmed her down as best I could, found out the name of the hospital and rung it.

Although I was worried I can't say I was surprised by her news. At the back of my mind I'd been expecting something like this, as Paul, like me, had a lot of unresolved conflicts inside him.

Fortunately I was able to speak to Paul himself. He didn't go into the whys and wherefores of the overdose he'd taken, but reading between the lines it sounded as though his action had been more a cry for help than an actual attempt to end his life.

I spent the rest of the evening on the telephone to Shene and Graham and my other sister, Maxine, and by the end of the evening I was exhausted. I flopped into the chair. 'This is all I need!' I thought. 'My brother attempting to kill himself on top of everything else!'

Then I cringed in shame at my self-centred attitude. I'll never make it as a priest! Never! Never! Never!

Chapter 18

Bleary-eyed, I stared down at my diary. My mind was a complete blank, but then it was only seven a.m., and I was never an early bird at the best of times. I closed my diary, pulled on my dressing gown, and quietly, so as not to disturb Lesley and the children, made my way downstairs for breakfast before John picked me up.

He was prompt, but then he was that kind of man. I sat silently beside him in his spacious car, abstractly watching a rising red sun struggling to throw some warmth on the cold, frost-bitten earth. He drove fast but competently up the motorway to Glasgow, talking about anything and everything in an attempt to put me at my ease, but I wasn't listening. I was trying to absorb the realisation that after all these years I was actually on my way to see Lindsay. I'd planned my opening speech over and over in my mind, but with each passing mile it became more confused by my nervousness.

I tried to pray, but my mind kept wandering, and in the end I gave up.

After an hour or so we stopped at a Little Chef for coffee and something to eat and I spent some time churning over what I ought to buy Lindsay as a 'thank you' for lunch. By the time we reached Glasgow I'd developed a throbbing headache, but I think it was partly due to the long car journey.

We wound our way through the city centre, following Lindsay's directions, until we reached a pleasant area in the suburbs and turned into a long, wide, tree-lined street.

'There! There's number twenty-four.' I pointed to a rambling but well cared for semi-detached house, just the sort I imagined Lindsay to have chosen, and John pulled up at the curb. Nervously I stepped out of the car, waited while he locked it, then followed him up the garden path, conscious of a small child peering curiously through the curtains at us. John gave me a reassuring smile as he rang the bell. At that moment I would have given anything to have turned around and gone back home again, but I'd come too far to do that.

A moment later the front door was flung open and Lindsay – my Lindsay – the woman I had loved all these years – stood in front of me. My opening speech froze to my lips and I stood awkwardly on the steps, staring at her. She still had that same full, warm smile that could turn my legs to jelly and that long tawny hair that sent my senses reeling.

'Come in! Come in!' She reached out and shook John's hand, then turned to me, and suddenly I was that adolescent schoolboy again, lost for words whenever she was beside me.

'Mark, how lovely to see you.' She spoke affectionately as she took me by the hand and drew me into the hallway. 'How long is it? Fifteen years?' Then she hugged me. The warm embrace only lasted a couple of seconds, but it brought back memories of the times she sat beside me helping me with my homework, smelling of talcum powder.

She showed us into the living room and introduced us to Geoff. He was taller than I imagined and seemed to have lost weight, judging from the photographs she had sent us a few Christmases ago, but he still retained his thick black beard and a full head of hair. He gave us a cheerful welcome and appeared to be a naturally talkative man who was obviously going to do his best to put us at ease.

We sat in the reception room, talking and drinking coffee. Fortunately John and Geoff seemed quite happy to monopolise the conversation, which was just as well, as the adolescent in me still couldn't find his tongue.

Eventually Lindsay brought out two very large scrapbooks from the sideboard and came to sit beside me on the settee.

'Remember these, Mark?' She opened one of the books. The familiar faces of Uncle and Aunty, surrounded by Gary, Robin, Lee, Rachael, the Clark brothers, Paul and me and a few others, greeted me.

I pointed to another photograph. 'There's one of our holiday in Mablethorpe.'

Suddenly there seemed so much to talk about. Memories to be re-lived, news of friends to catch up on, but even as we shared those precious memories, I was aware of the frustration of having John and Geoff across the room, half listening to our conversation. I desperately wanted to be alone with Lindsay, but social graces, it seemed, took priority over my desperate needs.

I found it very difficult not to stare at Lindsay as she walked in and out of the room, preparing our lunch of soup and rolls, then home-made pies and salad, and it seemed strange, crowded around the large family table with her children.

At one point John asked Lindsay and Geoff about their church, and I was surprised to discover they were both active Christians, but even though I would have been happy to talk about my own faith, I was conscious time was ticking away and that the main purpose for our visit had yet to be dealt with. It therefore came as a great relief when John sat back in his chair and said, 'That was a lovely meal, Lindsay. Thank you. Please allow me into your kitchen to do the washing up. I promise I won't break anything! Geoff can come and keep an eye on me if he wants. It will give you and Mark a chance to talk.'

Geoff agreed, then rounded up his children to help clear the table.

'Would you like to go for a walk?' Lindsay asked me, smiling.

'That would be nice.'

As we turned out of her driveway into the lukewarm autumn sunshine I couldn't help but reflect that the last time I'd walked by her side I hadn't been fully grown. Now, as we strolled side by side down the long avenue of trees shedding their leaves, I noticed I was slightly taller than her.

'I'm really pleased you came to visit us, Mark,' she said, setting the pace for both of us. 'But tell me, honestly, are you finding it difficult being here, talking to me?'

I was glad of her directness. It broke the ice immediately and enabled us to move towards discussing the real reason for my visit.

'Yes.' I kept my head lowered, watching our feet crunching on the brown leaves.

'Do you want to talk about it?' she asked quietly.

I gave a half laugh. 'Talk about it?' I repeated. 'Funny, but for years I've imagined what I would say to you if we ever met again, but now . . . ?' I shrugged. 'Now, I don't know where to start.' I raised my head to watch a plane rising above the gathering grey clouds, leaving a trail of white smoke behind it, and I thought enviously of the folk aboard who could afford to fly away from all their problems. 'I suppose Guy Fawkes Night is the place to start,' I said thoughtfully. 'The night you took us all to a fireworks display and bonfire on the village green. Remember?'

'Mmm. Vaguely.'

I told her all I could remember about that night. My disruptive behaviour in pinching her hat, flirting with her, and how, for the first time in the whole of my troubled life, I had felt emotionally drawn to someone I believed cared deeply for me. Then I told her of my hurt and confusion when, after my disruptive behaviour, she slapped me on the face on our return journey to the children's home.

She frowned. 'I can't remember slapping you, Mark,' she interrupted. 'I'm sure I wouldn't do a thing like that.'

'I don't think you meant to slap me hard, but you were angry, and . . . well, anyway, the incident sticks in my mind because it appeared like yet another rejection from someone I thought cared about me.'

She nodded in understanding and we left the avenue and crossed an open common with newly planted trees and bushes. Half a dozen neatly rounded flower beds lay empty, waiting for next year's flowers to bloom, as did a few pruned rose bushes. We were making our way towards a large pond, beautifully cultivated with reeds and bushes, and housing a few mallards and coots. I desperately wanted her to put her arm around me and tell me she was sorry, that everything was all right, that she had never rejected me. Deep inside I recognised the adolescent in me wanted to know he had been someone special in her life and that she had cared enough about me, but she was silent.

'And after Bonfire Night?' she prompted.

'After Bonfire Night...' A brown mallard waddled towards us, shaking her feathers, hoping for food. Her partner stood a few yards behind, colourful and proud, preening himself. We stood watching them while I told her how much I had grown to love her after that night but how my love had been seen as an obsessive teenage crush and had become a source of great amusement and teasing by the other children. I wanted to say more. I wanted to pour out the pain and anguish I'd suffered over their teasing, but Lindsay turned and smiled at me.

'Yes, it caused me a few problems as well. The superintendent told me on more than one occasion that I was giving you too much time and attention.' She pulled up the collar of her coat. The clouds were growing heavier and a chill wind had sprung up. 'To be honest Mark, I was young, just out of college and naive in the way I dealt with you.' When she turned and looked me fully in the face her eyes were sad. 'I'm sorry Mark. I really am. I knew you had a crush on me, but I didn't know how to handle it, or how to handle a boy with such a disturbed background as yours.' She smiled at me. 'You must admit, you were a difficult boy to handle, weren't you?'

I couldn't resist smiling. 'Yes, I was a bit, wasn't I?'

Lindsay chuckled. 'In fact, you were the most demanding, manipulative, awkward child I'd ever come across.'

'And caused more trouble than the rest of them put together,' I added, with a laugh. It suddenly felt good to laugh.

We stood silently, lost in our own private memories of those years at Ivy Cottage for a while. Then she said, 'Were you angry with the other houseparents for not understanding you, Mark?'

I kicked the leaves and the duck flapped its wings, alarmed, then waddled away, disgusted. 'I suppose so.

Their reaction to the way I felt about you made me feel . . . abnormal. As though there was something wrong with me.' I talked about my fears over having to leave the security at Ivy Cottage because of her and how I saw it as yet another rejection, and suddenly I realised Lindsay was walking slowly along the path around the pond and I was following, two paces behind, the way I had on so many occasions when she was a houseparent walking us to school and I was the adolescent schoolboy, and the moment of sharing was lost.

'There used to be a pond in the park near Ivy Cottage,' she said. 'Do you remember it?'

'Yes. Lindsay?' I hesitated. 'Lindsay? Can . . . I hold your hand?'

She stopped and faced me, raising her eyebrows questioningly with her head tilted to one side.

'Don't read anything into it,' I added, hastily. 'It's just . . . just . . .'

Whether she understood my desperate need to reach out and touch her, the way I had as a child, I'll never know, but she smiled as she slowly reached out, enveloping her warm soft fingers around mind.

'As long as you don't read anything more into this gesture either, Mark,' she said softly.

'I won't.' I had hoped this physical contact between us would make it easier for me to confide in her about the pain of loving her and that she would respond by comforting and reassuring me, but so many years had passed since I'd last walked with her like this and our lives had changed so much that after a few minutes I self-consciously withdrew my fingers. Neither of us were the same people any more. The young twenty-three-year-old houseparent, fresh from college, no longer existed. The mature woman who stood with me now had given birth to children of her own and had given her love to someone else, and I had Lesley and my children, and they meant everything to me.

'Memories, Mark?'

'I suppose so. Yes. The teenage boy in me doesn't want to let you go, Lindsay, because I've . . . I've loved you so much and for so long.'

She didn't say anything at first, but when she did she was obviously thinking carefully about her words. 'I'm . . . flattered and . . . honoured to have been loved so deeply by you, Mark, and it is something I will always treasure, but . . . but I think it is important for that teenage boy in you to let his love for his houseparent go, don't you? Fifteen years ago I gave you a little of what every human being needs. Love. You needed it, as did the other children at Ivy Cottage. It was given in order to help you in your growing up, not to be a twisted, distorted burden for you to carry.' Then she said softly, 'Let me go, Mark.'

I knew she was right, but my grief at having to separate from this person I had loved so deeply for all these years was too much to bear. I had loved so few people and lost them. How could I possibly let this one go? 'All these years I've kept my love for you to myself because I was always afraid the time would come when you'd reject me. There have been so many rej . . .' I couldn't go on.

She shook her head and a wisp of tawny hair blew across her face. 'I won't reject you, Mark, but in your heart you must know that the way you feel about me isn't healthy. Let me go, Mark. Will you do that?'

A heavy weight settled on my chest and the chill wind blew even more fiercely across the common, bringing with it the first drops of rain, which splashed into the pond, making ever-widening circles. Lindsay looked up and shivered. 'It's probably only a shower, but I think we better be getting back, don't you?'

I wanted to shout 'No! No! We haven't finished talking yet!' but she'd already quickened her pace towards the long avenue of trees leading to her home and I dutifully followed.

'But . . . we'll still be friends?' I sounded pathetic, even to my own ears.

She smiled at me. 'Of course we will, Mark, but not the same friendship of fifteen years ago. Instead, let's remember how we are today, and develop an adult friendship which will draw in our families.'

I pushed my hands in my pockets. I was suddenly feeling very cold.

Once inside the house it became clear that Lindsay was no longer mine. I'd had my time on the common. Now she belonged to Geoff and her children and to this comfortable old house in its tree-lined street, and I had to find a corner of the reception room where I wasn't in her way as she bustled around making tea for everyone.

After tea I took a photograph of Lindsay, Geoff and their children and another of John and Lindsay, then John began to make 'It's time for us to go' noises. I didn't want to go. What about all those unresolved questions? But I found myself pulling on my coat and chattering to the children while I wrestled with the pain of knowing this was it! The final break. I had to let her go and leave her to this place she called 'home', the man she called 'husband' and children who loved her.

There was a lot of shaking hands and goodbyes at the front door, then Lindsay, with her baby in one arm, embraced me, kissing me gently on the cheek. I wrapped my arms around her and her baby and returned her kiss.

'Goodbye, Lindsay . . . my love,' I whispered.

'Goodbye, Mark.'

I didn't want it to end this way. I wanted to scream 'I love you, Lindsay! I love you!' and hold her close, but I released her, and with tears stinging the back of my eyelids turned and made my way down the garden path to John's car.

This can't be the end! It can't! I cried inwardly. *Nothing's been resolved! I'm still hurting.* My hands were shaking as I fastened my seatbelt. John started the engine and it roared into life. I took one last longing gaze towards the woman I had loved all my life. She was standing waving to us from the front door with her family surrounding her. She was still as beautiful as I remembered her, but there were grey streaks in her hair now, more lines on her face and the extra weight of a woman who had given birth to four children. These things marked the passing of time, for both of us. I gave one final wave as John pulled smoothly away from the house.

The illusion had come to an end. The past and the present had met. My dreams of a loving reunion between the young girl fresh from college and the teenage boy had been shattered. She was no longer mine to love and could never be the person I had fallen in love with ever again.

Chapter 19

Sunday November 1st

The past and present came face to face yesterday when the teenage boy in me was jolted into the reality that the lovely young houseparent with the long tawny hair no longer existed. My illusion, my fantasy, created through a desperate need to be loved, has come to and end, and I'm moving into the stages of mourning as one would when grieving the loss of a loved one.

I was exhausted when I arrived home and my head was spinning with memories of the children's home. Lesley sat stroking my head reassuringly.

Really, my wife is so sweet. I don't deserve her.

My brother Paul rang after tea. Selfishly, I was relieved to hear he was feeling much better. I couldn't cope with Paul's problems. Not at the moment. He told me he has Christian friends who've offered him a room until he gets himself sorted out. I should have been delighted, but I couldn't have cared less. In fact, I couldn't even pray for him.

Monday November 2nd

Had a blazing row with Lesley after tea. It all started when I suggested she and the children might like to meet Lindsay and her family. Lesley said she couldn't even consider it until she'd worked through her own feelings about Lindsay. Then I put my foot in it. I wrongly accused her of not supporting me over this and suddenly we were yelling at each other. Lesley burst into tears and I ended up storming out of the house!

Thursday November 5th
Bonfire Night! It always brings back painful memories of the Bradshaws, who built our hopes up for adoption, then walked out on us after we'd invited them to our bonfire display in the children's home. I really believed they'd wanted us. The memories of their rejection still hurt.

Then, of course, bonfire night was the night I first fell in love with Lindsay.

I'm trying desperately to let go of the fantasies I've weaved around her all these years, but it is a terribly slow and painful process. Will I ever see her again? Spiritually I'm in a dry arid desert desperately looking for God. It isn't a very good place to be for someone training to be a priest.

I was reminded of a reading in Isaiah 35:1–2: 'The desert and the parched land will be glad; the wilderness will rejoice and blossom. Like the crocus, it will burst into bloom; it will rejoice greatly and shout for joy.' Will that ever happen to me? Can I turn this desert experience to my advantage?

Christmas and New Year seemed to pass without anything memorable to hold me to them. Not even the excitement on the children's faces on Christmas morning or the news that, after years of prayer, Paul had become a Christian stood out as being significant. I felt drained of emotion.

As the dark, cold days of winter came upon us Lesley began giving serious consideration to returning to teacher training college. I tried my best to be encouraging, but there was coolness between us, which hindered communication.

As the first warm days of spring heralded in lighter nights for the children to play outside and crocuses and daffodils pushed their heads through every garden on the estate but ours, my mood lightened. A group of students from the university had been given the opportunity to visit Taizé in France, a town where Christians from all over the world gathered regularly for prayer and meditation. I was very excited. This would be my first trip abroad.

It turned out to be a very moving experience, and on more than one occasion as I wandered through the peaceful French countryside I was aware of God reassuring me that he would bring his healing into those painful childhood memories. I returned from Taizé with a new resolve to work through these issues, regardless of how painful I found them.

Over the summer holidays, such a blessing to students and teachers alike, Lesley and I worked at developing more quality time together. We planned picnics and days out with the children, but although we enjoyed ourselves I was aware there wasn't the closeness we'd once shared.

I decided to apply for a placement with Social Services during the summer holidays as well, not only as part of my work for university, but with a view to confronting a few of my ghosts. I visited some of the most notorious estates in the area with Sue, a social worker not much older than myself. It was here I came into contract with children from broken homes, some with drug- or alcohol-related problems. Many of them were involved in juvenile crime or suffering from the blight of unemployment. The project I was involved with sought to draw alongside such young people, to befriend, counsel and explore their own potential by giving them access to the skills they needed.

As I was drawn into the hopelessness of some of their situations, I was confronted with images from my own childhood. Boarded-up houses on the estate where we lived, the local villains living next door. I saw myself playing in streets such as these, smashing grates over the drains just for something to do. I experienced again the pain of being referred to as a 'grubby little street urchin' by the social worker, then being labelled stupid and backwards throughout my school education. The people I came into contact with on this placement were people I could identify with because I'd been there. Their plight was nothing new, but an age-old fight for dignity and the right to stand up straight.

During that placement I found myself looking at the inside of a department I'd been at odds with for years. It was the Social Services Department that had first placed us in foster care when I was only three. It was the Social Services Department that had shunted us backwards and forwards between parents and foster parents and had decided what was best for us. It was this department that had cruelly taken us from our first ever stable home with the Tait family and then, without a word of explanation, had whisked us away from all we had come to hold dear. Our foster family, home, friends and lovely Christmas gifts. All my life I blamed a system, which I believed had abused my rights as a child and let me down, but now as an adult on placement with them I had the opportunity to see the system at work through the eyes of the professional carer rather than through the eyes of the confused, frightened child.

Sue talked me through some of the case studies they were handling and shared a few of the problems they had encountered. A particular incident that occurred towards the end of my placement stands very much at the forefront of my mind.

One night Sue had been called upon to go with the police to a home to check on the safety of a small child.

The mother had taken offence at their interference and in a spate of anger had pushed the child out of the door.

'Here!' she yelled. 'Keep him! I don't want him back!'

Despite years of experience, that incident had left Sue heartbroken. The child was hysterical, and she'd been forced to drag him, kicking and screaming, away from his home and place him with foster parents for the night.

Exhausted and still upset, she told me the whole story the following morning as we returned to the house to talk to the mother. We found her very disturbed.

'I can't cope! I just can't cope!' she cried, wringing her hands.

That afternoon discussions in the office centred on this family and what we could do for them. As I listened to the group earnestly making suggestions, planning and setting wheels in motion, it seemed as though a painful, long-buried incident was being brought to the forefront of my mind. I saw myself at the tender age of three being dragged, kicking and screaming, from my mother by the social worker. Another social worker carried my tearful little brother while my mother stood at the door, crying because she couldn't cope. That was the first time we were placed in a foster home.

I left the Social Services office in tears, heartbroken for that little three-year-old boy: the one Sue had taken into care and the one in me. But I was also aware that new light had been shed upon Social Services and the people who worked there, who were attempting to bring something good and positive out of very difficult situations.

It was a week or so later when Sue pointed out the high-rise car park in the centre of the city. She told me about an eighteen-year-old girl she'd been dealing with who had spent most of her life in and out of care. She knew rejection from her family and had struggled to find employment and worthwhile friends. The struggle had proved too much for her, and eventually one night she had jumped from the top of the high-rise car park. I returned home very distressed.

Summer Placement Reflections

I'm finding this summer placement harder than I imagined. I'm coming across so many people like me, rejected, misunderstood, ravaged by abuse of one sort or another and having to contend with their own negative forces.

I can't help thinking about the girl who committed suicide from the high-rise car park. It sounds blasphemous for me, a Christian, to suggest that pain can be so bad that death seems a welcome escape, but that's how it has seemed to me on more than one occasion.

My daily reading was from Isaiah 61 this morning: 'He has sent me to bind up the broken-hearted, to proclaim freedom for the captives and release . . . prisoners . . . to comfort all who mourn . . . . to bestow on them a crown of beauty instead of ashes, the oil of gladness instead of mourning, and a garment of praise instead of a spirit of despair.'

I think that's what's happening to me. God is ripping off the elastoplasts and exposing all the festering, wounded memories of my past and shedding new light on them from the experience I'm gaining with this summer placement.

Sores, if they are left untreated, can fester and that's what mine have done. I need my wounds to have their influence diminished over my thoughts and behavioural patterns of the present, otherwise I will never be a whole person.

I sometimes feel if I stand in front of a mirror I will reflect back some of the nightmares that encircle certain sections of the community. But as a priest I want to be a reflection of Christ, not of festering sores. It all sounds fine in theory, but it's quite another matter having your elastoplasts ripped off! However, I've resolved I'm going to see this thing through to the bitter end.

'When I compare myself with other colleagues training for the priesthood I'm filled with despair! I ask you, Lesley, what right have I got to be a priest?' My feet crunched noisily on the gravel around the university grounds. Lesley trotted along beside me, trying to keep up.

'Being a priest doesn't make you perfect or problem free.' Lesley sounded a little breathless. 'Anyway, it was God who called you into the priesthood, not some fanciful whim of your own.'

Her words were reassuring and just what I needed to hear. 'You're right. I think I'm just suffering from another dose of self-pity, but every now and again I have periods where I'm really tempted to give up.' Our feet stopped crunching as we left the path and cut across the lawns away from the university.

'Well, despite our . . . our difficulties, I won't let you give up, Mark,' she said gently.

'You won't?'

'No, I won't.' She paused. A strand of hair blew across her face and her pale blue silk blouse rippled gently in response to the breeze and hugged her shapely figure.

'You're a great person, Lesley,' I said, smiling down at her. 'And an attractive one,' I added.

She gave my hand a squeeze. 'It seems a long time since you've said that to me.' She smiled, obviously pleased with the compliment, and I couldn't help reflect she was right. It had been a long time since I'd said anything nice to her. I'd been too wrapped up in my work at university, my summer placement or working through my own emotions. She stopped suddenly. 'Would you mind slowing down, Mark? We're not training for the marathon, you know.'

'Sorry.' We slowed our pace, but still hand in hand wound our way out of the university grounds into a woodland area where the shade of the leafy trees cast cool shadows across our path.

Eventually Lesley asked, 'By the way, have you thought any more about contacting the counsellors John suggested?'

'Not yet.'

'I think it's worth a telephone call, Mark. These people are professional and experienced counsellors. They can give you the help you need.'

'I'll think about it.'

We lapsed into an uneasy silence because I knew what was coming.

'It's just I can tell the nightmares are getting worse,' she said quietly. 'I ended up having to sleep on the couch last night, you were so restless.'

I squeezed her fingers. 'I know. I'm sorry. I was dreaming of my old bedroom at Ivy Cottage and a frightening dark figure was bending over my bed. I woke up in a cold sweat with my mouth parched with fear. I tried calling for Brian, Richard and Paul, but no one could hear me. It took me ages to work out I was at home and not at Ivy Cottage.'

'In that case, I think it's definitely worth giving these people a ring, don't you?'

'Mmm,' I hummed uncertainly. 'It's just I'd rather not tell my story to a couple of strangers.'

She frowned at me. 'Give those counsellors a ring tomorrow, Mark. Will you?'

It was pleasant just walking and talking with Lesley and it was with some reluctance that we parted. I headed back to university to attend lectures and she returned home to collect the children from nursery school.

The counsellors that had been recommended to me were Dr Peter Ward and Reverend Anne Black. They and their respective partners had moved into an old and very large vicarage in the city centre, which they'd named 'The King's House'. The centre was opened up for weekly services, quiet days, teaching seminars, counselling and retreats. They and a team of volunteers dealt with problems such as depression, abuse, bereavement and other areas of personal pain and suffering. John spoke very highly of this couple who had moved from their professions of doctor and parish deacon to fulfil the calling they believed was from God. He was convinced they had the expertise to deal with my problems. I wasn't so sure. After all, I had friends to talk to, as well as my occasional visits to Rebecca, the psychotherapist appointed by the university to help me. Counselling seemed an added and unnecessary stress to those already pressing upon me.

The following day I didn't telephone the counsellors at The King's House because I woke up with a heavy head. It was a strange sensation, almost as though a thick fog surrounded me. I took a couple of aspirin, hoping it would pass, but by the time I returned from university at the end of the day my headache was considerably worse and everything around me had that strange surreal sensation that I'd experienced on various other occasions. It was a struggle to focus on the children's chatter through tea. In fact, it was a relief when they'd gone to bed and peace had descended upon our home. I took another couple of pills and stretched out on the settee with my head on Lesley's lap.

At first Lesley's talking revolved around the children, but then she commented on some event of the day and how she felt she ought to return to put right the wrong that had taken place. I made the odd monosyllabic comment, but as she talked images and incidents from the past started drifting in and out of my mind and I began to have an overwhelming desire to return to certain places of pain so I could put right the wrongs that had been done to me. As the minutes ticked by this wind of desire grew so strong it seemed to blot out the sound of Lesley's voice and dissipate the peace of my home. I put my hands over my face. My head was spinning. I couldn't think any more. I had the odd sensation that at any moment I could disappear into the whirlwind and be trapped forever in the nightmares of the past. I was sinking . . . sinking . . .

'Mark! Sit up! Mark!'

I found I was being pushed roughly into a sitting position. With a great deal of effort I opened my eyes to find Lesley's face peering worriedly into mine.

'Are you all right?'

I didn't answer. There was a battle going on in my head.

'Are you all right?' she repeated, giving me a shake.

'Yes. I mean . . . no.' My voice sounded thick, guttural. 'I feel dreadful!'

'You look dreadful,' she agreed, sounding worried. 'I think I better make you a cup of tea.'

I ran my fingers through my hair, and as she left me to go into the kitchen I tried to gather my fragmented faculties into some sort of working order. I didn't dare close my eyes again. I was scared of falling asleep. The nightmares were not only starting to invade my daytime but were increasing in frequency. I slumped my head into my hands and moaned. I was disgusted with myself. I'd turned into a weak human being who was totally unable to cope with his own emotional traumas. It was in total contrast to the masculine image I had of myself: someone who worked out regularly, enjoyed football and took his son to karate. I shook myself. 'Stop being a wimp, Mark! Stop it!'

Lesley returned with a mug of tea and suggested we watch television, but after a while my concentration wavered, so I made my way upstairs to write in my diary.

Tuesday October 26th

What's happening to me? I feel I'm losing my grip on reality! I really want to be a normal, whole person. I want to believe that when I read this journal next year that I will be different from the person I am now, but there are times I feel I'm going backwards rather than forwards. Trusting in God! That's the secret, but it's the hardest thing in the world to do.

I didn't sleep well that night and found myself joining the early birds in the university the following morning. My intention was to have a quiet word with John before lectures about these sensations of feeling trapped in the past, but he wasn't there.

I don't know how I managed to get through the rest of that day. In fact, I didn't. I skipped the last lecture and returned home in an emotional turmoil. I was tired, my head ached, my body was tense and I was depressed. I decided the best cure was a work out at the gym, so I raced up to the bedroom to collect my gear from the bottom of the wardrobe. It was missing. In a spate of anger, I hurled myself against the wardrobe doors. They slammed shut and my old brown suitcase fell off the top, on to the bedside light, smashing the bulb. I heard Lesley racing up the stairs.

'What's wrong?' she burst into the bedroom.

'Where's my gear?' I yelled at her.

She took a deep breath. 'In the wash, Mark. Now calm down and tell me what's wrong.'

'Wrong? Everything's wrong! I don't know why you bother staying in this marriage, Lesley! All I ever do is make your life a misery. You should get out of it before I destroy it!'

'Stop it Mark! You're being irrational and full of self-pity again!'

'I don't care!' I bellowed, knowing she was right, but totally unable to stem this flow of anger. 'I don't care about anything any more. Not my marriage, the priesthood – nothing matters any more!'

She came over to where I stood in an attempt to calm me down, but I angrily pushed her away and she stumbled back against the bed.

'I don't need you, Lesley! I don't need anyone! I can cope on my own!' I knew that wasn't true. Now of all times I needed my wife and friends who would support me.

Lesley bit her lip anxiously. 'Mark,' she said gently. 'Look, I had a word with Paul Holly this morning and we both think you should telephone the counsellors at King's House, the ones John suggested.'

I stared at her, horrified. 'You and Holly discussed *what?*'

She swallowed nervously. 'I was worried about you after last night's episode on the settee. I needed someone to talk to, so I rang Holly.' Her eyes filled with tears as she reached out her hand. 'Don't row, Mark. I just want to help.'

I ignored the outstretched hand. 'Help? Oh yes? And what's happened to loyalty, Lesley? My best mate and my wife going behind my back!'

'Don't be stupid! You're making it sound deceitful. We were concerned about you.'

'Uh-huh?' Furious, I turned my back on her and raced down the stairs to the telephone. A moment later Holly's deep, gentle voice sounded on the other end. I hardly waited for him to finish giving his name and number before I'd hurled a tirade of abuse down the telephone at him.

'Bugger off! Do you hear me, Holly? I will *not* have you and Lesley discussing me behind my back. It's none of your damn business who counsels me and who doesn't counsel me!' I slammed the telephone down on the cradle and turned to find Lesley standing halfway down the stairs, watching me nervously.

'What's happening, Mark? You're deliberately pushing us away when we're trying to support you,' she chided. 'I love you. I don't want to argue with you.'

I could hear the love in her voice and it seemed to drain all the pent-up anger out of me. My shoulders slumped and I leant back wearily against the wall. I was exhausted.

'I've got to get out of here,' I said, deliberately avoiding her eye.

'Where to?'

'I don't know. Anywhere. I'll go to karate.' I pushed passed her and, taking the stairs two at a time, dived into the bedroom for my karate suit. On the spur of the moment I grabbed the sleeping bag from the top of the wardrobe. I was aware Lesley had followed me back upstairs and was standing at the door watching me.

'Why don't you telephone Rebecca or John or Andy?' she suggested tentatively.

'I've told you. I don't need anyone! Just leave it, will you, Lesley?' I ran my fingers through my hair, frustrated by her pestering, but not daring to look her in the eye. 'Look, I'm sorry, but I need space for myself right now.'

She looked pointedly at the sleeping bag. 'So I see.'

'I'll just be at the university. OK? At least you'll get a good night's sleep.'

'If that's what you want.' The hurting edge to her voice filled me with guilt at treating my wife so badly, but I couldn't back down now. We stood in an awkward silence, avoiding eye contact, aware that once again there had been an unpleasant exchange of words between us. They were becoming more and more frequent.

'Right! I'm off!' I grabbed the sleeping bag and karate suit, pushed my way passed Lesley and hurried down the stairs. I desperately needed to get out of the house.

The room in the visitors' quarters of the university was small and claustrophobic and the bed was hard and uncomfortable. After tossing and turning for a couple of hours I gave up trying to sleep and went to sit on the basket chair in the corner of the room. I was desperately lonely and it was all my own fault. I'd bawled out my best mate, told my wife to get out of our marriage and in general behaved like an irrational fool. How could I have been so stupid? God had given me these people to support me. So why was I behaving like a complete idiot? If only I could get a grip on what was going on inside me, then these dramatic outbursts need never happen. Why was it taking so long for God to heal me? In fact, was I being healed, or was it all an illusion? Tears ran down my face as waves of self-pity flooded over me.

I don't know how long I sat in that small, hot, sparsely furnished room crying. It seemed like hours, but in actual fact I don't think it was that long. I hadn't bothered turning on the light, so I couldn't see my watch, and was only aware of the furnishings around me by the dim light of the moon. It was very quiet outside, except for the occasional barking of a dog or roar of an engine from a passing car, so I jumped violently at the sharp knock on the door.

'Mark? Are you in there?' It was Holly. Lesley must have rung him. I deliberately didn't answer. A moment later the door opened and Holly stood silhouetted against the corridor lights. He didn't say anything. I knew I ought to apologise for my abusive telephone call, but I was still in an emotional turmoil. Not even praying had helped my peace of mind. Holly walked over to the small bedside table light, switched it on, then closed the door and stood silently looking down at me for a long time. I was too ashamed to look at him, but that didn't seem to matter to Holly, as without a word he simply came over to where I sat and, kneeling down beside the chair, wrapped his arms around me.

I heard a great sob of anguish. It was me. It seemed to rack my whole body. I rested my head on his shoulder, sobbing like a child, and he just held me tightly, allowing me to cry, and somehow it was all right to do that with a man like Holly. It wasn't embarrassing and my macho image wasn't destroyed. Instead, his caring support bonded us together in a friendship that would last forever.

When I was calmer we sat talking quietly about what was happening to me and he tentatively suggested telephoning the counsellors from The King's House. I didn't answer. I was too scared to commit myself.

Holly moved away from my chair and started making the bed and packing my karate suit into the holdall. He obviously intended taking me home. 'Ready?'

'Yes, I suppose so.'

'Come on then.'

In the early hours of the morning Holly packed me, my holdall and my sleeping bag into his car and took us back home to Lesley.

Chapter 20

I arrived home from my parish placement Monday evening and the moment I walked through the door I knew something was wrong. Lesley was decidedly edgy.

'Go on! Tell me! You've bought a new dress and it cost the earth,' I joked. I gave her bottom a smack as she bent over the fireplace and she jumped, cracking her head on the mantelpiece.

'I'm glad you're in a good mood,' she said, straightening up and rubbing her head.

'Why?'

She looked at me warily. 'Because Holly and I have arranged for you to see the counsellors from The King's House tomorrow.'

Whatever good mood I may have possessed rapidly disappeared. 'You've what?'

'Arranged for you to see Dr Peter Ward and Reverend Anne Black, the counsellors from The King's House,' she repeated. 'We can't go on like this, Mark! You need help!'

'My wife and my best friend organising my life behind my back!' My body tensed as a sudden and unexpected surge of blazing red fury surfaced. My clawed fingers reached out to grab the first available object, our wedding photograph standing on the sideboard, and with all my strength I hurled it across the room at Lesley.

She screamed as it smashed against the wall, narrowly missing her face. For a moment we stood staring at each other, horrified by the intensity of my rage, then abruptly I turned and stormed out of the house. Storming out of the house was becoming a habit these days.

I didn't seem to have much of an option but to follow through their carefully laid plans. These counsellors had already discussed my case with John and he was encouraging me to see them, even allowing us to use his study for the evening. Then there were Holly, Nigel and Andy, who spent all day giving me what they called 'moral support'.

Dr Peter Ward and Reverend Anne Black weren't what I expected at all. He was a tall, distinguished sort of chap with not even a touch of grey on his head to show for his fifty years. That was probably due to his casual, laid-back attitude. He came over and shook hands with me, smiling warmly and putting me very much at my ease. Anne Black was small, pretty and vibrant with thick, soft, dark curls bouncing gently on her shoulders. They were comfortable people to be around and seemed genuinely interested in me, and despite the fact that I was still wary of them I must have talked for over two hours. I told them about Lindsay, from the moment she'd arrived at the children's home to my visit with John to Glasgow. Occasionally they interrupted to clarify a certain point or ask a relevant question and then we discussed my feelings about her in greater detail. I told them what she'd said during my last visit: 'Let me go, Mark. Let that mixed-up love go.'

'And can you do that?' Anne asked.

'I want to. It's just . . .' I shook my head.

'But you *want* to?'

'Yes.'

'Is there anything you'd like to say to Lindsay before you let her go?' Peter asked.

I thought about it. 'I once wrote a letter telling her exactly how I felt about her. I found writing it all down helped.'

'Would you like to do that again, Mark?'

I nodded and, because I wanted to do it straight away, they gave me time to write my letter. It wasn't long. After all, I'd had what I wanted to say in my mind for years. All my feelings of love, pain, rejection, bitterness and anger poured out in my short letter.

'What would you like to do with these feelings, Mark?' Peter asked.

'I want rid of them. They're part of my festering sore that can never be put right. I don't want to spend my entire life remembering them and being pained by them. I want to let Lindsay go.'

And so, as a symbolic gesture, Peter lit a match and silently I watched my letter, with all my feelings written on it, burning in the waste bin.

Before they left, they made a number of positive comments, telling me how courageous I had been in sharing these painful issues with them and in wanting to tackle them.

When I arrived home I wept in my bedroom for well over an hour. I wept for the deep loss I'd encountered in finally letting Lindsay go. I wept for the inadequacy in me at never having been able to say 'I love you.' I wept for the children I'd seen taken into care during my summer placement and the loss of parenthood and love their small lives would have to encounter.

Thursday November 5th
Bonfire night! A difficult day, but strangely enough not as difficult as previous years. I no longer feel rejected or grieve over

Lindsay and for that I'm grateful to everyone who has been willing to listen to my story.

Those deep, painful emotions I'd carried for my houseparent all those years were like a stronghold in my life. A stronghold that needed demolishing, because it was more in control of my life than God.

God is holy and he will not tolerate any other god or stronghold in his place. I've discovered that demolishing these strongholds means enduring suffering as we come to terms with the past and do battle with the stronghold. But then God has proved by overcoming death that he is able to overcome all strongholds. I really feel my love for Lindsay is one stronghold that, with prayer and discussion, has been demolished.

Nevertheless, each bonfire night the painful rejection from the Bradshaws is the memory that soars to the forefront of my mind and I can't stop myself reliving every minute of that fateful night. The blazing fire crackling, spitting and sending red and orange flames high into the night sky. The fireworks, roast chestnuts, hot dogs, soup, surrounded by my friends and the image of Mr Bradshaw standing with his hand on my shoulder. 'These presents are for you, Son,' he'd said, handing me a parcel.

That Bonfire Night held a promise of people who would love my little brother and me and I'd been the happiest child in the world. Then they'd walked away! No explanation, no goodbyes, no 'sorry'. They'd just disappeared out of our lives after months of building up a relationship of trust. Is it any wonder I'm insecure?

This November 5th, however, I met with Anne and Peter, and instead of burying my memories I examined my festering wound and 'owned' my deep disappointments, my confusion, the pain of rejection, the sense of worthlessness it had left me with and the pain of wondering what was wrong with Paul and me. Then I wept over all the suffering I had experienced because of the Bradshaws. When I'd calmed down somewhat, Anne held my hands and we prayed for God to bring his healing into those deep, deep places of pain. Then Peter read a verse from the Bible: 'Do not conform any *longer to the pattern of this world, but be transformed by the renewing of your mind' (Romans 12:2).*

My expectations for pain every November 5th were now being addressed and the mindset patterns were being changed. As I said before, a difficult day, but not as difficult as previous years.

Saturday November 7th

Lesley is being wonderful at the moment. She's a real tower of strength. It's marvellous how she manages to keep the children from knowing the traumas I have to work through.

It's difficult to tell how my parish placement is going. I enjoy the work and get on well with the vicar, but I'm hoping my present state of mind doesn't influence my work.

Sunday November 8th

Had a very bad night! Voices from the past, houseparents, foster parents, my real parents, arguing, scolding, screaming, crying, all became distorted as past and present merged into another frightening nightmare. I tried to pray but I couldn't! There is no awareness of God in this deep pit of despair I find myself in and I wonder how I could possibly call myself a Christian.

Then I remembered Psalm 40: 'I waited patiently for the Lord . . . He lifted me out of slimy pit, out of the mud and mire, he set my feet on a rock and gave me a firm place to stand.'

I tried to tell myself this was where faith had to take over, but I was tense, my breathing was heavy and laboured, so I just curled up in bed, crying like a baby. I'm ashamed of my weakness. I feel less of a man and wish I could find the strength to assert my masculinity again. Is there something wrong with me? I hope I don't have a nervous breakdown and end up in a psychiatric hospital again and I'm frightened that it will only be a matter of time before everyone gets fed up with me. O Lord! I want to trust You more!

I want to believe You'll lift me out of this miry pit!

I hadn't intended telling Anne and Peter about the suicidal tendencies that had come upon me over the years, but somehow as our counselling sessions progressed and I became more comfortable with them it seemed to slip out. I thought they'd be shocked that someone like me, training for the priesthood, should have even contemplated such an act, but they didn't seem shocked at all.

'Would you like to tell us about it?' Peter asked.

So I did, focusing primarily on the last one, the incident on the bridge while I was on retreat. My pain that night had been so bad that in a moment of despair I had turned on God and all that he had done for me. 'I might as well be serving the devil for all you care!' I'd screamed at him.

When I came to that part I broke down in tears of shame over my abusive language towards God. Deep sobs racked my body. I wept for my weakness of mind in listening to the tempter's voice of destruction urging me to end it all by taking my own life, and I wept for my sinful weakness in attempting those suicidal acts.

Anne reached out and stroked the back of my head, reassuring me that it was all right to be angry with God. He knew how I was feeling anyway. Then she began praying quietly and that seemed to calm me down somewhat.

When I was more relaxed Peter took a small wooden cross from the mantelpiece and began praying for God's supremacy in this inner battle in which I found myself and these recurring temptations to end my life. I must have clung to Anne and Peter for nearly an hour while some form of spiritual battle raged on inside me. Then, although I was still in an emotional turmoil, I sensed the presence of God and reached out, crying for him to forgive me for denying him, abusing him and for listening to the voice of destruction calling me to end my life.

We were silent for a long time after that emotional outburst and, although I can't say I experienced any deep emotional healing, I was very aware that the weight of guilt that had hung over me for years seemed to have lifted from my shoulders. I also felt reassured that those times I had been angry with God were all right. My anger had had to go somewhere and it was better it went to him than became rooted within me, as had happened in my childhood and adolescence. He died to take all our ungodly emotions upon his cross.

The following night I'd hardly fallen asleep before I was awakened by a severe nightmare. My mind had been wrestling and screaming with images from my childhood, unresolved areas of distress and physical and mental pain. I shot up in bed, soaking with perspiration. The room was crowding in on me! On the spur of the moment I leapt out of bed, grabbed the sleeping bag and with some form of garbled explanation to Lesley, shot out of the house and made my way to the university, where I curled up in a bed in one of the visitors' rooms.

I tried to sleep, but it was hot in the little room, and for some reason, despite all the prayer we'd had the previous night, the memory of abusing God and contemplating suicide when I was on retreat continually haunted my thoughts. I seemed to wrestle all night with frightening images of the inky blackness of the rocks below the bridge and a flashing thought kept crossing my mind that what I had failed to do then I could do now, *if* I had the courage to go up on to the roof. It was almost as if this was the enemy's counter-attack!

Time seemed to stand still as hour after hour I dragged my frightening, suicidal thoughts through the night. My only prayer was a cry: 'Lord Jesus, Son of God! Have mercy on me, a sinner!' I hoped Holly would come and rescue me like he had the last time. I was scared to be alone, but no one came, and the long night of wrestling continued until the early hours of the morning, when a watery sun penetrated through the grey skies and the university started to come to life. Only then did I drag my weary body out of bed. I hadn't eaten much the previous day so I was physically weak and very hungry. I stared at my dark, unshaven face in the mirror. What a state I was in! So much for all that praying! What good had it done?

I snatched some breakfast in the canteen, then joined the other students for early morning communion in the chapel, wondering why I was bothering. Surely it would be much easier to work in a shop, a factory.

It was only as we were singing the chorus – 'Here I am Lord. Send me' – that a strange sense of peace started to penetrate through my awful tiredness. A calming influence seemed to soak slowly through my battle-torn mind and deep, certain knowledge filled my whole being.

I was called to be a priest! That was why I was here!

As John stood up to speak to the early morning worshippers, strength seemed to flow back into my body.

I was called to be a priest! That was why I was here!

It's times like this when I realise life is not all black but that strangely enough some form of healing and restoring is taking place. I walked through the chapel doors after the service with a lightness in my step I never expected to be there, feeling surprisingly better.

Some of my counselling sessions with Peter and Anne turned out to be very challenging. There were times when the distinguished gentleman with the soft, gentle voice and the pretty deacon with curls bouncing around her shoulders turned into monsters, especially when they seemed to sense I was erecting a barrier. Their counselling techniques would change from the comfortable 'get it off your chest' to picking up on odd words I'd said and asking astute questions about their meaning for me. I didn't like that. It made me uncomfortable. I felt they were about to rip the elastoplasts off my festering wounds and I wanted to stick them back on again. I told them so.

'And what do you think would happen if you hid your pain away again, Mark?' Peter asked gently.

I shrugged, annoyed by the way he had me relaxing one minute, but would throw pointed questions at me the next.

'I don't know! Go back to the way things were, I suppose. Look, I'm really not in the mood for facing your issues today. Let's finish it. OK?'

'They're not *our* issues, Mark,' Peter said softly. 'They're yours. We're just helping to bring them to the surface so you can look at them, but it's up to you whether you want to continue or not.'

'Yes, well. Whatever!' I said grudgingly. Suddenly I didn't like this man who confronted me with something every time I opened my mouth.

Peter stirred in his seat. 'Mark, would you consider yourself to be a responsible adult?' I sensed he was backing me into a corner. That made me angry. Not that I was any less angry with Anne! She had been gentle and sympathetic all evening, and look where I'd ended up!

'I am a responsible adult. Yes,' I snapped. 'Otherwise why would I be here?'

'Not all counselling is comfortable, Mark,' Anne informed me. 'Sometimes painful issues are brought to the surface, but no one will make you face them. The choice is always yours. To deal with them, or not.'

I wasn't listening. I was tired and upset that evening so I retaliated the only way I knew how. I exploded into another one of those blinding rages. 'Get off my case!' I bellowed. 'You're finished!'

I expected some sort of alarmed reaction at my outburst, especially from Anne, but there was none. In fact, they made no attempt to move, but continued to sit passively, waiting for me to calm down. I leapt to my feet, knocking my chair to the ground. 'Get out!' Still no one moved. 'Well, if you're not going, I am!'

Peter crossed his legs. 'That's up to you, Mark! You can stay and see this issue through, or you can leave.'

I left! Slamming the door behind me.

A freezing fog had settled upon the town for the night and the cold seemed to seep through my clothes. My mood didn't improve any when I arrived home to see John Pritchard's car outside my front door.

'I just wondered how you're getting on with Peter and Anne?' he said by way of explanation as I entered the house. He couldn't have chosen a worse night to ask a question like that!

'Would you both like a bite of supper while you're talking?' Lesley asked.

'That would be lovely,' John replied, and my heart sank. The last thing I wanted was to sit making polite conversation with John for the next half hour or so. He made himself comfortable on the long settee where I usually sat and I slumped down opposite him in the cane rocking chair.

'I don't know whether I want to go back to them,' I said bluntly.

John frowned at me. 'Of course, it's up to you, but I would strong recommend you don't back off now. If Peter and Anne can't help you it may be you'll need some sort of psychiatric input.'

I stared at him, horrified. 'No way!' was my immediate response. 'I'm not that bad and I'm not going down that road again!'

'I'm not saying you will. I'm just saying you may have to consider it,' he said hastily.

'I have considered it and the answer's the same. No!'

John didn't press the subject further and after we'd finished our toasted sandwiches Lesley saw him to the front door.

Tuesday December 14th

I'm so close to the edge I don't know how I don't flip completely! After leaving Anne and Peter the other evening I stood on the bridge in the freezing fog for ages, watching the great wide river swirling beneath me as it wound its way to the sea. I was reminded of the James Stewart film It's a Wonderful Life *and tried to imagine what it would have been like for the people around me if I hadn't been born. It wasn't difficult to come to the conclusion that their lives could only have been better if I hadn't been around to bring them so much misery.*

Christmas Day

It should have been a good Christmas with Shene, Graham and the children visiting us, but I've been distant with them because I needed time to think.

Saturday 8th January

Andy's wife invited Lesley and me for a meal. I think I had my first good laugh this year. Andy laid out a challenge as to who could lift the heavy table above their heads the most times. I did it twenty, but of course Andy had to go four better than me! Stupid, but good fun!

Sunday January 9th

Good service at church tonight. The speaker talked about pruning. He said that sometimes we have to enter a dormant period and during that time we're cut right back, like rose bushes, cutting back the dead or old growth to allow fresh growth for the next season (John 15). Oh Lord, this pruning is taking so long, and it's so painful! When will you grow in me and allow me to be fruitful for you?

Friday January 14th, eight p.m.

I took four sleeping tablets last night. I thought they might help. They didn't. I've been tired all day. I feel as if I'm in a spiritual desert again.

I've tried hard looking for God by praising, praying, reading the Bible, but He remains elusive. Eventually I lay down on my bed and when I was almost asleep Psalm 40 came to mind again: 'I waited patiently for the Lord; He turned to me and heard my cry. He lifted me out of the slimy pit, out of the mud and mire; he set my feet on a rock and gave me and firm place to stand. He put a new song in my mouth, a hymn of praise to our God. Many will see and fear and put their trust in the Lord. Blessed is the man who makes the Lord his trust.' I must stay focussed on God! I must!

Monday January 31st

Had some dreadful dreams over the weekend, which left me tired and nauseous, but I struggled into university anyway. It didn't help that it was snowing and traffic was almost at a standstill.

When I eventually arrived home Lesley was upset and gave me a mouthful for not spending quality time with her and the children. I knew she was right, but at the moment I can't seem to help it. Be patient with me, Lesley! Be patient! I'm very confused at the moment.

Friday February 18th

Woke up sobbing for mummy. Oh God, I pray I get put right soon!

I put down my pen. There was the sound of someone crying quietly downstairs. I crept out of my study to the top of the stairs. Lesley was sitting in the chair, lost in her own private grief, while through the window behind her the snow continued to fall gently to the ground.

Chapter 21

I wandered downstairs and pulled on my coat. It was still wet from my walk earlier that evening. Lesley stood at the living room door, her face streaked with mascara from crying.

'Don't go out,' she implored. 'It's blowing a gale out there.'

I ignored her. Wordlessly I closed the front door behind me and wandered aimlessly around the cold, white streets, ending up by the old bridge near the town centre. I rested my arms on the wet stone wall and, leaning over, watched the snowflakes swirling downwards towards the river. Some of them landed on the riverbank, but most of them seemed to end up in the river, washed away into oblivion, into nothingness. If I'd had the courage it would have been a welcome relief to join them. I shivered. I didn't want to struggle with the pain of suicidal thoughts again. I didn't have to. Not only did the image of my family's warmth and love hold me back, but it seemed as though those self-destructive thoughts were no longer part of my life.

Eventually I pulled myself away from the edge of the bridge and reluctantly tramped home through the thick snow. The roads were almost deserted and what cars had ventured out were skidding and sliding all over the ungritted roads.

I walked into the house, drenched through and shaking with the cold. Lesley didn't say a word. She just took my coat and hung it over a radiator to dry, and then, avoiding eye contact with me, said, 'I've rung Peter and Anne.' I was too exhausted to argue with her. I caught a glimpse of myself in the hall mirror. My clothes were dishevelled, beads of perspiration stood out on my forehead and my eyes were bright and glaring.

They came. Peter and Anne that is. They arrived cold and extremely stressed by their hazardous twenty-mile journey through the blizzard-swept hills. I don't know how they managed it or why they even bothered. A few weeks previously I'd been inexcusably rude to them and had dismissed them, yet they'd been willing to turn out in the most atrocious conditions just for me. Of course, I didn't appreciate it. I was too absorbed in my own intense pain. Everyone else's discomfort and inconvenience came second. But they stayed with me, letting me talk until well into the night. At one point Peter began praying. As he prayed, a memory of a lady with a large stick reared its ugly head. They were memories I'd tried to blot out because they were so frightening, but many a night I'd woken up in a cold sweat because of them. However, this particular night, Peter encouraged me to stay with the memories.

I was in a foster home, I was pretty sure of that, and I must have been about three, because I remember Paul was only a baby. He was standing up in a cot, holding on to the sides and crying. I lay in a small bed in the corner, frightened because I'd wet it again. A big, tall lady stormed in through the door. 'If that kid doesn't stop bawling . . . !' she shouted threateningly. Horrified, I watched her approach my baby brother, wielding a huge stick. My throat seemed to dry up.

'You must look after your baby brother, Mark!' they'd warned. Terror wrapped its icy fingers around my whole body. If I didn't look after him and he was hurt it would be my fault. *My fault!* I screamed and she turned from Paul to me. Her face was grim, her voice angry, and the stick was raised. 'I'll teach you to cry in the middle of the night!' Wham! Across my buttocks. 'You and your brother can lie and rot in a wet bed!' Wham! Wham!

Tears of compassion ran down Peter's face as these memories surfaced and my feelings were allowed expression. Then he and Anne prayed for the abuse I'd suffered at the hands of that lady and once again I visualised the Lord walking into the situation. As I lay on the settee weeping I heard him speak softly into the deepest part of my being. 'Let me take your pain, Mark,' he said, and in my mind's eye I could see the torn, bleeding whiplashes as the soldiers flogged him. Wham! Wham! The twisted crown of thorns was thrust on his head and the sharp needles dug into his forehead. Blood intermingled with sweat ran down his face. He had been whipped, scourged and set upon like me, and he knew the eyes of anger and the loneliness of rejection. So it was all right to hand over my worst nightmares to him, because he could understand my suffering the way no one else ever would. I knew the memories would remain forever, but the sting was being taken out of them. Never again would something that was said or done trigger off a Godless response in me, because healing was taking place.

These, I discovered, were the root causes of the fears I had of being 'dumped'. Fears that had been built upon over the years by parents, Social Services, foster homes and individuals. I'd had years of the same thing and knew the consequences would be pain. Was it any wonder I had become irrational and even suicidal with fear?

Eventually sheer exhaustion took over, so Peter and Anne left after a short prayer, and agreed to see me again on a regular basis for counselling. By now it was almost one thirty in the morning.

February was a difficult month! I blamed myself for the way my life had turned out, for not continuing counselling with Peter and Anne. If I had, it might have eased the pressure on Lesley and made a world of difference to our relationship, but miserably I realised I couldn't undo what had already been done.

I remembered Peter Haywood explaining to me that because I hadn't been able to cope with my feelings in the past I had in effect built a brick wall around them. The work of chipping away the mortar and exposing a few of those feelings had really started with Pastor Coombs, the first man to have genuinely cared for me and given me his time. The dismantling continued with Peter Haywood and his team at the Anglican church, with Rebecca at the university and with friends who'd been willing to listen. The wall was now in a precarious state and unable to withstand the professional counselling and ministry of Peter and Anne. During February the strongholds came tumbling down, exposing many more deep emotions. But instead of taking pills to suppress them again, as I had at the psychiatric hospital, with the help of Peter and Anne I was able to look at each festering wound and accept it as being mine. And because I didn't want to bury it in the deepest parts of my mind again, we prayed, asking God to take it and bring about his deepest healing.

During the cold, wet and windy month of March, Peter and Anne helped me look more closely at why being rejected so terrified me. I talked through my attitude towards my parents and the way I blamed them for dumping me on to Social Services. As I talked I was able to come to terms with the deep fear I experienced every time they placed Paul and me into foster homes.

One night as I talked I found myself curling up in a foetal position. I was remembering when I was a child of two or three, and, like any little boy, I wanted my mummy. I wanted to be loved, to feel secure and safe, but instead I remembered being dragged from my mother's arms, kicking and screaming. But it was not for my mother I was screaming: it was Paul.

'Paul,' I head myself whimpering. 'Paul, where are you Paul?'

'You must look after your baby brother, Mark!' Those words, which my mother had instilled in me, were so deeply imprinted in my mind that I became terrified of being taken away from home because of the added responsibility of looking after Paul. It was too much for me. I shouldn't have been asked to shoulder a burden like that. I not only had to try to fend for my own emotional needs, but Paul's too.

Anne came over to sit beside me. 'Would you like someone to help you shoulder that responsibility, Mark?' she asked softly.

Tears started running down my face at the compassion in her voice. 'Yes.'

She stroked my head, the way a mother does with a small child. 'We love you, Mark,' she said quietly. 'We love you and God loves you.' Then she quietly prayed for God to walk into those memories and take the weight off my young shoulders.

The past couldn't be undone and the memories would always be there, but as I lay, visualising God walking into my past, I was warmed by his deep sadness. I didn't understand what happened next. All I knew was that as

Peter and Anne continued to pray for me, telling me they loved me and that God loved me, and I sensed a great weight lifting off my shoulders, and I knew, really knew, that I was totally free from the heavy weight of responsibility I'd been forced to carry all my life. A moment later a deep sense of peace flooded over me. Difficult to describe, really, because it was too deep and meaningful. The 'peace that transcends all under-standing' (Philippians 4:7) is the way the Bible describes it, and that's a pretty accurate description. That was the point at which I knew God now had a far greater control over me than my fears and pain.

By April the first daffodils had pushed their way through the ground to herald the coming of spring. Strange how nature can give you a sense of encouragement to keep going. Peter and Anne continued enabling me to come to terms with the painful memories of my youth. I found counselling physically and mentally exhausting, and at times I wanted to give up, but Lesley encouraged me to persevere.

Going back to university after the Easter break was traumatic. I was terrified of facing friends and fellow students who'd heard about my counselling, but Peter and Anne were very encouraging.

'You've nothing to be ashamed of,' Peter said.

'Hold your head up high, Mark,' Anne said.

I never thought I'd be able to do it, but I did.

John was never far away. He firmly believed that my first two years at theological college had been very successful, despite having so much upset. I'd even managed to attain reasonable grades in my exams and that in itself was a shock. I was convinced I had failed. Then John brought a detailed report of my progress around to the house late one night. I recorded parts of it in my diary as a confidence booster for when I'm feeling really down.

Mark has natural pastoral gifts and is particularly good at listening and talking . . . He also showed considerable flair at preparing for the liturgy and setting out worship space.

By rolling up his sleeves and getting involved, individuals have been able to relate to Mark, especially members of the congregation who come from a lower social/economic background. Mark relates to them more effectively than any other student who has been here on placement.

Mark also preaches well and enthusiastically and his sermons have been well received. He has contributed greatly to our Christmas celebrations by making a splendid life-size nativity scene which produced stunning results and highlighted Mark's particular talent in enabling people to worship . . .

In conclusion, it is clear that given the right environment and encouragement Mark will flourish in his ministry and be a good curate and priest.

I should have been in high spirits after such a good report, but then John said the only reason he'd shown me it was to prove I'd been doing well regardless of the traumas I'd faced this past year. Then he dropped the bombshell: in his opinion another year at university would be in my own interest! I was devastated. He went on to explain that because there were still important issues to be worked through with my counsellors, another year of study and working towards getting emotionally fit would greatly benefit me and prove I was able to cope with the responsibilities of ordained priesthood.

I chatted it through with Lesley, and I knew it made sense, but I was pretty depressed at having to do another year when Holly, Nigel and Andy were all going forward for ordination.

By May we seemed to have been dealing with forgiveness for weeks! There was a big knot of bitterness inside me, directed at individuals like the Clark brothers, who'd bullied me when I was in the children's home; Mrs Robins, who'd come with Miss Vernon to take us away from the Tait family; my dad, for not being there for me even when I'd run away to find him; the Bradshaws, who'd built up my hopes for adoption then dumped me. There was even the Social Services system, which had shunted Paul and me between parents and foster homes and had decided what was best for us. I'd always felt the system had abused me and let me down until I'd had the opportunity to see the other side of the coin during my summer placement. It had been a strange experience, being part of a team attempting to draw alongside children from broken homes like myself, or with drug- or alcohol-related problems, and I'd realised the difficulties of working as part of a system in an imperfect world. I talked through all these thoughts and experiences with Peter and Anne. There were so many people I needed to forgive!

As the warm summer months of June and July came upon us and the roses bloomed around our estate, my sessions with Peter and Anne became less frequent as I was able to take up the reins of my own life again. My general and mental health continued to improve and I began to feel whole, despite the fact that a huge question mark hung over my career. Lesley and I continued to receive support from the handful of friends who believed in my vocation as a priest. It was particularly difficult seeing some of my friends ordained and saying goodbye. Holly was almost in tears as he hugged me. He and his wife moved to the south of England, where he took up a position as curate. I missed that guy!

Over the summer holidays I found myself relaxing more. Healing really was taking place.

By October Anne and Peter had finally withdrawn from the scene and had left me with words of encouragement about how brave I'd been and how well I was doing.

By the end of the year I was worrying whether I could really be true to my vows of ordination.

Chapter 22

She sat on the grass with her arms wrapped around her knees, her head slightly tilted, squinting in the warm sunshine. She was watching Fiona and Jonathan squealing as they paddled in the river, trying to catch fish with their fishing rods, but there was no gentle smile playing around her mouth the way there usually was. She looked sad, my Lesley. Absorbed in some train of thought other than her children. I stopped in my tracks and, hidden under the shelter of the trees, watched her. She'd let her hair grow recently. It fell in soft brown curls around her pale face. I liked it that way, although I don't think I ever said so – in fact, I don't think I had made any comment at all when she had come back from the hairdresser's!

The children were now more intent on negotiating the slippery stones underfoot as they wandered further upstream. Lesley roused from the depths of her thoughts. 'Don't go far!' she called, and Fiona waved in acknowledgement, her head bent low beside her brother's as they pored over some unfortunate creature caught in their fishing rod. When was the last time I'd been totally absorbed in their world instead of my own?

It seemed as though I stood under those trees for a long time, trying to capture that scene, so I could hold it in my memory for ever. The old tartan picnic rug littered with sandals, towels, the thermos flask, and the picnic basket, with the remains of the sandwiches I knew they'd saved for me. Lesley reached out and idly picked a daisy, twirling it around in her fingers, but I could tell she wasn't really seeing it. She seemed to have reverted to the train of though that had so absorbed her earlier, because there was that look of sadness across her face again. There were one or two other families picnicking, but not near our spot. This was our place. Quiet and sheltered, where the river was shallow enough for catching tiddlers and paddling without fear of the children getting out of their depth. Lesley stretched out her legs, pulling her skirt up a couple of inches so the sun could brown them, then she rested back on her arms and stared at the blue sky. What was she thinking? In truth, I didn't know. In fact, I suddenly realised it had been a long time since I'd known what she was thinking or how she was feeling. I'd been so wrapped up my own journey that I'd almost forgotten the person who'd walked faithfully alongside me all these years, who'd picked up the pieces when I'd fallen, who'd encouraged me when the going got tough. My Lesley! What had all this done to her? I had no idea. The realisation didn't make me feel good at all.

I took a deep breath and, squaring my shoulders, left the hidden shelter of the trees and hurried down the gentle slope towards her. 'Hope you've saved me some grub!' I called.

She turned and smiled but her eyes didn't twinkle the way they used to. 'How did you get on?'

'Got it!' I waved the envelope at her, then flopped down on the rug beside her.

'Open it!' There was a slight sign of enthusiasm.

'I think I should eat first,' I teased.

She threw me a box of sandwiches and snatched the envelope from me.

'You've already opened it,' she reprimanded.

'Uh-huh.'

'Cheat!' She pulled the three-page final report from my consultant psychiatrist from the envelope and started reading. I sat quietly, munching my cheese and pickle sandwiches, waiting for her to finish. When she came to the end she grinned at me. 'Mark. It's marvellous! Don't you think so?'

I nodded happily and bit viciously into a hard green apple. 'Marvellous!'

In short, the report from the psychiatrist, which had been sent to John, stated that in his opinion I didn't have an enduring mental illness and that the emotional problems I had displayed in the past were consistent with a disruptive family background and difficult upbringing. In his opinion, he concluded, I was likely to complete the academic programme satisfactorily.

'Are you pleased?' she asked.

'You've no idea how much.' I grabbed another sandwich and for a while we sat discussing the report and how much it meant to me and how difficult it had been discussing my childhood experiences with the psychiatrist. In fact, it wasn't until I'd finished the thermos of coffee that I realised every conversation Lesley and I had these days was about me. How *I* was feeling? What *I* was doing? I shuffled uncomfortably on the rug. 'I think I'll check on Fiona and Jonathan. Make sure they haven't drowned themselves,' I said, throwing the dregs of coffee on the grass.

'Mmm.'

I left her as I'd found her. Quiet and contemplative. As I wandered upstream in search of my children it occurred to me I should have asked her if anything was wrong, but I brushed it aside. It could wait. It was about time I gave my children some quality time and here, in the river, seemed an ideal place to start. I pulled off my trainers and socks and, rolling up my jeans, joined the children in the water with their fishing rods and jam jars. Strange how a simple pleasure like this reminded me of the happy days in my childhood. For the first time in my life I found myself telling Fiona and Jonathan about those two short years with the Tait family, when David, Laura, Paul and I used to take our jam jars down to the dyke at the bottom of their big garden to catch tadpoles. I found myself laughing as I recounted the fun Paul and I had riding on the combine harvester and feeding the cows at the nearby farm. It seemed a long time since I'd enjoyed myself so much with my children and I joined in their cries of excitement as we filled our own jam jars with fish. It came as quite a surprise to hear Lesley calling and to realise we had been engrossed in fishing for so long.

As we bundled our belongings into carrier bags and set off walking home I knew I had reached the point in my life where the focus of my attention needed to move from me and my needs to my wife, children and my vocation as a priest. There was only one final hurdle to overcome: my need to be certain I had forgiven everyone in the past who had hurt me.

I had the opportunity to discuss this issue with the Archdeacon a week or so later as we sat in the gardens of the castle where a group of us had been staying for a three-day retreat. I had a lot of respect for this man. He always had time to listen.

'Do you, in all good conscience, feel you have done all you can to forgive those who hurt you in your childhood, Mark?' he asked gently.

'Absolutely everything!' I said vehemently.

'Then put it behind you. Let it go.' He smiled at me, then patted my shoulder in a fatherly manner. 'Go forward and be ordained in all good conscience, Mark.'

I sat in the garden for over two hours after he left, thinking over what he'd said. He was right. Of course he was right! I was reminded of the festering sores I'd had and the elastoplasts that had covered them. There were no elastoplasts now and no festering sores. Perhaps the odd scab, but if I kept picking at that scab it could end up in being a nasty sore again. 'Let me go, Mark,' Lindsay had said, and I had. 'Put it behind you, Mark,' the Archdeacon had said, and that was what I had to do.

The vision of Lesley sitting on the riverbank while the children played, absorbed in some sad train of thought, suddenly flashed into my mind and it occurred to me that perhaps I was spending too much time thinking about me again when my wife ought to be the focus of my concern.

This wonderful old castle with its beautiful gardens and peaceful countryside surroundings was the ideal place to get the solitude I needed to put all these thoughts into prayer, but I discovered that for the remainder of my time there it was Lesley who filled every waking thought. I remembered the way she had taken my ranting and ravings, tears and moods. The encouragement she'd given me with my counselling, supporting me when I felt I couldn't keep going. The hours of prayer she had spent with me and for me and the financial sacrifices she'd had to make in being the wife of a student. On top of all that, she was a mother, with all the responsibilities that entailed. Life hadn't been easy for her, but she'd survived, with God's help. But what about me? When had I been there to help her with her own emotional, physical and spiritual needs? That last day on retreat left me feeling not too good about myself, but resolving to do something about it.

I returned home to find a bucket full of dead fish. The children didn`t seem overly concerned, however, more enthralled by the gruesome insect that had eaten them, so words of comfort weren't really necessary, just a masochistic interest in the insect. I did, however, have to perform a burial service for the fish later in the week because of the smell from the bucket.

Lesley seemed quieter than usual and because, for the first time in a long time, I was more focused on her needs than my own, I was aware she had lost some of her sparkle. There were longer periods of silence between us than usual. I debated whether to ask her about it, but decided instead that perhaps what she needed most of all was what she called 'a bit of TLC'.

We were sitting in our favourite restaurant when I approached the subject. I say 'favourite' as if we were never away from the place, but the truth is we didn't come very often because eating out was a luxury we just couldn't afford.

'Are you all right?' I asked her. 'You've been very quiet lately.'

'Mmm. Just tired, that's all.' She took a sip of wine and I refilled her glass to the top. 'Whoa! You'll have me intoxicated!'

'That was the general idea,' I murmured.

She gave a half smile. 'This is a lovely night out, Mark. Thank you.'

I didn't say anything, and we were quiet for a while as we ate our steaks, but it was a comfortable silence. Occasionally I glanced up at her. Her hair was neatly curled around her face and the dim orange lighting of the restaurant and the wine had given a warm glow to her cheeks. The candle on the table shimmered, sending streaks of silver across her white beaded blouse. I couldn't remember having seen her look so lovely.

'We're going to make it, Lesley. You and me, I mean,' I said softly.

She looked up and smiled and I was surprised to see how easily tears sprang into her eyes. 'Do you think so?' The doubt in her voice shook me.

'Is there any reason why we shouldn't?'

She lowered her eyes and continued eating. 'Lesley? Is there any reason why we shouldn't?'

She shook her head dismissively. 'Don't let's talk about . . .'

'Yes, Lesley. Let's talk about why you don't think we are going to make it,' I said firmly, but I reached over and gently placed my hand over hers. She didn't respond. 'Lesley?' I prompted. She hesitated. Unsure of herself? Of me? I didn't know.

She shook her head and I was shocked to hear the venom in her voice when she said, 'These have been the worst two years of my life!'

I didn't say anything. What could I say? I'd been the one to make them the worst two years of her life.

'I don't really want to talk about this,' she reiterated.

'Please, Lesley. I love you,' I said, squeezing her hand. To my concern, tears started running down her face. 'What's wrong, love?'

'Mark, I . . .' She struggled to regain control of her emotions, her knife and fork on the plate, dinner forgotten.

'Talk to me, Lesley. You've always been here for me. Please let me be here for you.' There was some sort of battle going on inside her. It was painful to watch.

She hesitated, then said, 'Mark, if I ask you something, I don't want you to answer straight away, I want you to think about it carefully and when you do answer I want you to be truthful.'

This sounded serious. I nodded. 'What do you want to ask?'

There was a pause before she said, 'I always found your relationship with Lindsay difficult to understand, Mark.' She looked me squarely in the eyes. 'Can you reassure me that . . . that it's over? Completely over now?'

Lindsay! Lindsay again! Was she forever to be imprinted on my mind? I dropped my eyes from Lesley's penetrating gaze and stared thoughtfully at the flickering candle between us. A couple of times I glanced at the pain in my wife's face and my heart bled for her, but I didn't rush to reply because I knew a lot depended on my answer. Eventually I raised her hand and brushed her fingers with my lips.

'There was a time in my life, Lesley, when I needed Lindsay,' I said quietly. 'I did. And I think I grew up expecting her to fulfil all the things my childhood lacked. I grew over-dependant on her. She made me feel good because she was willing to spend time with me.' I twisted Lesley's engagement ring around her finger. She tried to withdraw her hand from mine, but I held on to it. 'For a while she was the most important person in my life, Lesley, because she represented something I needed. A mothering figure, an elder sister figure, a mixture of all those things. I was confused, mixed up and in pain, but, Lesley – Lesley, look at me.' I put my finger under her chin and forced her look at me. 'I've always loved you. A healthy love. The way a husband should love his wife!' I kept my finger under her chin and wouldn't let her turn away until she'd looked into my eyes and seen my honesty and love for her. 'It's over, Lesley,' I said. 'Lindsay was part of my past and my past is over. Over.'

She searched my face carefully, then slowly smiled at me through her tears. 'I believe you.' Untangling her fingers from mine she sighed and sat back in her chair. 'Your steak's getting cold,' she said, and there was a flicker of that impish grin that I loved so much.

It was at that precise moment that I felt it. A stirring deep inside me. I was in love. Deeply, deeply in love. I sat watching her cutting her steak, pouring on more gravy, and I couldn't take my eyes off her. It was the strangest experience, as though I was falling in love all over again, and it was wonderful!

She glanced up and raised her eyebrows. 'What's up? Why are you smiling?'

I shook my head. 'It doesn't matter.'

'Yes it does. What are you thinking?'

I picked up my knife and fork before answering. 'I was thinking I would like to say sorry to you and also thank you.'

We looked deeply into each other's eyes and she knew what I meant. She knew it was an apology and a thank you for the past two years, but she asked anyway.

'Thank you and sorry for what?'

With a sombre expression across my face, I said, 'Thank you is for coming out with me tonight, Lesley, and for bringing the family allowance money, and sorry is for having to ask you to dip into it because I've decided we should treat ourselves to some of that chocolate gateau on the sweet trolley.'

The contours of her face relaxed and her mouth broke into a wide smile. 'Aren't we being a bit indulgent? You haven't starting earning yet, you know.'

'I don't care. Tonight, with the help of the family allowance, I'm celebrating the fact that I've fallen in love with my wife all over again.'

Chapter 23

The sun shone through the small, multi-coloured panes of glass in the corner of the cathedral, making a rainbow effect on the stone floor. I walked slowly towards it, my footsteps echoing around this magnificent building. At the moment it was empty, with the exception of an elderly lady arranging a colourful display of flowers near the altar, but soon throngs of worshippers, friends, relatives, priests and the hierarchy of the Anglican church would be gathered to celebrate the handful of young men being ordained.

Silently I stepped into the rainbow of colours and watched them dancing around my shoes. I debated whether or not to go outside and join Lesley and the children in the grounds, but it was hot outside, one of the hottest Junes on record, and not a day to be standing around making polite conversation with relatives and friends. I couldn't face that. Not at the moment. Besides, it was cool here, inside the cathedral, and I needed space for myself right now.

I moved from the rainbow of light to a seat in the corner. Here I was out of sight of the lady doing the flower arranging. I sat down. The highly polished wooden seat was hard and smelled of beeswax. I closed my eyes, enjoying the peace and quiet of this holy building. Quiet, that is, except for the occasional echo around the rafters as someone closed a door, or whispered voices elsewhere in the cathedral as last-minute preparations were made for the service later that day.

This day was one of the happiest days of my life, yet a small black cloud continued to hang over me. With a background like mine, was I really fit to be a priest? There was no doubt about it, I was more positive in my outlook these days, more confident in myself as a person and more stable in my walk with God. Even my marriage seemed to have been turned upside down as the pain and hurt I had put Lesley through in recent years was resolved between us and the initial love we'd had for each other was allowed to blossom and develop in a way I had never thought possible. I was a very fortunate man. So why did I still feel as though I was not worthy to take these vows? After all, I even had the Archdeacon's blessing!

I don't know how long I sat quietly in the cathedral. I think at one point I must have dropped off to sleep, because I was suddenly awoken by a loud bang as someone slammed one of the doors. I opened my eyes and looked around. The lady arranging the flowers had long since disappeared, and one or two early arrivals, or those unable to stand the heat of the midday sun, were making their way towards the rows of chairs set out for relatives and guests of those being ordained. I stood up. I was stiff after sitting on the hard seat for so long. I stretched my legs, brushed a crease from my long black robe, ran my finger around my dog collar and tiptoed out of the cathedral to join Lesley and the children for a few minutes before I went forward for ordination. Despite that brief moment of sadness, I was at peace. The confident peace of a man who knows the way ahead of him is that of God's calling into the priesthood.

The organ swelled and the procession, led by the Archdeacon, moved slowly into the main body of the crowded cathedral. Bishops, visiting clergy, lay representatives and those of us being ordained or priested followed them down the wide aisle in our black robes or cream and gold vestments suited to our office. My hands trembled under my black robe. This was it! This was what I'd been waiting and working for all my life! The total giving of my life into God's service.

My eyes flickered across the tanned faces of the smartly dressed congregation as we passed. A number of them beamed their encouragement, but I was too nervous about tripping over my robe to smile back and concentrated on matching my footsteps with those of the priests in front. I could see my colleague beside me was doing the same. I couldn't resist smiling to myself. The last time I'd formed a crocodile like this had been on my way to school when I'd lived in the children's home. Strange how the pleasant memories of my childhood were starting to emerge. The children's home! They'd never believe that the disruptive lad they'd had to deal with was about to take his vows as a deacon of the church.

As we moved towards the centre of the cathedral the sunlight streamed through the stained glass windows, catching the golden staff carried by the Archdeacon. It sent a rainbow of colours shimmering around the stone walls. I felt proud to be part of such a procession. We walked slowly up the steps towards the altar. A gleaming golden cross dominated the centre and a golden plate and cup symbolising the Eucharist stood neatly at the side.

I caught a glimpse of Lesley and the children sitting in the front row near the choir stalls with the other friends and relatives of those taking part in the service. She looked beautiful in the new pale green summer clothes I'd bought her especially for the occasion. She smiled and me and I held her gaze, gently smiling back. There was no need for words. Not at that moment. The look of love and understanding between us said it all. Fiona and Jonathan stood beside her, their faces wreathed in broad grins at the sight of their father in a long black robe. They were both spruced up and looked very smart in their new outfits. Crisp yellow ribbons held Fiona's hair neatly in place, despite the fact she'd been racing around the cathedral grounds for the last couple of hours, and for once Jonathan's thick, dark, unruly hair was slicked neatly back. I was very proud of my family.

The music climbed to a crescendo and the procession broke away from its uniformed line, each of us taking our designated seats to allow the service to begin. I took a deep breath, trying to calm the nervous flutters in my stomach. I was sorely tempted to gaze around the congregation to see who else had come to support me being ordained. I knew Shene and Graham were somewhere in the congregation, I'd seen them earlier, but now wasn't the time to start looking.

As I stood with the congregation to sing the first hymn, I drifted deeper into worship, my heart swelling with a sense of joy more profound than I had ever known before. I breathed a grateful prayer of thanks for his faithfulness in bringing me through not only three years of long theological study and training but also a painful exploration into my own background until I was strong enough to take up the reigns of my life again. But then I realised I was experiencing something I had never really experienced before. A strong, supporting parental love. It seemed to wash over like a wave of reassurance. 'I will not leave you as orphans; I will come to you' (John 14:18).

The hymn finished and I sat down on my hard wooden pew. I was warm inside. Warmed by the feelings of being loved so deeply, so perfectly – *by my Father!* ' You are not "Nobody's Child": you are My child!' My heavenly Father's voice seemed to speak deeply into the recesses of my mind and every prayer that was uttered, every reading from the scriptures, every hymn that was sung and the sermon seemed to echo those words. 'You are not "Nobody's Child": you are My child!'

As I moved forward for the Bishop to take me through my vows, my love for my heavenly Father and the knowledge that he found me worth calling into his service as a priest in his church was almost overwhelming. I knelt down before the Bishop and as I made my vows I surrendered my childhood into his care and once again I knew that peace that transcends all understanding.

I seemed to move through the rest of the service in a dream until I heard the voice of the Archdeacon say 'The Peace of the Lord be with you' and the congregation respond with 'And also with you'. I realised the congregation, priests and ministers of the church had moved from their seats and were mingling, shaking hands, hugging and murmuring 'The peace of the Lord' to each other, as is the custom of the Anglican church before the Eucharist. I joined in, mingling with the crowd congregated in front of the altar, while trying to make my way towards Lesley and the children.

'Mark!'

I turned at the deep, vaguely familiar Scottish accent and came face to face with a man I hadn't seen for almost seventeen years. I stared at the figure in front of me, speechless, but only for a moment. 'Uncle! Uncle Andrews!'

He seemed to have shrunk, or was it that I had grown taller? and his hair was much greyer, but then was that any wonder after what I'd put him through!

'Uncle, this is great! Just great!' I stammered, grasping his hand and pumping it up and down. 'What are you doing here?'

'I came for your ordination, Mark.' He beamed at me, obviously delighted at my pleasure in seeing him. 'Shene, she wrote and told me.'

'And Aunty?'

His face clouded over. 'She died two years ago, Mark.'

I grasped his hand even tighter. 'I'm sorry,' I said sincerely. I wanted to say more, but people were making their way back to their seats again. I felt a tug on my robe and turned. It was Shene.

'He's come all the way from Scotland,' she hissed. 'Just for you.'

I found the very thought of Uncle Andrews travelling all those miles just to support me extremely touching. I kept thinking of how badly I'd behaved when I'd been in his care in the children's home and it dawned on me that if it hadn't been for his influence in sending us all regularly to church I might not be here in this cathedral today!

Strange how once again positive issues from my past were rising to the surface of my mind instead of the painful ones.

It was very difficult trying to concentrate on the task in hand, which was administering my first communion to the congregation. One by one the people formed a queue in front of me, other newly ordained deacons and members of the clergy, who were placed strategically around the cathedral.

'The body of our Lord Jesus Christ . . .' I murmured to the bowed head in front of me as I handed her the bread from the golden plate.

'Amen,' she murmured, then stood up and moved over to my colleague to receive the wine.

'The body of our Lord Jesus . . .' The bowed head of the young man in front of me looked up and dark eyes mirrored the likeness of my own. 'Paul!' I mouthed his name, then slowly, choked with emotion because this was the first time we had ever worshipped together as Christians, I administered the bread into the waiting palm of my brother's outstretched hand. ' . . . broken for you,' I concluded, and then I let him go to receive the wine from my colleague.

Shene, Graham and my nephews followed Paul a few minutes later. Each one appeared quite taken with the idea of having me administer communion to them and either grinned broadly at me or surreptitiously winked. Either way I was not in a position to respond the way I would normally have done and was forced to bestow my best ministerial smile upon them instead.

And then it was almost over. I resumed my seat for the final hymn and breathed a sigh of relief, allowing my eyes to wander over the faces of the congregation for the first time.

Lesley and the children were sitting with Shene, Graham and my nephews in the choir stalls and to my surprise my other sister Maxine and her husband Robert sat behind them. I couldn't believe they had travelled such a great distance just to support me at my ordination. Beside her sat Lesley's sister with her husband and their children and behind them were Lesley's parents. All my family. I don't think I'd ever seen them all together before. I stood up as the organ swelled for the final hymn and my eyes wandered towards the back of the cathedral. There was Uncle Andrews, watching me, one of his boys, with a look of pride on his face. Paul sat a few rows in front of him. They obviously hadn't seen each other yet. I looked forward to the end of the service and the surprise reunion between them. My eyes continued sweeping across the sea of faces and with some astonishment landed on the familiar faces of Peter and Anne, my counsellors. I caught Peter's eye and he solemnly winked at me. Anne was beaming from ear to ear as she sang, looking really pretty in a pale blue summer dress. And there was John Pritchard further along the row, throwing himself into singing the last hymn with great gusto. In front of him stood a lady with a straw hat and a pale pink flowered dress. She looked vaguely familiar. If she would lift her head so I could see underneath the straw hat I might be able to ... As if in answer to my unspoken request she looked up and directly towards me. It was Jane Haywood, and beside her stood the Reverend Peter Haywood himself. I hadn't recognised him without his clerical robes. Delighted, I smiled across at them, and they smiled back. They couldn't have come all this way especially for me. Could they?

It seemed as though in the middle of that hymn, with the congregation's voices raised in song, there dawned a deep quietness in my soul and in that quietness He spoke again. 'You are not "Nobody's Child". I am your Father and you are my child and belong within my family.'

The hymn finished, the benediction was given, the organ swelled and the hierarchy of the Anglican church drew together to form the procession which would lead us out of the cathedral. I took my designated place, catching Lesley's eye as I passed. Annoyingly, she gave me a wink, which she knew I didn't dare return.

As I walked out of the cathedral into the warm sunshine I reflected on those words. Over the long, painful years of feeling poor in relationships, rejected, lost, not belonging, God had in fact always provided me with someone. People like Pastor Coombs, Peter Haywood, John Pritchard, Peter and Anne, and, yes, even Lindsay. People who were in his family, my brothers and sisters. People who had supported me, believed in me and pulled me out of the pit when I'd been sinking.

Fiona and Jonathan were the first to reach me and give me a hug. 'You were great, Dad! But when do we eat?'

I laughed. There's nothing like children for bringing you back to earth with a bump. Paul came over and we both let out a cry of excitement and slapped each other on the back.

'Have you seen Uncle?' I asked.

His eyes opened wide. 'He's here?'

I nodded and as Uncle came over to join us Paul let out a whoop of delight and, like me, began pumping Uncle's hand up and down and plying him with questions about our friends in the children's home. I realised with surprise that I looked forward to catching up with the news myself later.

My nephews came to join us and we moved across the grass to a quieter part of the cathedral grounds so that the children could be noisy without disturbing the other family groups.

Peter and Anne came over. Anne took my face in her hands and whispered, 'We're so proud of you, Mark.' Then she kissed me gently on the cheek and Peter shook my hand, echoing similar words of praise.

Shene, Graham and Maxine were all chattering in my ear about the lovely service, Jane Haywood was crushing her new straw hat by trying to give me a hug and John Pritchard was introducing himself to Peter Haywood.

A lump materialised in my throat at the party of people gathered around me. Nobody's child? Not me! I was rich in people who loved me!

'Hi!' Lesley stood in front of me looking remarkably cool and beautiful amidst the heat and clamour around us.

I wrapped my arm around her shoulders. 'Hi yourself.'

'What were you thinking just now?' she asked. 'You had a very pensive look on your face.'

'Oh, nothing really.' Now wasn't the time to start telling her.

'Lindsay?' she persisted.

I shook my head. 'Definitely not Lindsay. All that's behind me – us now, Les.'

By the way, Lindsay and Geoff have sent you a card of congratulations.'

I grinned and squeezed her shoulders. 'That was nice.' At one time a card from Lindsay would have had me dizzy with excitement, but now all I felt was a warm glow of friendship for her.

'There were also cards from Andy, Nigel, Holly and their wives with apologies for not being able to attend because of commitments within their own parishes.'

'That was nice as well.'

'Oh, and Jenny has sent you a present and card and says how proud she is of you.' I nodded. It gave me a special thrill, hearing from Jenny.

There was a scream from Fiona as one of her crisp yellow ribbons fell and was ground into the dust by her brother and cousins, fighting for the privilege of taunting her with it. I glanced around at my friends and relatives, gathered in the hot summer sunshine laughing, chatting and enjoying themselves, and I gave a sigh of contentment, squeezing Lesley's shoulders.

'You're the best thing that's ever happened to me, Lesley. Have I told you that?'

She chuckled. 'Only recently. Before that you were tied up somewhat.'

I smiled and, raising my face to the warm sunshine, squinted in the bright light. 'What now, Lesley? What has God got in store for us now?'

She gave me a hug and didn't reply for a while. Then she smiled and said, 'Who knows?'

I didn't answer. I knew what she meant. My God was the God of the impossible. I just stood contentedly with my family and friends around me.

The King's House

The King's House begain in 1993 when the Revd Anne Black, an Anglican Deacon, and Dr Peter Ward, a GP, bought an old vicarage on the outskirts of Gateshead and supported by their spouses, began work among people with problems such as addiction, depression, broken relationships, abuse and many other areas of personal pain and suffering.

Today, clergy and an ecumenical ministry team trained in counselling, listening skills, teaching, spiritual direction and pastoral care run The King's House in Washington, Tyne and Wear. It continues to provide non-residential retreats, training courses and there is always someone there to listen to *your* problem.